Beyond The Veil

BURGS

Other books by Burgs -

The Flavour of Liberation Volume One & Two:
**Healing Transformation through Meditation
and The Practice of Jhana**

The Flavour of Liberation Volume Three:
**The Practice of Vipassana and
The Path to the Deathless State**

December 2014
All Rights Reserved

For more information please visit
www.theartofmeditation.org

ISBN 978 0 9568917 4 7

CONTENTS

Prologue

To all you brave souls out there who are reading this I have just one message for you and that's: "Go for it!" Get out there and make your life everything that it is meant to be. Don't sit there waiting for your stars to line up, and definitely don't keep putting it off for later. Don't be one of those folk with a bucket list a mile long while you watch the seasons come and go. Just do it.

This is your life and you have waited a long time for it. There are dreams in your heart that are waiting to be lived. Stand up and breathe some life into them, and do it even though you do not know where they will lead you. It doesn't matter. What matters is that you set off on the way.

There is no map that can tell us what even the simplest of journeys may entail once we actually set out. It can merely hint at the way. Only the testimony of those who have walked the road can tell us what we might expect to encounter upon it, and even then we will not know how it is, until we walk the road ourselves.

For some journeys a map may well suffice, but there are others of an entirely different kind, for which the call of the heart is the only pointer to the way. And even though we will need some guidance and navigation we will still have to find the courage to walk terrain that we have yet to chart for ourselves.

Some journeys we are cast upon against our will, others we may or may not choose. But there is one journey that calls out to all of us, and that is the one that leads us out of the lowlands of confusion, doubt and fear to the high-plains of freedom, trust and love. And though it has called to each one of us since we first arrived here upon this earth, many of us may never set out upon the way.

Many people ask me: 'What was it Burgs, that called out to you so strongly to make you give up all that you had in search of something which you had no idea that you would find?' In truth, I have asked myself that same question many times. In the end I stopped asking and came to accept that it doesn't really matter what it is that calls to us, what matters is that we answer the call. The only thing I do know is that I had faith that if the way had been walked by others, in time it could be walked by me.

So here is my story. It is for those of you who honestly wish for more time, whose hearts long to walk the road home. Consider this; to gaze upon a landscape unspoiled by man, to see the light change and the mist rise at daybreak and feel the world wake from its sleep. To glimpse such a thing for an instant is enough to justify the nine months of becoming in the womb.

Oh, that you had any idea how rare and precious is this world and your human existence. Then you might savour each timeless moment as it is and not seek to consume yourselves with anything more than this. When a moment such as this is all the intoxication you will ever need, then you are ready for the knowledge that such a moment contains. In the gap, the silence, the space from which such beauty arises, is the truth your hearts yearn for. It is for you, who can taste in the wind what I speak of, that I write this book, in the hope that it may open your heart to the way.

CHAPTER ONE

It Was Just An Ordinary Night

I met my first teacher quite by chance. I might easily have not. It was an ordinary mid-week evening in Bali. I had been living there six months of the year since moving the production for my clothing label out to Indonesia. It was 1993.

I had finished my work and left the factory where I was sampling. I parked my bike outside Krakatoa Café in Seminyak and was about to go in to rent a video for the night.

Two voices shouted my name as I got off my bike.

I turned round.

"Burgs. Burgs. What are you doing tonight?"

Two friends pulled up in a jeep and leant across, shouting at me.

"Do you want to meet a miracle man? We are going to Denpasar to hear an amazing healer speak. It's the first time he has spoken in English. His teacher has just died. Do you want to come with us? We're off there now."

"No, that's OK thanks," I replied. "I'm gonna chill and watch a video. I've only just got back from the factory."

"OK. Enjoy. See you later."

"Sure. Let me know what he has to say."

And off they went.

I was almost into the café when I stopped. I don't know why. I looked up the road as their tail lights faded.

"Why not?" I thought.

I jumped onto my bike and followed them. I had no idea where we were going. They led me to an office-like building in the heart of Denpasar. There was a simple flier on the entrance announcing that we were in the right place. We walked up to the second floor to a small conference room where the lecture had begun. We crept in and sat on mats on the floor.

The speaker was a Chinese-Balinese man with a heavy limp. His name was Merta Ada and he had had polio as a child, which had left him permanently lame. He told me later that this was his blessing in disguise for if he had been limber and agile like his brothers then he would have asked their teacher to instruct him in Kung Fu and not meditation and medicine.

He was thirty-seven years old and ten years my senior.

He talked that night of his story. How he had met his teacher Tiyah Balian, a master yogi and extraordinary healer. He told of how Tiyah would sit for forty days and nights on a tiny deserted island without food. How he had perfected his meditation and developed the state of one pointed concentration known as samadhi and how from this his healing powers had emerged.

I realised that night amongst other things that the ability to heal and its potency was not the result of this or that technique but simply a by-product and reflection of the level to which one has trained one's mind and focused its consciousness. It is concentration and mindfulness that makes potent the healing ability and brings it to fruit.

When I myself started teaching and healing I would often be approached and asked to teach healing to my students. My answer was always the same: "Go and master your mind and I will teach you how to heal in a day."

Tiyah hadn't taught Ada how to heal and he didn't teach me. They taught and practised their meditation till their ability revealed itself. It seemed that it was something that was latent in our operating system, like a program that, though installed, needed to be activated. I simply followed in their footsteps.

In the years that followed I was approached by many who assumed that they would be able to heal others simply as a by-product of learning to meditate. Although this is not the case, it most certainly is true that the ability to keep one's own body in balance becomes hugely improved.

At one level we can see sickness as a reflection of incoherence in the system. Meditation is quite simply the most powerful and effective way of restoring the systems natural state of coherence. Doing this for oneself and doing it for others however are different things.

That night as I listened to Merta Ada talk, I knew I was meeting my first great master. He talked of things I had never heard before, but which lit a flame within me. He explained the role our mind plays in making us sick, what is the true cause for the arising of sickness and how might we eliminate it. He showed us plants and herbs and asked us to meditate and try to feel their energy.

He called someone from the audience up to the stage and sat them on a chair in front of him. Then he closed his eyes and just seemed to drop directly into another state. His body occasionally twitched but he didn't seem to breathe. After about three minutes he opened his eyes.

"Thank you," he said.

He then began to explain what he could see and feel in his meditation.

"Your heart is weak because your unconscious mind is always disturbed. You worry and obsess about so many things. Even when you sleep your mind doesn't stop shaking. You need to trust things more. You have so many allergies because your mind is so reactive. If anything isn't the way you want it to be you get frustrated and angry. This is exhausting your nerve system and your heart."

"Wow," said the man. He was a western ex-pat like me. "That's weird. How do you know all that?"

"Because I can feel it in your body. Every time your mind appears it produces an impression in your body. Over time this energy accumulates. Every organ and tissue and bone in your body carries the vibrations of your mind. This is why we have to take care of our minds. This is why if we meditate we can take out all the bad reactions from our mind and body and heal ourselves. Please, if you would like to try meditating for eight weeks with me all your allergies will go away and you will start to sleep properly."

He checked a number of people that night. Some with cancer, some with diabetes and others with heart conditions. Every time he was able to diagnose the conditions and explain why they had appeared without any prompting. Each time he brought the information up from his meditation.

4

This was extraordinary. This was far more than intuition. This man could feel directly inside the body of someone in front of him, and every time he was spot on.

I was impressed. During my time as a monk in Burma some years later we would have to meditate on the body parts of the monk in front of us in the same way. By then I could understand the mechanism of direct perception*, but right now, this evening, I felt I was watching a wizard at work.

I had never really meditated before. I had vision quested with an Ojibwa Shaman in Colorado the year before while scouting for a retail outlet in Vail, but never tried anything structured. We had spent that winter walking the Rockies together as he showed me how to read the energy of the land. But I sensed most of his ability was inspirational and intuitive. I did not feel he had the capacity to feel directly, the way Ada did. One day he had picked a leaf from a tree, it seemed like a random act. He placed it in my hand and said

"This leaf has your medicine in it. It can heal whatever sickness is in your body right now."

When I quizzed him as to how he chose this particular leaf and this particular tree, he had winked at me.

"My son. This tree contains your medicine because I told you so. You just have to believe me. It is your faith that heals you, not the leaf or me."

He was talking about the placebo effect; the healing power of faith. It was the faith that instilled the leaf with its magical healing power.

There is no doubt that faith is powerful medicine, but this evening Ada was talking about something totally different. He was talking about making a direct connection to the energy of the plant and matching it to the energy of the patient. In many ways it was quite shamanic, but he wasn't extracting his guidance through dreams or visions. He was feeling the energy of each plant and each patient in his mind by a faculty of direct perception.

Later on in the evening Ada put a herb in my hand and asked me to try to feel in my body where it was working. I closed my eyes and concentrated on the herb in my hand and the feeling in my body. To my surprise I could actually feel it. It was making my stomach warm. When I told him he seemed pleased. "Well done," he said.

But while I sat and focused my mind something strange had happened to me. There was a rather large middle-aged lady sitting beside me to my right. The herb was in my right hand. As I concentrated on it I suddenly found myself looking inside her body. I was completely taken by surprise. I could hardly believe what I was seeing. Could it be possible? I saw the organs and bones inside this woman's body, and the energy of them. And in her heart I saw a rather disturbing olive green colour.

I mentioned this also when I finished. She seemed startled. "Hey, that's incredible. I was told by a healer only last week that my heart chakra is a muddy green colour. Can you see that too?"

"Yes, it's the same colour as the carpet," I said.
I had no idea then how I could see and feel this. It was something of a shock.

I guess Ada had seen it too because after he finished and we were all leaving he approached me.

"Would you like to come back to my house for some tea?" he said.

"I'd love to."
The evening had sparked a flame in me. I was

thirsty for this knowledge that he had.

We went back to his house and sat up late talking about life and the Buddha and his medicines and what he wanted to do now that his teacher had died.

His knowledge was deep and real and tangible and in no way sensational and all of it made perfect sense to me. I tried again feeling the energy of plants, and he told me of his plan to start teaching healing meditation.

I was in. I was so in. I knew that evening that I had found what would fill the gap that would be left behind when I finally packed in my business and walked away from the madness that my life was becoming.

It was the beginning of an extraordinary friendship. We shared so much together over the next five years. I became his first and most committed student. He taught me as his protégé. Every time he ran a retreat I would be there beside him assisting him. Serving the best I could and always doing what I could to be as close to him as I could be. I became like a younger brother to him. He mentored me and I advised him. I watched him work, heal, teach. He was an impeccable example and role model. Exemplary in everything he did.

His abilities inspired me and I knew I wanted to follow his example and take teachings such as his back to my country. I knew from the first day that this was my way. And Ada must have known it too.

We travelled together. Teaching anywhere we could in remote Javanese villages, in old Catholic nunneries, in Buddhist temples, in the cities and in the forests.

The first retreat we did was in an old deserted house in Denpasar. We went in there with his maid and cleaned the place up. There were eight students. We sat in the living room. The men and women slept separately in the two bedrooms and Ada and I slept on the floor in the kitchen. Some of them were sick, a couple very, but everyone got healing as they learned Dharma*. Two of that group went on to be Ada's main assistants and continued to serve him long after I had gone on my own mission overseas.

CHAPTER TWO

Doing Time

Soon after I met Ada he started encouraging me to practice meditation intensively and suggested I go away to a monastery in Borobudur to sit and learn formally.

So I took a bus from Bali to Yogyakarta in Java and made my way to the monastery that sits beside that vast ancient temple of Borobudur. When I arrived I was met by a very old woman who spoke only Javanese, and after a brief tour of the monastery I was ushered to my quarters. I was given a bedroll and a small space on the floor underneath the main meditation hall.

There was no food after midday so I went to sleep hungry that night. I was the only westerner there, but I was clearly not the only lay yogi. Others slept beside me on the floor of this big room, and that became my home for a while.

I was awoken at 3.30 the next morning by the sound of a gong. I followed those around me upstairs to join the monks who were already sitting.

There were no instructions, so I just sat and did the meditations that Merta Ada had already taught me. At 6am there was another gong and I followed as everyone made their way to the food hall where we were served rice gruel and sweet tea.

We started meditating again at 7.30am after a short rest to walk and shower. The bathroom was just a concrete outdoor space with large barrels of cold water and smaller buckets to ladle from. As with everything about the daily routine there I took my lead from those around me, and we bathed together in our sarongs.

The routine was rigorous. I had never had to sit for so long and so consistently throughout the day. We took lunch at noon and at 1.30pm I was told to go for interview with the teacher, who until that time had sat like a Buddha, utterly unmoving and silent before me in the meditation hall.

He was a slight Sri Lankan monk, with a stern but kind face. And thankfully he could speak English. In fact, to my surprise I learned later that day, that he was to give all the teachings in English which were then translated into Bahasa for the Indonesian audience. It seemed in the end as though I might have some advantage being the outsider.

Despite the ease with which understanding had come to me, my progress in the early days was painful. Many years of negligence had left a heavy toll. When I came to sit long hours, the decadence of my youth and the years of 'Making Madness a Way of Life' played back at me.

I thought the pain would never end. Every cell in my body screamed as I sat ten or even more hours a day, peeling away the ignorance. But I gritted my teeth and pushed on. There was no giving up. No turning back. I was in for the duration now. I had no doubt about that.

I will be honest and admit that although I felt my

mind cutting deep into the Dharma, the Dharma was cutting deep into me. For years I had been wild and unrestrained; the freestyle pioneer. I had an aspirational sports fashion label and shops in some of Europe's hottest spots. 'Revel Without a Pause' had been the message I printed on my gear. 'Make Madness a Way of Life' had been our motto.

I was paying dearly now for instilling such recklessness in others. I had been in every way the opposite of the restraint I now had to find. But the soft voice of the teacher drew me in and I was intoxicated with what he was telling me.

He would chant:

"Sabbe sankhara annicca ti.
Yada pannaya passati.
Atha nibbindati dukkhe
Esa maggo visuddhiya."

"All conditioned things are impermanent.
When one can see this with
mindfulness and wisdom,
One grows tired of suffering
and sees the way to end it."

The truth of these few words, so straightforward and obvious, changed my life forever.

It was in that moment that I began to let go. I no longer cared what would become of me, or what my friends and peers would think. I could not even wait for approval from my father this time. This was my path. I was sucked into it inexorably and I would walk it to its end.

Nothing else mattered.

As I prepared to leave the monastery and go

back to see Merta Ada I found myself quite incapable of expressing my gratitude to my teacher. This slight, unassuming monk had such depth of presence to him. I knew he would find my testimony sentimental and self-indulgent. I knew he knew what had happened to me on my cushion. So I simply wrote a brief note and put it in his hand as I said my farewell.

It read, "I know that something truly important has begun here. I pray that in years to come I may repay my debt of gratitude to you by bringing this Dharma to many others."

After the long days on the hard stone floor, eating only once a day and rising at 3.30am my body was tempered and strong. I took the bus back to Bali instead of flying. It was a whole day. I sat in my bliss, too big by far for my seat and delighted in the love that I felt for each and every person who got on board along the way.

Two travelling minstrels jumped on for half an hour. They played the ukulele and sang Bhajans. Now I could see the joy in their young eyes. For a bowl of rice they sang their little hearts out and their songs were of love. I knew for the first time that what we really needed to be happy was so far from what we were brought up thinking.

I finally knew why I had not joined the milk round after school. It wasn't so that I could forge my way as a self-styled fashion designer. It wasn't for the years revelling in the mountains and skiing my pants off in the back-country of Chamonix. It was for this: to come to this point of total surrender, a sense of complete abandon.

My wallet had never been emptier and my heart never more full. I felt unshackled for the first time in my life. It didn't matter a jot where that bus was heading that day. At one point I just got off with the minstrels and sat with them while we waited for the next one.

I called Merta Ada en route to tell him I was coming back to Bali. He congratulated me and told me that another of his teachers had died while I was away. The famous monk Bante Giri had been the head of the Indonesian sangha* for many years. His funeral and cremation was that day. Merta Ada had been charged with organising the whole thing and there were many visiting dignitaries from neighbouring countries.

He asked me to go directly to Brahma* Vihara, the monastery in North Bali that Bante Giri had built in his hometown. It was here that the ceremony was to be.

When I arrived the place was a throng. He was loved by many well beyond the Buddhist community and hoards of devotees had come to pay respects. I was ushered to the front of the main Dharma hall and sat behind Ada. I had only time to tap his arm and nod before the ceremony began.

A group of monks began chanting. Many of the congregation chanted too. I listened. I was swept away by the sound, transported to an ancient time. The voices of the monks struck a chord so deep. I listened and meditated as they chanted over and over. And then I started too.

These chants are called the Paritta*. It means protection. The language was Pali*, a Sanskrit dialect from North Eastern India at the time of the Buddha. Most of the Scriptures are recorded in Pali and it was in Pali that they now chanted.

And I knew it. I don't know how I knew this ancient language. While I sat my retreat in the days leading up to this, my teacher would occasionally chant a few lines while elucidating some point but now I was hearing the intonation and inflection and this ancient language came to life in my mind.

I recognised it, and I started chanting along.

CHAPTER THREE

Rex

It was Bob Dylan who first challenged me to push the boundaries as the heady rush of adolescence took hold. I spent hours listening to his songs at school, identifying with the unexpressed rebel, the misunderstood heroes he sung of.

As I grew through my teens, beyond the girls and the booze and the parties, there was always something more deeply yearned for and I first learned of it from Dylan's songs. Even at school I had felt a hunger for knowledge that lay beyond the classroom. I didn't know what it was that I sought.

It was something whispered secretly in the gap between lessons and sport: hours in the woods smoking roll-ups, thinking it was the cigarettes we yearned for, when actually it was the space and the solitude.

It's a great shame that so many kids feel angry, let down, not feeling understood as they grow up. Parents get driven to distraction trying to find the key to their kids' happiness; feeling it was they who let us down, they who should have done more or should have understood us better. Blame it on our childhood, split families or over competitive peer groups, but no one ever really seemed to understand.

But one man did understand. It took me years to realise what an extraordinary man my father was. I had long left home before I even began to appreciate all he had done for me. It's often the same that we never truly appreciate what we have had until we have lost it. Dad always understood when I needed him to. For all the challenges he faced in his life he never failed at that.

Our family took a heavy knock when I was turning thirteen. I had just been made head boy at my prep school. Our fortunes as a family had been on the rise for some years. Dad had an exciting business turning high-end furniture from black oak found from the peat bogs of Ireland. It was a perfect mix of craft and business. Making beauty from things lost and buried. Not one tree was cut to make his furniture for it had all lain hidden in the peaty swamps of Ireland for centuries.

Years later when I discussed with my students the idea of right conduct and right livelihood I would say: "For those of you fortunate enough to have the chance of a life free from suffering, there are only two things to remember to safeguard your passage. Be totally unwilling to harm yourself and others in the pursuit of your desires and don't expect to take out more than you put in."

The idea that Dad's beautiful furniture had all come from trees long lost appealed greatly to me. I was so proud of him one Christmas when he took us to see his first display in Harrods.

But the pride of youth is a fickle thing. Nine months later he had lost the lot. A fire at his factory claimed his entire stockpile. Each log took ten years to dry and cure before use. There was no way to replace it. The insurance company suspected arson and Dad was bankrupt. Our family home and the cars all had to go.

We moved into a caravan in mum's friends' garden, and the pride turned to shame overnight. No longer collected from school in Dad's fancy sports car, I would walk to the end of the drive so the other kids wouldn't see the old banger that came to pick me up.

Dad's health suffered tremendously from the loss, but he picked himself up and went back to work. But two years later his heart valve collapsed and he was set back once more by major heart surgery. I was called down to my tutor at school to be told that Dad was seriously ill, and that was the first time I began to appreciate the sacrifices a father so often makes.

I had grown up seeking heroes in all kinds of places, and almost always amongst the extraordinary. As I sat outside his hospital room the first time I went to see him, I saw for the first time how easily true heroism can go unnoticed.

He was a rebel at heart, a seeker, longing all his life for spiritual truth and a sense of meaning. He had played harmonica in a skiffle band as he grew up and ran adventure camps for disadvantaged kids from London's docklands when he finished his time in the army.

It was Dad who first read me 'Grey's 'Elegy' and played me 'Like a Rolling Stone'. He read me 'The Jungle Book' and 'The Wind in the Willows', and it was always the story of the quest, or journey that enthralled us both. He understood, and every book he gave me told me that he did.

Every Christmas or birthday message hinted at a secret knowing we shared. It was an understanding that we would not speak openly about for years, but he knew, and I knew he knew, and he knew I knew he knew. He never sat me down to tell me about the birds and the bees, he knew where we learned about that stuff, but when I was thirteen he gave me my first Blues Harp. Yup, Dad understood alright.

The year I started my clothing business his birthday card read: "Go forth son. Bring golden opinions from all kinds of people." He often quoted Shakespeare and always knew that my work lay not in the business but the message it conveyed.

"It doesn't matter what you do son," he told me, "as long as it means something to you and sets an example for others."

So when I was suspended and sent home from school, it was Dad who came to pick me up. It was mid-morning and everyone was in class. My shame was bottomless. Mum and Dad had given everything to send me to one of the country's top public schools despite his bankruptcy. The one thing that wasn't compromised by the loss of Dad's business was his kids' education.

There I was, standing outside Great Gate waiting to be taken away from the place Dad had fought so hard to send me to, and for stealing chloroform from the chemistry labs and getting high in the woods. A good number of us had been busted. Some of us sent home. Me indefinitely.

What was there to say?

Nothing.

I just got in the car and he drove away.

Silence.

Then suddenly he stopped. I half expected him to drag me out of the car and beat the living daylights out of me. But he just looked over at me and said, "I don't know son. What do you want? We have tried to give you everything we can. The best education available and the best start in life, and look at you. I give up. Tell me what do you want?"

"Honestly Dad?" I asked

"Yes. Straight up."

"I just want to go to the Grand Canyon, play my blues harmonica and hear it echo back at me."

More silence. I held my breath. It seemed to be an age. And then finally he smiled.

"Well, if that's what you want, that's exactly what you should do."

I was stunned. He really did understand. He was no pushover. This wasn't him just giving in to his spoiled unruly kid. This was him telling me to go out and blaze my trail, and to do it for him as much as for me.

He was giving me permission to find my way.

I knew from that moment on that whatever I would do with my life I would do it in honour of my father. I owed him my freedom, the freedom he granted me in that moment of unconditional trust, understanding and love; the moment he gave me permission to be myself.

Twenty years later he was on his sickbed, days from his death.

We sat alone in the night. I held his hand. We meditated in silence and I chanted the Metta* Sutta* for him. He squeezed my hand tight. I cried. We were beginning our goodbyes.

The next day I dropped in on my way to Devon where I was to teach a week-long meditation retreat. I knew he could go at any time. But equally he knew how much it meant to those who had taken time out to come and learn meditation. He had insisted I didn't cancel the retreat.

19

"I have told the nurse to take me off the heart drugs. They make me feel so spaced out," he said. "I'm dying of cancer and they are stimulating my heart to keep me alive. If my heart isn't strong enough to support me on its own then I would rather go that way than the cancer take me slowly."

Mum was distraught. She would have the doctors do anything to keep him alive as long as they could. The nurse led her away to counsel her and Dad and I were left alone for the last time.

"I love that lady so much." he said. "You make sure you take care of her. I will never forgive you if you don't."

He didn't need a reply.

"I was thinking again last night about your idea to go away to the Himalayas and live a simple life. Promise me you won't run away. Not this time. Think of all those monks still in the forest where you were. You owe it to them at least. Think of all the love and care and special efforts your teachers have made to share with you the precious knowledge you have. It will mean so much to them.

I know you see so much darkness in this world. I feel it too and I can see a fraction of what you can, but remember this: there is no way that God in all his love will ever let this world come to grief. You need to mix a little more faith in with that wisdom of yours."

Mum reappeared with the nurse. He squeezed my hand.

"Go on son. Get going. You have got work to do."

I hugged his frail body one last time and kissed his forehead. I knew I was in the presence of someone great who was about to pass, and it hurt. I so wished I could have stayed and spent every second with him. But duty called. And that's the thing about duty. When we fail to answer its call we have lost our way.

I kissed Mum and left, and that was the last time I ever saw my beloved father.

The next day I was sitting in silence before thirty yogis on the first day of their silent meditation retreat. I had received a text from my brother: "Dad's heart is failing. It looks like he is on his way. Don't know if you want to try and make it here. We know you have duties. Love you. Grant."

Phew.

It hit me hard even though I had known it was coming.

Five years before I had made the decision to move back home from Asia to be near my parents. I had realised that Dad would not be around forever and I should take the chance to be as close to him as possible. I returned home from many years in exile and began to teach him meditation as I started teaching others. He drank up the Dharma like a parched man coming in from the desert sun. Few of my students showed the commitment he did. Every day without fail he had risen at dawn and sat for an hour before doing his Chi Kung. But his body was not strong. From the time of his first heart valve collapse he had had to work hard to keep his body going.

Many, who I was not close to, had won their fight against illness such as this. Some of them were in the room with me now on retreat. And now there was my own father in this terrible position. No one was dearer to me than him and yet I knew he would not win this fight.

When Dad was first diagnosed it was assumed

that he would be OK. He had seen me help others face illnesses like this. Why should he not expect the same? After all, he was every bit as committed to his practice as they had been.

He wasn't offered any viable medical solutions and so the decision to go it alone was easy. But the cancer was strong and the pain came on quickly and once the morphine stole his mindfulness there was little chance for him to heal himself. He was unable to reach down deeply enough into his unconscious to feel the force that was breaking his body apart, or where it was coming from.

The healing Dad needed was to find the courage to accept his life of poor health and allow it to become his teacher. From it he learned real courage, acceptance, and unconditional love. The point was not to take the sickness away but for him to reach a point of peace with the things that had made him sick. Somewhere inside I think he understood this, even though he prayed daily for healing.

Over the years that I have worked with people seeking healing, I have come to see a clear dividing line between those who are able to accept that at a conscious or unconscious level they may have played a part in their sickness, and those who are unwilling to acknowledge the connection between the body and the mind. Some would come asking me as a healer to take their sickness away, others would come asking what they could do to heal themselves.

Dad would not find the obvious cause of this suffering by reviewing this life. He had lived an honest man, battled with his demons as courageously as anyone. Memories of suffering lay hidden deep in his unconscious. Though he never accessed them directly in his meditation they were a felt presence that haunted him all his life. He carried hidden within him a sense of shame.

Although he was afraid as he approached his own death, he accepted his suffering in this life with humility and grace. Never once did I hear him complain about how unfair life had seemed to be to him. He knew this was his lot and he accepted it. What he feared was that he hadn't done enough, lived well enough, to grant him safe passage. It wasn't until later in my life, when I felt the crippling effects of shame within myself, that I came to understand how important it is that we find a way to forgive ourselves for the mistakes we make along the way.

Somehow he seemed to see only his mistakes and had failed to recognise the immense field of merit that his life had been. There was no physical healing I could give him, but even if I had it would not have meant as much to him as finally finding forgiveness and love for himself.

It was entirely on account of his unwavering support and devotion that I had found the courage to go out and seek the teachings and practices that were now helping others. My merit, if there was any, was his. That evening in hospital I retold the story of the day I was kicked out of school and it was the first time he had ever seen the true merit in his life.

He thought only in terms of his failed business and the hardships it inflicted on his beloved family. He smarted from the failure, felt himself unworthy. Yet for all his inner turmoil he never once stopped loving. I remember peeking through the door to his room just days before he was taken into the hospice.

He was listening to Kedrov's Our Father. His

eyes were tight shut and wet with tears, but he sat in a state of deep rapture and joy with a smile of pure love on his face. For all his pain, I knew he had access to his heart, and in his quiet moments all alone he made peace with himself.

Mum knew the goodness in him and so could never understand why he remained so haunted inwardly. She could be forgiven for thinking that life had been so unfair on him, for she hadn't meditated for long enough to understand how it could be like this.

Only when we allow ourselves to accept that things are what they are, do our challenges become transformed into our teachers. Dad understood this unequivocally and met it with dignity.

The Buddha had said that three things are hard to know; the cause for the coming into being, the future destination of beings, and karma*. We have become so used to looking at the appearance of things for a sign on how and why they are, that the causal process by which they come to be that way, or the basic ground for their being, remains a mystery, leading to a conviction that we are essentially living in a material world of which consciousness is merely a by-product.

Well, Dad had not reached the level where these things could be seen and known directly, but he sensed clearly that his suffering was to be owned, accepted and passed through with forbearance and love. In the end he found both of these noble qualities by the boatload.

Now he was dying. His hard fight was coming to an end and I could not be there to hold him as he embraced his final challenge.

I didn't go to him.

I sat and reflected. I looked at those who sat in

front of me and knew how important it was for them to be here. One young lad had brought his own father, brother and sister in the hope that the Dharma would heal them as it had him. I recalled the first time my own father had sat and how it had marked a milestone in his life. There were two others in the group who were fighting a brave fight with cancer and winning.

Dad wouldn't win that fight and I knew he would be better served by what merit I could share with him from the help and service I could give here. The decision not to be by his side as he passed on was the hardest I ever made; yet I knew he would not have had me do otherwise.

"You take care of your students, old boy." he had said as I left him the day before. "They need you more than I do."

And so even at the end he had given me permission to do my best. He had sent me on my way to do the work I had to do, and it was in honour of him more than anything else that I decided to stay.

I sent Metta all morning and felt his light pass. I cried silently and at lunch break got the message from my brother.

"Just to let you know that our dear Dad has gone on his way. It's about 12.10."

I was grateful for the two-hour lunch break. I had time to honour him with my tears. I lay curled in my bed holding my pillow. And only one thing reflected in my heart: his beaming toothless smile burning bright through his sunken eyes, illuminating his whole being, even on his death bed. This had been my last image of him before I had left him the day before.

"Give us a hug son," he had said.

I held his frail body so tight. I knew it was the last time. I squeezed his cool hands.

"Oh Dad. I love you so much. Thank you."

"Thank you, old boy. I don't know how I will ever thank you for all you have done for me. I am so proud of you. Now go forth and do what you are here for, but remember, there is more love in this world than you know yet. Keep your faith."

I had spent years teaching my father the wisdom of the Buddha and here at the end his own wisdom shone brighter than anything he had learned from me.

So I had driven away that night and left him to die in my mother and brother's arms.

I decided to tell my students what had happened. I knew it would be hard for them. I knew they would feel guilty that I had stayed but I didn't have the strength to carry it silently. I had just lost the most important person in my life.

We began our sit after lunch as usual and as we settled into our concentration I told them:

"I feel I need to let you know that my dear father passed away while we sat before lunch. I know that some of you will feel I should go to be with my family but I have thought it through and decided that the best thing I can do for my father now is to do my best for you. This is what he wanted. He would hate to think that you lost your chance to learn Dharma on his account. So let's keep our heads down and do our very best. And get the full benefit from our time here."

His presence was felt in the room that week. He was there at the end when we shared merit with him and he stayed around me till the next retreat. It was on Metta day six weeks later that he finally

26

took his leave. That was Dad all the way: a sucker for loving kindness. He just had to be there one last time, and then he was gone. He had been around me so much in the six weeks following his death. I had dreamed of him and sat with him and told him all the things I had wanted to tell him.

But when he did go, he really went. He never again appeared beside me while I sat and meditated or chanted, and the feeling that he might walk into the room at any time never came back. He had done what had to be done and had earned his safe passage. He had found the peace he longed for. And he had earned every bit of it.

Karma is indeed hard to understand and one of the things the Buddha said was most hard to see. Because there is no obvious sign that our actions now may have future effects upon us, it is easier to come to the view that what we say, think and do does not ultimately matter at anything other than an ethical level. The rejection of the principle of karma allows us to believe we are not responsible for our predicament or accountable for our actions.

When the Buddha spoke of Karma, he was not talking of a belief in some kind of reward or retribution for our past acts both wholesome and otherwise. He was pointing towards a universal law by which things come into being, the very creative principle itself by which things only come into being dependent upon a cause for them, and never come into being without such a cause.

What he perceived when he looked deeply down into the causal process of life, was not a judgemental universe that favoured some over others, but a deep quantum process by which consciousness and the material world are interdependent and conditioned by each other. It is a fundamental principle that runs so deeply through our lives and is so little understood.

Dad's physical weakness and his misfortune in this life were due to past karma and he was able to understand and accept that. This was the final life of his affliction and somewhere inside he must have known it, for he never once complained through all his long years of bad luck, accidents and illness.

His life after forty was a long series of setbacks. No sooner would he recover from the loss of his business than his heart played up on him. A second time he was left redundant as he clawed his way back to health. Then the garage collapsed on his leg and left him lame for life.

In the end jaundice from his long years of heart medication and the wrong drugs prescribed finally gifted him an aggressive cancer of the pancreas. But through all of this his love was boundless.

My mother had found his misfortune harder to accept.

"But he is such a loving man." she would say, "It all seems so unfair. Never once in his life did he get a lucky break. He never had any ill will for anyone or complained about his bad luck. I just don't know how he ever remained so positive."

I have always felt there is wisdom within some of us well beyond our knowing. We just get clouded and lose our way. Dad had such wisdom. He knew he carried the energy of a past he could not see into and worked it through in the hardships faced in life. He had no bitterness in him, only the fear that he might not have done enough to avoid going through it all again.

The patience and commitment he showed to his spiritual recovery was an inspiration to me and an example to all those who sat with him.

He would join our silent retreats and work tirelessly through the anguish and agony that presented itself. But always, always there was love: oceans of it.

At the end of a retreat one time when sharing with the group he cried:

"I was born a Christian and all my life I have prayed, but for many years I had lost faith that we were looked over and cared for. Today in this room I felt a love, stronger than I have ever felt. And I know now that God is always and everywhere with us, in the hearts of each and every one of us when we sit still long enough to feel the love we have forgotten."

Older by far than any other yogis in the group he would always be a motivation and inspiration to others. If he could do it, seventy years old and lame then how could they give up when it got tough?

That week on retreat everyone was touched in some way by him. Many of the old students knew him well. Others just put respect to their teacher's father. But we all left that retreat moved in ways we could not speak of.

Beyond the Dharma they had listened to, and their work on the cushions, we all took inspiration from the example that he had set, and worked harder by far than we might otherwise have done.

His love healed a part of all of us that week. And for me it was a rite of passage. My mentor was gone.

As my first teacher, Merta Ada, had said to me: "You know Burgs, you will one day have to fly alone like an eagle." I had left my teachers one by one and now my father had gone. That time to fly alone had come.

When the retreat was over we all honoured the gift Rex had sent us by sharing our merits with him. Then we went our separate ways knowing that we would always be connected by the time we had shared that week. I drove back home to my mother and brother.

The first thing I did was go to see Dad in the chapel of rest.

He looked so handsome. It is an amazing thing, death. The anguish and turmoil, pain and suffering that many experience as it closes in leaves completely with our final passing. Mum had told me that at his passing he had simply held her and Grant's hand and said.

"I love. I love. I love." Just that. It wasn't directed at anyone, just a pouring forth from his heart. And then he was gone.

CHAPTER FOUR

Revel Without A Pause

I looked down at Dad as he lay in the chapel of rest and saw only love on his face. His hair was immaculately parted as it had always been and there was the gentlest of smiles on his lips. Not a trace of the hardship he had just gone through remained.

And what should he be wearing? His old 'Mad Rags' shirt. The one he loved the best. "Cowes 96: Make Madness a Way of Life."

Mad Rags was the clothing label I set up off the back of my ski-bum days and Dad had loved it with a passion. He had been a wanderer and a romantic in his youth and it called to the free spirit that he left behind once he took up the reins and responsibility of fatherhood.

The last book Dad had ever read to me, before I was considered too old to be read to, was Laurie Lee's 'As I Walked Out One Midsummer's Day.' It was the first time I really felt the road beckon to me, and I answered its call as soon as I could. I was fourteen years old when Dad read it to me. Over the next year I re-read it three times and the following year when Dad asked me what I wanted for Christmas I said, "I want a ticket to Spain. I want to go walkabout."

I took the train to the airport from Victoria station on New Year's Eve, having seen in the New Year at Trafalgar Square with all my buddies from school.

I was off on a mission. I had no idea where it would lead but the dusty foothills of the Spanish Sierra Nevada drew me towards them like a parched man to an oasis. I was so hungry for adventure I could burst. My friends walked with me to Victoria and bade me farewell and off I went, travelling alone for the first time in my life. I ditched my trainers for espadrilles at Alicante airport and hitched inland towards the mountains in a battered milk truck.

I spent an ecstatic week of solitude walking from village to village. It was January and the air was cool and moist. I slept in olive groves and beside rivers and spent the night of the Three Kings drinking calvados with the father of a pretty young girl I had tried to chat up at a village fiesta. Having banished his daughter to bed he pulled a dusty bottle from a shelf in the kitchen, and we sat through the night, smoking filterless cigarillos and drinking his powerful hooch.

I had little grasp of the Spanish language and he knew even less English, but with the help of my pocket dictionary he asked me if I was serious about marrying his daughter. Needless to say I left town early enough that morning to not be spotted even by the farmers on their way to the fields.

In many ways I felt it was a coming of age as I rambled alone through those purple hills. When I returned home I knew a fire had been lit in my heart that would call me back to the road until finally, years later, I found what it was leading me to.

So I left school a rebel and a dreamer. I was clearly in search of meaning, even back then. I had no idea where it lay, but that didn't matter because I knew I would not stop looking until I found it. I knew I wasn't going down the route offered up to me as the end of my school days approached.

I took to the road again after school with the wild abandon of a young seeker given his first taste of true freedom. This time there was no new school term to come back to, it was an open ticket. For months on end I slept on beaches or on boats and buses. I was finally free.

After years of schooling, parents and teachers, for the first time in my life there was no one to answer to. It was a glorious celebration of life at a time when we really are free enough to actually be free. I trawled my way from country to country, from isolated beach to mountaintop, from city to city, making friends and falling in love along the way. Spending precious moments with people I would leave the next day and never hear of again.

Apart from a brief spell working in a windscreen laminating factory and another in a sawmill outside Jerusalem, my two buddies and I were constantly on the move.

When I finally arrived back in England, I had been out of contact for months and it was too late to accept most of the offers I had received from universities. I had however been offered a place at Manchester before I had gone travelling, and so that was where I headed in early October.

I am not quite sure why I went. One of my best friends was going and he was driving up from near where I lived. I think I just went along for the ride.

And so a week after coming back home, having missed the registration for my degree, I arrived in Manchester to spend three years of my prime seeking higher education.

Manchester itself appealed to me. It was the early Eighties and house music was just being born. Manchester was the epicentre of it all. After a year on the road I found Manchester's clubs claustrophobic, but the people were warm and friendly, hip and creative, and the music kicked.

The student scene didn't impress me so much however:

I had left school with my mind honed and bright, but at university that changed from eight hours work a day to eight hours a week. There was a real danger these bright young minds of ours would stagnate, lose their edge and become dull. While our parents thought we were engaging in the highest form of education, I felt myself drift into apathy over the first two terms.

Once the novelty of the parties and the dance music wore off I did indeed feel myself stagnate. What we learned in three years could have been done in six months, and we could have been given back the other two and a half years to get stuck into life.

I wasn't cynical when I arrived, and there were many who were working hard to open the door to a profession and career that they truly aspired to; would-be doctors, lawyers, accountants and engineers, seeking professional qualifications as a bridge to a career.

The rest of us were out living life too large or being angry with those who were, and all of us whittling away those years when we first get the chance to put some experience behind the still heady and tireless energy of our youth. How much might we really achieve in this precious time in our youth, if we could only get over our preoccupation with being seen and heard?

Instead we revelled in the booze and the parties and the promiscuity, as we got lost in our ideas of ourselves, thinking that we were truly living life. Whether we were out getting drunk or protesting on the union steps, it seemed as if we all just needed to make as much noise as we could.

But something didn't ring true. We were led to believe university marked the start of our adult life, but I wonder how many of us would have really coped back then if we had had to support ourselves the way most people did. There we were protesting when grants were cut yet spending most of the hand-out on booze and partying.

In our oversized sense of entitlement I don't think we ever stopped to ask ourselves why anyone should be paying for us. I think in some twisted logic we all managed to convince ourselves that our university education was a basic human right rather than the rare privilege that it was.

Whatever it was, I got the feeling that most of us didn't really appreciate it. Like so many of the things in our lives, we had already started to take it all for granted.

Yet in spite of all this, my generation was perhaps the first to begin to sense the impending crisis in the system of values and aspirations we had inherited from our parents. I was growing up to a totally different world to them.

In the few brief years between my adolescence

and manhood I noticed a sense of entitlement creep up on me. The bicycle I was given for my twelfth birthday was cherished until I left school. I knew how to repair and service it and washed it devotedly every weekend.

To this day I still have the cricket bat my Dad bought me when I was made captain of my prep school team. For all the attachment I had to it, I valued it and appreciated it. I remember what a big deal it was when I got my first digital watch, and then my first stereo cassette player. These things that came into our lives, did so with a sense of wonder.

But slowly we were becoming spoiled. Slowly the novelty wore off and the appreciation paled. By the time mobile phones appeared on the scene they were nothing more than an appendage to be cast aside as soon as a newer model came out.

The little luxuries that had added joy to life were starting to be taken for granted. We started to need more. Slowly the little things stopped satisfying and gradually these privileges became consumerism and meaningless consumption.

What is more we started to borrow the money to pay for it. Our society became one built on services and credit. We chose to pay others to do for us what we would prefer not to do ourselves. Nothing wrong with that, but that is a luxury normally afforded to one who had surplus enough to pay for it.

But gradually in our indolence we started to pay for all these goods and services we took for granted with borrowed money. We took credit and gradually our society went into overdraft. We were living a life of ease that we couldn't afford to pay for, while our factories and mills became inefficient and began to close. Quite simply we were no longer producing enough to pay for what we wanted to consume. What did we think we were doing?

As I have said, I didn't find my path immediately on leaving home. It took a fair few years of living life too large before I finally developed any sense of responsibility. There were a few side-tracks on the way. I left university having spent my final year setting up a ski tour business.

I called it Ski Mania. Coach loads of university students out in Val d'Isère and Chamonix having it large. We had a mobile sound system that we would take up the mountain on a skidoo and set up shop for the day, with barbecues, dancing and crazy ski races.

Within two years it had evolved into an inter-resort dual moguls and freestyle competition which we called the 'Boss Des Bosses'. It became one of the highlights of the season in Chamonix during the 1990's where hoards of ski-bums from across the Alps converged for a day of freestyle ski races and partying.

The kids wanted to join us rather than their parents, and the parents trusted us enough to send their kids away so they could go skiing in peace. It was a good deal. Everyone was a winner.

At the end of the second season I designed a sweatshirt and printed it up to sell to the seasonal ski-bums. The motif on the back read: "Val d'Isère 90. The Powder and the Glory. Make Madness A Way of Life."

I sold the lot in one evening and they were trading second hand at the end of the season for more than their original cost.

It was the birth of what went on to become Mad

Rags. I quickly realised that selling sweatshirts was both more profitable and less work than running ski trips. We were on a roll. Over the Summer I took the gang to North Cornwall and South Devon and we took Rock, Salcombe and Cowes by storm too.

We lived on the road. We would sleep on the beach or in grounded launches, occasionally being taken into people's holiday homes. We had an old ex-army minibus and a printing shop in Yeovil a good two hours away. At times we were selling so much gear we would have to drive to Yeovil and print through the night in time to be back on the beaches and in the bars the next morning.

That Summer I took the crew to Glastonbury. We printed up eight hundred shirts and it rained the whole time. There was no way we could pitch in the torrential rain, so we stashed the gear in our tent and partied.

I woke at dawn on the Monday morning. The sky was clear. In a few hours everyone would be heading home. We had a window. It was a small window, maybe a few hours, but a window nevertheless.

I woke the guys. They were messy. We had only just gone to sleep an hour before. A couple were still up round the fire. If ever there was a time to make madness a way of life this was it. It was utter insanity. We sold all eight hundred shirts in two and a half hours while the official merchandisers were off-loading two for a fiver. That evening we were in the Evening Standard Magazine. There was a new way of doing things and there weren't any rules.

These were the nineties. We were coming off the back of the Thatcher era; the Sloane Ranger had given way to the Yuppie some years ago and it was time for something new. I knew it, the gang knew it and everyone around us knew it. It was a time to push boundaries, get outside the box and ask a few questions.

It wasn't about the ski holidays or the gear I was making. It was about attitude. It was time to question how we might live. The New Age was just being born, it was time for some fun, time to put our hands in the air and scream, 'I'm alive.' I was twenty-three and that is exactly what I was going to do. It was the scene that people bought into, not the clothes.

We took the mobile sound system and rotated our beach parties along the coast all summer long.

I remember one night we were packing up on Rock Beach. It was 5am and the last revellers were heading to their homes. I was loading the van. The local police had been in the car park all night. But they had left us alone. I was approached as I packed up.

"Is that the last of them gone now?" he said, referring to the youngsters who were heading home.

"Yup. We are the last ones off the beach," I said.

"Good job." he said.

"Thank you. So tell me. How come you don't bust us? Beach parties are illegal," I said.

"Because when you guys throw a party we know where all the kids are. When you don't they are all over the place and we have to try to keep an eye on them. You seem to be keeping better control of them than we ever could. Just don't let it get out of hand."

"Hey," I said "Trust me. I know the score. The kids are safe."

And they were. And for some reason the parents

knew it too. I half expected to see a parents' revolt, a petition to have us banned from Rock and Salcombe but somehow they knew the spirit of adventure we stood for was good, and they recognised we had the balance right.

There is a part of every parent that wants to see Tom Sawyer or Huck Finn in their kids. Mad Rags stood for that. The pioneering spirit latent in the heart of every young soul, waiting to be kindled and nurtured into life. It was the fire of this spirit that we were lighting in the young hearts of those who jumped on the bus.

We toured the Alps in the winter and the Coast in the summer. Within five years we had thirteen retail outlets of our own and a factory in Java with a hundred and twenty machinists. It had grown at such a pace I hadn't had a chance to catch my breath.

And then even more suddenly than it had begun it was over...

It was the last night of the Cowes Week regatta. Our shop on the high street had just taken seventy thousand pounds in ten days and the gang were out celebrating big time.

I was playing blues harp with the band on the main stage in front of a crowd of five thousand. The energy was intense and we were rocking. I turned to the guitarist to indicate I was going to finish my solo and then as I turned back towards the crowd something hit me right in the middle of my chest.

A few minutes earlier the scene had been a glorious celebration of energy and exuberance and as I played I felt utterly alive within it. But now all I could see was insanity, everywhere. What was I looking at? Countless people drunk to the point of lunacy.

It was a pure expression of the herd instinct in a display of complete mindlessness. It was as if somehow the mirror was turned round; from a total sense of vibrancy and connection to isolation and separation within a split second. Time froze for an instant and I glimpsed a reality so totally alien from the one I thought I had become the master of. It was no longer a celebration of life I was looking at, but the pulsing throbbing sea of sheer delusion.

So this was how we came to celebrate our life? By intoxicating ourselves to the point where we had no idea of who we were anymore. There was no light in the eyes of these people who were celebrating their finest hour, just a glazed fog of intoxication to which they were completely surrendered.

It was me I was looking at, every one of them was me. I saw the years of my youth in that split second. Banging out my message: 'Make Madness a Way of Life.' I remembered dancing on the dunes with my hands in the air screaming; 'I'm alive!' and really feeling in that moment that I was. Ten times, a hundred times, countless times. How long does it take to make that point?

I'd been there. I had revelled without a pause for one gig too long and suddenly the bubble had burst. In that moment my life changed so unrecognisably that it would take me the next few years to understand how.

In time I came to see why the Buddha had turned away from his life of excess. It wasn't just abhorrence at the impermanence, as many would have us believe. It was because he had filled his cup and drunk from it and there was nothing more that sensual desire could bring him. He had taken it to the end and it held nothing left for him. He didn't struggle to walk away. It was a choiceless process. There wasn't anything else he could do. He just knew it was over, and in that moment so did I.

I had drunk of my cup and refilled it over and over. The sweet nectar it had contained had grown tasteless and flat. It no longer meant anything to me. That season we took over four hundred and fifty thousand pounds and I hadn't once stopped to ever ask how much money we had made. I didn't care. I didn't even care that so many people wanted my gear. I had made my point and banged out my tune. I had flattered my ego one last time and I just had to get out. I could hardly breathe.

I turned round to the guitarist,

"I just gotta get out of here. One last solo and I'm off."

"Are you nuts? Look at them. They are all over it."

"Sorry guys. I gotta go."

I turned and threw my harmonica into the crowd and jumped off the side of the stage into a skip full of plastic beer glasses. I pulled the lid closed and sat there with my head in my hands. It was over. In that moment whoever Burgs thought he had been died.

It is extraordinary the momentum our ego gathers as we trawl through life. We become so defined by it that we get to a point that the pantomime we play out in our search for love, admiration or even acceptance consumes us. Eventually we arrive at the point where there isn't much else to us but the pantomime we are playing out.

42

The ideas that we cling to and seek to express in our efforts to win ourselves the place in the world we think we deserve, become the only kind of identity we have. Almost everything we do is an effort to uphold our pantomime, to project to the world the way we would have it perceive us.

Even our darkest and most confused patterns are rooted in our need to feel expressed in one way or another or a reflection of our lack of that same sense of expression. What is it about us humans that we will lose all sight of our heart in our vain attempts to win acceptance from others? Why do we need so badly to be noticed?

I realised later in my life that the only acceptance I had really needed had come from my granddad when he gave me my first cigarette and my father when he gave me permission to play blues at the Grand Canyon. I often wonder what was the real cause of my giving up a life that seemed like a dream come true.

Was it really because of the pull of my soul towards a higher quest, or was it simply because I had been gifted my rite of passage and been accepted by my elders years before. All I wanted was for people to have a good time. I foolishly thought that by doing what we were doing, we could make people happy. I just hadn't yet learnt the difference between the pursuit of pleasure and happiness.

It's true that for all our success with Mad Rags the fact that so many people wanted what we did never really touched me. I didn't even on occasion stop to reflect on why it didn't really mean anything to me when on paper it was everything a twenty-five year old could dream of.

The obvious answer was that I had always had

the higher call of the quest buried latent within me, waiting to be ignited and brought to life. That would be the more romantic answer. But I think perhaps the answer was in fact less exotic.

I just didn't seek the admiration of my peer group, because deep down I knew I had been given it by the only two people who really mattered. My Dad and my Granddad.

I don't even think either of them understood the significance of the permission they granted me but I have come to reflect on how much hurt could be saved if every father could just bring himself to say "Hey son. You're a good kid. I think you are the best."

That's all it takes to set your kid's heart free for life. What kind of paucity of spirit is it that makes a mother or father incapable of bestowing on their children this priceless gift? They might struggle and save to buy the next bike or ipod, but this gift is free and lasts forever. Maybe they are so caught in their own pain that, without meaning to, they hand it on down the line to their kids.

CHAPTER FIVE

Innocence Lost

In my day I was a pioneer breaking the mould, rejecting the milk round and heading off to the Alps to set up my clothing business. Even then I had no idea of what had gone into giving me these opportunities. I was lucky enough to be able to revel in the novelty of being a non-conformist, and yes, I took it all for granted.

Perhaps mine was the last generation that could be excused for such self-indulgence. Seeking to express myself, sing my song, play my tune, I never stopped to reflect on just how rare was my good fortune, and while I did deeply appreciate it, I know I took it for granted. I didn't know what the answer was, but I knew where I wasn't going to find it.

I was lucky enough to grow up in that brief period when the sky was the limit, and everything was acceptable in the name of self-expression. It was the absolute tail end of the great expansion that was sealed in its coffin when Al Gore spelled out to the world the Inconvenient Truth.

I could be forgiven for first seeking expression in hedonistic gratification before I finally yielded to a higher sense of purpose. It wasn't quite time yet to wake up and smell the coffee. But it wasn't far off.

How lucky I was. I have often mused what an extraordinary time it has been to be alive. Kids leaving school now don't have the same luxury of being able to pretend they don't see. If they turn to hedonism, it is often to numb themselves rather than as a celebration of life. There is a world of difference.

When we discovered ecstasy and stood on the roof of our cars at the first ever raves screaming, 'I'm Aliiiiive,' we really knew we were. Sure there was a casualty rate back then, as there always has been for taking more out than we had coming to us, but things are so different now.

I remember a lad of twenty-five being brought to me for help by his friend.

He was extremely bright and from a good family. He first got involved with drugs at school. First pot, then cocaine and then during his time at university, heroin. He was bright enough to muddle through in spite of the daze the drugs left him in, and qualified with a first class degree.

He went on to become a head-hunter in the city and made ludicrous amounts of money whilst drunk and stoned at his desk. Crack cocaine kept him high enough to cope with the pace at which he had to work and heroin got him to sleep at night. In his first year he earned a hundred thousand pounds and spent every penny of it on drugs.

He ended up living in a squat in Hackney spending up to five hundred pounds a day on his addiction, and when his money was all gone and his overdraft at its considerable limit, he would beg.

The first three attempts to meet up with me failed until one day he turned up at a café in Chelsea to tell me his tale, and ask for my help.

I sat him down and asked him what was up. He looked at me blankly and then rolled his eyes as his mind searched for an answer to justify his position. I knew he was sizing me up. I touched my finger to my head and said:

"Don't even try to understand."

There was a pause. Although he was stoned I knew that he felt he was in control of the situation, and was trying to approach me the way he had approached all the counsellors he had been to before.

"Forget it." I said. "You have no idea what this is about, and don't try and tap dance me."

He refocused. He was smart. He needed to know I couldn't be fooled. He breathed deeply and sipped his lime and soda. I could see he felt safe enough to start to open up. His eyes began to water and a tear ran down his cheek.

"OK," I said. "So what is it all about?"

"You tell me." He replied.

"OK. So you are so confused about who you think you need to be that you have invented this rudeboy whiz-kid who thinks he's smart enough to break all the rules and win."

He stared at me.

"So are you winning?" I asked. "Are they buying it?"

"I think they are." He said.

"Really? Clever you. So where does it go from here?"

Silence.

"You choose. You go to the Priory and get treated for depression and addiction with your schoolmates, or you end up in detention centre with the real rude boys…"

"No? OK then, your mate gets a call to say they

47

found you dead in a back alley with a bag of crack and a knife in your neck, right?"

"And he calls your parents, who never understood you, and finally they do...Right?"

"And it's all over, you made your point. Right?"

Pause.

"Wrong. What do you think happens next...the moment after you bleed out in the underpass? Huh? What you reckon?"

"Whatever pain you are feeling, whatever wound you are using to justify your position is nothing compared to what happens next if you die in this state. What kind of mind do you think will carry you on from there? Huh? The wise crack rudeboy with a silver spoon who died in the gutter?"

"And how will we remember you? Don't tell me. Facebook: Burberry cap, gold chain and a purple velvet jacket. Bottle of scotch in one hand and a cigarette in the other. The big man. Close?"

He looked into his glass.

"Not far off." He smiled

"And which picture will your Dad keep on his desk to remember you by? The rudeboy in the purple jacket or the scholar on graduation day?"

We sat in silence as people ate lunch and sipped rosé around us.

"Well." I said. "It's a big hole you dug, kid. And wise up. No one's coming to dig you out but you. So where do we go from here? You want to start digging?"

He began to cry.

"OK. I'll tell you what. I'll help you. I'll get you off the gear and help you out of your hole but on one condition. We do this at your home, your family home, with your Dad there. I'll stand beside you, but this is your fix and not mine. I need to know your family are behind you. Deal?"

A long pause

"Deal," he said.

I knew then that he knew he had no choice. He was smart enough to know that whatever smokescreen he had hidden behind had just become the mirror.

"OK." I said "I know your world doesn't make sense to you, but that's no excuse. Like it or not, it is what it is, and it's all you've got. So you had better start trying to make sense of it or you'll be choosing this hole until they bury you in it. One thing is for sure, however bad it is, there's countless other folk out there in a far bigger mess than you. Some of them will be made by the challenges they face and others will be undone by them. I'm not going to pretend this is easy. You are going to have to dig deep, but in doing so you might just find something inside you that you feel is worth loving. Are you up for it?"

We sat in silence. I think it was the first time in his life that he felt met.

"So are you up for it?" I asked again.

He looked at me and nodded.

"Yes. I am. Just tell me what I have to do."

"Call your parents. Tell them where you are at and ask if we can stay with them until this is done. I'll stay with you as long as it takes but the moment I think you're not pulling your weight I'm gone."

"And one last thing. Before you pack up and leave Hackney spare a thought for all those who didn't have a choice to be there. "

I paid the bill and we left.

Five days later I was waiting for him at Moreton-in-Marsh station. I agreed to pick him up from the train out of Paddington and drive him to his

49

parents. He missed three trains and was arrested for shoplifting along the way and finally arrived in the late afternoon. He was in a really bad way.

I drove him into the town and we sat on a bench. I didn't want his Dad to see him like this. He couldn't speak but gestured that he wanted to write something. I pulled a pen and paper from my bag and handed it to him.

His hand shook uncontrollably as he wrote:

"I no longer know if I can or want to go on."

"It's OK." I said. "You are safe now."

I left him there and went into the newsagent and bought some tobacco. I came back and rolled him a cigarette.

"Here," I said handing it to him. "Just one step at a time. It's OK."

We sat in silence as he smoked. Although he almost hadn't got there, I think we both knew that the decision to come was the hardest step he had to take.

He was addicted to heroin, crack cocaine and Valium, and was drinking a bottle of vodka a day. It was a rough ride. We stayed up on the top floor of his house, him in his childhood bedroom, and me in his brother's.

I sat in the next room for five days, meditating and sending him healing while he went through his rite of passage. He was brave. I think one of the reasons I stood by him was that I didn't know if I could have gone through what he did and come out the other side.

Two weeks later he attended my week-long meditation retreat.

In the sharing session at the end a psychotherapist who worked at a drug rehab centre stood up to speak:

"I have been in this business for most of my professional life. If I hadn't seen for myself what has happened here this week, I would have said it was medically impossible. This has practically re-written the rule book on the approach to drug addiction."

Seven years later he remains drug free and doesn't consider himself to be either an addict or a victim. He wasn't a bad kid. Nor did he have a chip on his shoulder. He was a good kid, who was too bright to pretend that he didn't see that the options presenting themselves to him didn't add up.

I remember asking him some time after his recovery where he thought it all went wrong. Before his recovery he had insisted that it all stemmed from his mother dying of cancer when he was fourteen. But he quickly learned that there were untold orphans out there getting on with life without burying their heads in drugs.

Now his head was clear and he knew that the victim stance wouldn't wash. He told me that even when he was sixteen he began to see that the world he was growing up in couldn't last, and that what he felt he was expected to do with his life made no sense to him at all. The drugs, he said, had numbed him enough to toe the line.

These days so many kids come to my classes totally lost. I am horrified by how many exceptionally gifted and fortunate kids turn up with hollow eyes and a prescription for anti-depressants. They are often burned out and yet they haven't even begun to really live life.

These are not the casualties of living too large. They are the casualties of not living at all. The drugs are stronger, they are starting to take them younger, and it's not a celebration of life they are engaging in but an effort to numb themselves.

The privileged are ending up in clinics with Valium addictions and the less privileged in hospitals with knife wounds or worse. Or even worse, they are numbing themselves in their virtual world so that they stop having to feel all together.

There is no real rite of passage from adolescence to adulthood these days and no mentors to show them the way. In years gone by we came of age in the forests and fields beside fathers and elders.

Today it's about how many drugs they took at the festival, or who they smoked in the gang scrap and many of today's kids are doing it in rehab, as they get over their first round of addiction or detention centres, after they draw first blood.

So when they turn up on retreat and hear the Dharma for the first time it cuts deep. Somewhere deep inside they recognise it as their invitation to take back the reins and set themselves free.

They realise quickly enough that just being angry or disappointed or feeling let down isn't going to get them anywhere. They know in their hearts that the victim never comes out victorious.

Having pointed the finger of blame everywhere they can, suddenly they are left naked and asked to look inside for the answers. Somehow they sense that finally they are being recognised as adults capable of working out their own stuff.

"Work out your own freedom from suffering with diligence."

Those were the final words of the Buddha. And today they are calling, loud and clear, to those kids whose hearts are still connected enough to recognise that something has gone astray.

In the world they are growing up in, self-expression has been squeezed into the virtual world of their laptops and iPads. On Facebook they can re-invent themselves to win admiration from their peers, but they know somewhere inside that the person that puts their head on the pillow each night is finding it harder and harder to uphold the image they feel they need to project. They know it isn't enough.

Many numb themselves, often with drugs, both prescription and recreational. But more and more have had enough and are asking new questions and looking outside the box for their answers.

In the deeper part of their hearts they understand the law of karma and realise finally, that the real life work is not done on the trading floor of the banks or fighting over postcodes, any more than it is in the race to win friends on Facebook or the most hits on Twitter.

Today, twenty-five centuries after the Buddha died, the age of the yogi has come around again, as we realise that the modern age has brought much wealth but little contentment and much numbness.

What exactly was the cause of my epiphany on the main stage at Cowes Week that day I threw my harmonica away, hardly matters. But what it did do was propel me headlong into the journey that would finally bring me home. I'm not talking back home to roost, I'm not even talking about back in touch with ancient roots that lay buried in Bali, India and Burma, although it did indeed do that.

What I mean is that it set me off on the journey back to the heart that I had come close to losing all contact with, in my bid to make a name for myself. Whatever I thought I had been looking for since I began my quest, I finally knew that it didn't lie in personal glory or the rock and roll lifestyle. I had looked under that stone good and proper and found no hidden treasure there.

It wasn't easy to just walk away, however. Mad Rags had a lot of energy behind it and it took me two years to fully extract myself. I agreed to return to Indonesia to design the next season's range with the understanding that I would play no more part in the retail end. We passed most of our shop leases over to our competitors and I bid my farewell to the fashion industry.

I remember that autumn I was back in Bali sampling my final range of gear for Mad Rags. We were up on the Bukit at the mother of all full moon parties. The sun was coming up over the lagoon of Benoa and the moon was setting to our right, over the temple at Uluwatu. It was a vision only God could have created. I was monstrously high. We all were.

To an onlooker it looked like a glorious but deranged celebration of life, but in fact we were drowning our sorrows. A friend and mentor, who had been the driving force behind one of Australia's great surf brands, had been found hanged in his room two days before. The house was burnt to the ground with him in it.

My two friends, George and Muz, and I were comforting his distraught fiancée.

In front of us, on the dry earth below the balcony we were all raving on, a lone cow was tied to a tree. Its eye shone like a diamond as it caught the rising sun. Suddenly I felt appalled. The innocence of this young animal cut through me like a knife. I jumped down to the ground below and walked over to the cow. I held its head in my hand, "I am so sorry. I am so sorry. What have we done to you?" I whispered.

I looked back at the throbbing mass behind me and suddenly the bass and the noise stopped. Silence. What were we doing? Celebrating as if we had won some kind of victory. But what had we achieved?

I held that calf in my arms and cried from the depth of my soul. I was twenty five years old and I thought I was a man.

I had not long before met a beautiful free spirit called Nancy and fallen deeply in love with her. She was a refugee, orphaned at two in the uprising in Czechoslovakia, raised by her brother in Paris. She was wild and free like the wind and we had jumped headlong into our adventure.

But less than six months later she had died in an Indian prison where she had been locked up after being arrested carrying a small amount of cannabis in her backpack into Goa. It had shattered me. I could not bear the idea of her dying all alone. It was my first glimpse of how fragile this beautiful life is, and how easily it loses its light.

And now a man I admired as an inspiration for what I myself was trying to achieve had taken his life out of despair. And I thought I was a man of the world, The Big Man. I cried for the loss of my innocence and the knowledge that the world would never be the beautiful place I had grown up hoping it to be.

As my tears fell on the golden skin of that young animal it looked at me and I could feel its confusion.

"But I'm just a kid." I cried, "We are all just children. What have we done? What have we done to your world? I am so sorry." I untied it and shooed it away. I slumped to the ground at the foot of the tree and cried myself to sleep.

How fast I had run in the scramble to grow up and be a man. How I had shed my youth like a snake its skin, discarding it in my wake. But in that moment I knew I would never have it back.

I longed for the bliss of innocence. I longed to not know what I had come to know. It's terrifying how quickly we want to be done with our innocence and youth. Grow up as fast as we can, ashamed to be kids. Girls wearing make-up at ten, boys smoking fags and looking at porn behind the bike sheds, losing our virginity or feeling ashamed that we haven't, getting drunk in our teens, getting stoned at uni.

Aren't we all so big and clever? Our parents are out of touch, they don't get it, right? How could they understand? They were never our age, were they? The arrogance of it all. To think that we have any idea how the world is or who we are. We become so utterly convinced that we know it all at the grand old age of twenty-five. We know nothing but how to undo ourselves, and we don't even know that we are doing that.

I was done with being the Big Man. It was over. I had no idea what I was going to do next; my whole world had been defined by Mad Rags and the lifestyle it symbolised. And then chance played its hand and dealt me a new set of cards, and I met Merta Ada.

CHAPTER SIX

Rite of Passage

As I said, my meeting with Merta Ada came quite out of the blue, on an ordinary night in Bali. I was all set for a quiet night in, and had my friends passed the cafe just sixty seconds later I would not have gone to see him that night. Some might say it was fate, others perhaps that I probably would have met him sooner or later one way or another. Me, I am not sure that really matters.

But what did matter was that that first meeting was a spark that lit a flame that would light my way on the long journey ahead.

In the early days he made me a small room in the back of his own clothing factory, which later he would transform into his meditation centre and clinic. I had my factory in Java at that time and a small house in Bandung where I lived alone.

I had let my house in Bali go, so whenever I returned, I would plot up in the back of his factory, if we were not travelling around running retreats. I have always said to my students, as he said to me, that continuity of practice is the key to making progress.

In many ways it is like getting fit. We can

meditate so that we can bring the mind to a quiet place, but to develop the penetrative capacity of insight, concentration and direct perception that is necessary to feel the subtle currents running in the background of our lives takes a lot of sustained effort.

It becomes clear that we mostly use our mind to fill in the gaps in our perception with ideas. This is on account of our inability to pay sufficient attention to feel and perceive beyond the mere appearance of things to the energetic processes that are the cause for their appearance. This is what the Buddha called Dependent Origination, the very ground for the arising of things.

Tiyah Balian was clear that if we wanted to truly understand how and why sickness appears in the body we would need to delve a little more deeply than simply looking at how it appears to be, for there is always a causal chain behind anything that comes into being, be it harmonious, beautiful and balanced, or dysfunctional.

So the first years of my training were spent meditating deep into the night. Initially, Ada asked me to use the breath as the object upon which to develop my initial concentration, but once my mind became sharp and bright he asked me to start meditating upon the organs and internal structures of the body.

For three years, I meditated in all my spare time. I would come home from my factory and sit on the porch of my house, and late into the night on the floor beside my bed. I would spend weeks just on my teeth or the bones of my hands, until I could feel every tiny detail.

Initially, I also had a very clear visual impression of my own body internally, but I came to realise that this was a way of attention to be left behind. It was the actual feeling within the body that marked the point of contact between the mind and body, and so ensured that the mind's wholesome qualities impacted the energy of the body in a powerful and constructive way.

I came to learn that the way we perceive things is largely defined by the way in which we pay attention. One of the faculties I had to develop was what we call wise attention, overcoming its opposite of unwise attention. This was one of the most important things I learned.

I recognised how keen the mind is to come to ideas about its experience, and how in doing so we stop short of directly perceiving what is actually there. It was so easy to get lost in an intuitive sense of things rather than allow the gap in perception to remain until it is filled in with concentrated, clear awareness that actually sees, feels and knows.

Most of my training, and most of what I later went on to teach others was to work patiently to develop this combination of concentration, mindfulness and wise attention that leads in stages to what is called clear comprehension or insight knowledge. In essence, the practice of meditation became about allowing this knowing and seeing mind to gradually take the place of this thinking, view-forming, intuitive mind that speculates.

My early days on the cushion were painful. I had not treated my body kindly. Although I only battled with restlessness very early on, and genuinely did delight in sitting, I had to fight with the years of negligence and disrespect I had shown to my body. But clearly it was the effort I had to put forth to sit with this and stick it out when my body was screaming with pain that broke the back of any restlessness and formed the basis of my strong determination to persevere. Gradually the body eased, finally becoming comfortable and later blissfully so.

My mind was becoming bright again for the first time since my school days, but with it, as the vital energies came online more strongly, my body was being transformed. I had always been active, skiing most winters and surfing in my time in Bali, but something other than fitness was developing within me.

I was sleeping only a few hours a night, eating only twice a day, and only light food: fruit and rice. I'd been studying an Indonesia martial art called Silat and Yoga. My body was lithe and supple and the pain I had experienced when I first started meditating was gone.

I had broken my back and neck in separate skiing accidents skiing moguls in my day, and had carried other injuries that initially I thought would prohibit me from sitting effortlessly. But as my concentration developed, I felt the impedance in my nervous system reducing, until gradually I got to the point that I could sit quite effortlessly for two hours or more with no pain. My neck and back remain crooked to this day, but the energy flow through them opened up again and my injuries stopped being a bother.

It was fascinating to watch my mind and body changing over time. Sometime later, I spent five years with a Burmese healer and shaman who taught me alchemy as part of my training. The practice involved slowly tempering base metals so that they transformed from volatile unstable substances, to stable non-toxic ones that could remain solid and stable at temperatures that would even melt gold. It was clear that the process of meditation was bringing about in me a kind of internal alchemy that was transforming my body, perhaps not in such a dramatic, but certainly tangible way.

It always astonished me how, after doing a week or 10 days of intensive practice, taking no real exercise and doing no yoga, my body would be far more supple and flexible afterwards even when I was doing the most regular asana practice. I learned gradually that so much of the pain we experience in our body and nerves is produced by the resistance in our mind that produces and then impedes the currents of life force that flow through us. The clearer the mind, the freer the flow. I think this was one of the most wonderful things of all the many benefits I gained from my practice.

On the way back home from north Bali I asked Ada what he thought I should do next. I had picked up a copy of the Visuddhimagga* at the monastery in Borobudur and asked if he thought I should study it.

"Well, that's pretty heavy going," he said. "You won't be able to just read it straight off. You will have to meditate on it section by section. If you are willing to do that then you certainly should."

The great thing about having total faith in your teacher is that you can surrender your personal will to his guidance.

I now had a mandate for my next endeavour and so I headed off to the tiny island of Gili Nanggu between Lombok and Bali to begin my Visuddhimagga studies.

Access to the island is only by fishing boat from the harbour of Lembar in Lombok. This place felt suitably remote. There was a single hill in the middle of the island on the top of which was a small temple and an annexe with simple but clean quarters for monks. For a small donation I was allowed to plot up there and continue my meditation.

The island was tiny. In twenty minutes you could walk around the whole thing. This I did at sunrise and sunset every day. Apart from this and my midday meal I spent my entire time studying the Abhidhamma and the Visuddhimagga or meditating on it. One hour sitting, one hour study; all day, every day. I drank it up.

Here, in these texts, every question I could imagine was answered, if not explicitly then in meditation upon the texts. My mind was clear and bright now. The fog of my youth had burned off and my Dharma eye was opening. Again there was a familiarity. I soaked it up.

My concentration deepened but for now it was mindfulness and wisdom I was honing as I cycled between one hour study and one hour sitting and reviewing what I had read.

Clear comprehension appeared and my doubts were overcome, and the language of the Visuddhimagga changed from an archaic dialect to the most incisive, direct, and explicit exposition of the way things are.

They say we all know the truth somewhere inside. This is the reason I give for the high number of people who feel it is like waking up out of darkness when they first hear the Dharma. It is either this or they have learned it before and it is like coming home to meet a dear friend.

I knew so deeply there was truth here that was way beyond anything I had heard in my long and expensive education. I was intoxicated with this truth. I had answers to things I longed to understand.

How does this mind work? What produces this body? How do we die and what happens to us when we do? Where do we go and what determines our destination?

All these and many other questions answered themselves in the long hours spent sitting. Not because I was reading the Buddha's explanation of life, but because these processes began to reveal themselves to me directly in my meditation as I unravelled these pithy texts.

Reflection and contemplation are subtle states but deeper by far is the faculty of direct perception or direct knowledge. As the wisdom and concentration faculties of the mind are honed, so its ability to see into things directly appears in stages.

A month later I had almost finished. It was the rainy season and apart from the one family who lived permanently there, the island was deserted.

One evening I was preparing to go back to Bali to join Ada for a retreat that was due to begin. It was raining particularly hard as I walked from my kuti* to the temple to chant Paritta one last time and share merits.

I climbed up the steps to the temple I realised I was out of breath and feeling quite week. I sat and began to chant the Paritta. My head was like lead, my mind fogged and all my bones ached. I battled through the chanting and staggered back to my room. I lay on my bed gasping. It felt like a fever coming on.

I don't remember anything else that night but I awoke in the morning soaked with sweat. I could hardly raise my head off the pillow.

I had no idea what had happened to me. I was exhausted. I had no energy to make the journey home and had rest up for the day. But the next day I was weaker still. I could not hold down food and was fast becoming dehydrated. The fisherman I had arranged to come for me had gone back. There was no one to help me. A month ago I had arrived and felt the bliss of my solitude. I even reflected that I would be happy even to die out here alone. Now I was beginning to wonder whether that might fast become a real possibility. And of course, I was faced with the question, could I really delight enough to surrender to such a fate?

I lay on my cot fighting to maintain a semblance of serenity as I felt the sickness run riot though my body and derange my mind. It was clear that the romantic idea of passing away quietly in a state of peace and bliss and dying of a tropical fever in a state of delirium would be very different experiences.

And it was in that moment I clicked what the Buddha was really trying to teach us. I had read it often enough: "That which is of the nature to arise is of the nature to pass away. Decay is inherent in all compound things." I had always felt that his conclusion that life itself is suffering was somewhat drastic.

I could of course recognise how easily we can turn life into suffering, but I had always personally maintained the conviction that life is truly awesome, and it is up to us to take care of it enough to experience it as such. Since first learning Dharma I had felt that if we could only learn to take care enough of ourselves and others, life could be something far more amazing than even our wildest dreams.

Now here I was, doing what I thought was best. I was following my heart and hopefully was not being an inconvenience to others in the process. Working hard to tidy up a mind that I had allowed in my complacency to become extremely messy and self-absorbed. Doing my bit to try to stop being a burden to others and then...suddenly ...Bang...Out of nowhere...Side-swiped, off my stride, knocked for six.

I was helpless, there was no one I could go to for help. I lay there all day and all night for three, four five days? I can't remember. And in that time, all alone on that tiny island, my own personal paradise, I went through hell and back. In short I was put in front of myself and there was nowhere to hide.

Up to that point I thought that I wanted nothing more than to be left alone to work out my stuff, figure it all out and open myself right up. I thought sitting in temples and monasteries with healers and monks would do it. But no. Alone on a deserted tropical island in rainy season, sicker than I had ever been, that was where I met myself.

I thought my mind was becoming equanimous. I thought I was progressing well in the direction in which the Buddha pointed. I could sit for hours, I wasn't restless, my mind was calm, and I had let go my old life. Surely I couldn't be far from being truly free as he would hope.

But that time in Gili Nanggu, I got it. I saw why the Buddha taught what he did. I had never really experienced hardship. I was one of the rare few who had coasted through life on a wave of good fortune. And of course I had come to assume that life was always like that. Although I had been moved by the suffering I had seen others going through while living in Java, it was all too easy to feel the kind of compassion that can't even begin to imagine it happening to me.

But the Buddha was looking for a solution not just to his predicament, but to the predicament of us all, and that means all those who aren't experiencing any comfort, who have no security of food or shelter, poor companionship and live in a place and time that is full of strife. They would not be able to let go blissfully to the sound of monks chanting or delighting in the sunset over the ocean. And now perhaps, nor might I.

I saw now that the equanimity that frees us from suffering is that which is able to find forbearance, patience and grace in the face of all suffering, as Jesus had done in the moments before his death. I saw that the way out of suffering was a far deeper path than I had bargained for up to that point.

As I lay there exhausted in my bed, the fever, the sickness and wherever it had come from became my real teacher. There was nothing I could do to change it. No comfort I could seek, and no one to take it away. It simply was what it was and I had to be with it. I had no choice but to let go, and to do so without knowing even if I was going to survive.

Now I saw the grace of those who had asked myself and Ada to teach them meditation on their deathbeds, the grace they had found in their passing. I saw how their sickness, and the way it had ended their life, had been their teacher. From it they had learned what otherwise they may have not. I asked myself many times in those days whether I would be able to find such grace were I to find myself in such a position.

Suffice to say, I did make it through, and eventually made it off the Island and back to Bali.

But they were bleak days there all alone. I had been so absorbed with my practice up until then, but sick, exhausted, hungry and alone; I was really put in front of myself.

I reviewed my life in those long wet nights, I thought of Nancy, dying alone in an Indian jail. The pain of it felt unbearable now. I remembered waving goodbye to her at the airport in Bali. The last time I ever saw her. We had come straight from the beach. She was in a sarong with sand in her hair. As I left it felt as if we would be that young and beautiful forever. I thought of Phillip alone in his room that moment before he kicked away the chair. However did he lose his way? I saw how easily I might have lost mine.

It felt almost as if that fever might just be my body casting off the years of excess and indulgence, recklessness and selfishness. I cried for all of us, for Nancy, for Phillip and for myself.

I thought of the Buddha the night he left his home at twenty nine to walk alone on his rite of passage. I know he faced hardships that almost killed him and that it was the passing through the storm that was the making of him.

In those long, lonely nights on Gili Nanggu, I saw the last traces of my childhood and adolescence come to pass. I would have to stand alone on my own two feet from now on. The time for leaning on others was over. It was the beginning of my rite of passage. I could never again pretend that I hadn't seen and come to know the things I had. There would be no hiding from myself any more, and no turning back.

CHAPTER SEVEN

India

Merta Ada had often said to me that he felt it was necessary for me to go to India. He had a strong feeling that much of the knowledge that was now coming to me in this life had been acquired originally in that ancient country. All the time that the Dharma was crystallising in me, a sense of a more hidden knowledge was also coming through in ways I could not easily explain. Whenever I discussed this with Ada he would say he felt it had come from ancient lives in India.

Bali is a Hindu island, the roots of its spirituality originally coming from India and though I resonated deeply with its culture and people it wasn't the religion or spirituality that drew me. I wasn't attracted to India because of its obvious spiritual tradition - it was more a sense of the energy of the place that pulled me.

Ada had said that if ever I taught meditation in India countless people would come to learn. He had wanted to travel there with me, but when the time did come for my first adventure, his commitments in Indonesia meant he was unable to take time out. His own mission had picked up at a tremendous rate and there was clearly a deep spiritual thirst in his own country. It seemed there was little chance for him to travel.

I had a good friend who had been going through something of an epiphany of his own. The last time I was back in England he had called me up while I drove back to London from a retreat I had been teaching. I was in the car on the motorway back from the West Country when he rang.

"Burgs. It's George. Mate, I need to talk. I think I am losing the plot."

"Where are you?" I said,

"In London."

"Can you leave?"

"Yes."

"OK, well I am coming up from Devon. If you leave now we can meet half way. Call me when you get out of town."

"OK, I am on my way."

It was late summer and we met up at Avebury in Wiltshire as the evening drew in. We walked around the ancient circle of stones as he explained to me where he was at.

I first met George during the heady days of Mad Rags. I had a seasonal chalet in Verbier and he had ended up renting a room there for the winter. It was just after New Year and I had come over from Chamonix to check up on things. My brother Grant was in charge there and I hadn't heard anything for nearly a month. He had come to Verbier himself to keep an eye on my operation. By the time I arrived on the scene there was quite a gang of reprobates hanging out in my chalet. I didn't know most of them but it was clear they had made themselves quite at home. I left Chamonix early morning and arrived in Verbier around eleven. The place was a bomb site, bodies everywhere. Empty bottles of booze littered the floor and half the furniture was broken. I rummaged around looking for Grant who it seems had been the only one to make it up that morning. It was a powder day and he had gone off to get some fresh tracks. I decided not to wade in there and then and went skiing myself with my buddy Tom who had come over with me from Chamonix.

That evening, I met up with Grant in the Pub Mont Fort. He had a troop of ski-bum mates with him, many of who now lived in my chalet. They would trawl the bars during après-ski selling my gear. They had quite a scene going and seemed to be selling loads of stuff. The only problem was that almost all of them seemed to be living exclusively from the revenue this provided. So they would pretty much spend all the money they made during après-ski over the course of the night in the bars and clubs around town.

"Well what do you expect?" said Grant when I quizzed him on the proceedings, "You told us to create a scene, to make madness a way of life."

Well, I couldn't really argue with that. It had been the ethos that had shifted container loads of gear already that season. The only problem being that I needed some of the revenue to be coming back in my direction.

Anyway, I surrendered to the situation and went to the shots bar to buy everyone a round of drinks.

"What will it be?" asked the bar man.

"Ten Kamikazes." I replied.

Standing next to me was a dazed looking individual with his head lolling over a row of half a dozen shots of tequila. He was obviously impressed that my order had exceeded his own and lifted his head and nodded at me in a bedraggled kind of way.

"George," he said, offering me his hand.

"Burgs," I replied, taking it.

I carried the drinks back to the waiting posse and saw no more of him that evening. That is, until I got back to the chalet.

It was way late by now and the clubs were turning out. I had told Grant that I wasn't expecting to sleep on the floor in my own chalet and he had assured me there was a room for me.

When we got back there was a frenzied period of a few minutes while everyone vied for beds. Grant had already told them all where I was sleeping and to keep out. He showed me to my room, but the bed was far from empty. Where I was expecting a fresh bed and crisp laundry I was greeted instead by the totally comatose and mostly naked lump that had introduced itself to me as George at the shooters bar.

There was by now no reasoning with him so Grant simply and unceremoniously rolled him off the bed and onto the floor.

"All yours," he said with a wave of his outstretched arm.

The next day George and I skied together and that was the beginning of a long and dear friendship that has lasted to this day.

In the years that followed George had become involved in my clothing label before going his way to start a dance music label with my brother, called Flying Rhino.

When I suddenly announced that I was quitting Mad Rags there was a sense amongst many that I was letting the side down. Our operation had stood for a way of life that had changed attitudes in many places. What I had set out to do in The Alps and along the south coast, George and Grant were doing their way on the festival dance scene. It had been maybe three years since I had quit when George called me that day. I knew immediately he was having something of an epiphany of his own. As we walked around the ancient stones I let him talk.

A friend of ours called Tiger had recently been killed in a car crash on the London embankment. Tiger was one of those special people that everyone loved. He was infuriatingly good looking with a heart as big as an ocean and an intriguing twinkle in his eye. Tiger had time for everyone. He had been part of our gang since the early days of Ski Mania, but had gone into the city a year after leaving Oxford. He was one of those people who you always knew would fly in life. He was earning big bucks and had just bought himself a brand new Porsche. One morning at eight-thirty, he was driving to work. He opened up the throttle to overtake the car in front in the morning rush hour. It was the last thing he ever did. He was twenty-six years old.

George had been in Cape Town where he had been organising parties when he heard the news. He had met up with a friend who told him of Tiger's tragic death. His initial response was a mixture of grief and anger. He got drunk. He found himself sitting before a row of drinks, alone at a bar as he had been when I met him in Verbier. As he looked down at the bar he had a flash of the scene on the embankment, a car crash and the end of a beautiful person's life. He suddenly felt deeply sick in his stomach. Not from the booze. He felt sick with life, disgusted, angry and let down.

He had returned to London to the office of his record label, but something had changed. He felt empty yet overwhelmed, claustrophobic, and suffocated. I remembered my own feeling when I threw my harmonica off the stage in Cowes. I remember the feeling I had when I got news that Nancy had died in an Indian Jail. I was hearing now for the first time of Tiger's death. And I remembered the last words of the Buddha before he died.

"Decay is inherent in all compound things. Work out your own salvation with diligence."

I listened to George's story carefully before replying:

"What do you want to do now?" I asked.

"I need to get away. I need some space, some silence. I need to figure out what this is all about. Where it's all going, what we are doing all this for. I want you to teach me how to meditate."

We sat for a while in silence. Although I had been teaching meditation for a while now, this was the first time one of my friends had asked to learn. Until now most of them had found it hard to come to terms with the changes I had made and the new way of life I was living. I had been in Asia most of the time and came home only occasionally to teach. Most of them still saw me as Burgs whose mission had always been to 'Make Madness a Way of Life.' They were mostly still some years away from settling down and getting married and the party was still on.

"OK." I said. "You want me to teach you meditation? Do you want to learn properly?"

"Yes. I want to learn what you learned. I want to know how you made sense of all this."

"Well," I replied. "I am off to Bali to run a retreat with my teacher Merta Ada in a couple of days. When I am finished why not come to India with me. We can stay there a couple of months and I will teach you what I know."

George had always been easy to mobilise and so the stage was set for my first retreat in India. We parted and went our separate ways. The next time we met was in Delhi.

I flew into Delhi from Jakarta and we met at the Intercontinental: our first and last taste of what luxury India might have on offer.

That evening we discussed plans. We decided to head north towards the mountains and try to find a remote place where we could sit. So we went first to Dharamsala and from there to McLeod Ganj, where the Dalai Lama resided, to find our feet and get a feel for things.

The moment I had stepped out of the airport into the madness of Delhi I fell in love with India. I was intoxicated with the energy of the place; the smells, the sounds, the colour. Ah, this was what I had been missing. From the very first moment I sank so deeply into India that I thought I would never come up for air. For all the impossibility of it, the apparent chaos and even insanity on display all around, there is a timelessness to it that simply melts away all concern for anything but the present.

It seemed to me from the outset, that meditation might simply have been a direct response to what India is at the very core. There would be no other way to live in India than by total surrender. We are so used to being able to exert our will on our life in the west. Not so there. The only way to get anywhere in India is to simply allow oneself to get carried there by the current of things.

I guess somewhere inside I figured this from the outset, for we never really made a plan. We just allowed the country to unfold us.

We befriended a Sikh taxi driver. He was a mountain of a man called Singh. In my wisdom I convinced George that we should let him drive us the twelve hours to Dharamsala. It was a bad move. His taxi broke down two thirds of the way in the middle of the night in a remote area. We slept in the back till daybreak when he walked off in search of a mechanic. They did what they could to patch up his Vintage Ambassador and we limped on a few more hours before finally he gave up his quest. He had shown noble determination but eventually set us down at a bus stand in some village we couldn't even find on our map. He waited with us till our bus set off and smiled hugely as he waved us goodbye.

To this day I have no idea how he ever got his cab back to Delhi but six weeks later when I returned to fly home I looked for him at the Intercontinental and there he was sitting outside the lobby as big and as bearded as the day we had met. And of course he was delighted to see me.

After several changes of bus we made it into McLeod Ganj. We had spent two days doing a journey that should have been twelve hours. We were dusty and happy and checked into a small guest house to take a shower and sleep. Over the next few days we scoured the scene in McLeod Ganj. The Dalai Lama is without doubt the most prolific voice of Buddhism alive today and countless people are drawn there to be close to him. There was a buzz about the place but I knew it wasn't the place for us. We were looking for a quieter backwater for our retreat.

While we were there we visited a couple of meditation centres including one called Tushita, named after the heavenly realm where the Buddha had abided as the Bodhisattva* in his last life before being born in India in 500BC. It was, like much on offer there, a Tibetan influenced place and as we milled about the courtyard, we were approached by a Tibetan nun, who introduced herself as Kundrel. I have no idea what drew her to us but she just approached us directly and asked me if I knew anything about hepatitis. She explained that she had contracted it from drinking poor water on retreat and her health had been failing for some time. It was quite out of the blue and appeared most random.

Anyway, I told her of the meditation I practised and taught and that I had come to India with my friend to teach him. Without the slightest hesitation she asked if she could join us. I smiled to myself remembering what Ada had told me before I came. However did she know that I could teach meditation and why should a nun be approaching a lay person like me? Anyway, providence moves in strange ways and equally without hesitation I agreed. As it turned out she brought us much good fortune for she knew this part of India and it was on her account that we gained access to places we certainly would not have otherwise come to.

For all the progress I had made with meditation I longed to taste the authentic way of the real yogis of India. I had travelled to India with only six sarongs, six white tee-shirts and a copy of a shaolin jacket that my pattern cutter had in my factory in Java and had given to me as a present. His grandfather had been a kung-fu master and I had been learning from him for a while. It was a replica of the jacket he

77

wore.

I wanted to sleep on the earth and wake up with the dawn's cold air. I wanted to be far away from all the quaint little health food restaurants and the tantric yoga classes, from the gap year students with dreadlocks and the bragging about how much hashish folks were bringing out of the Manali Valley. I had the Heart Sutta rolling in my mind. Om Gate Gate Para Gate…beyond, beyond, utterly beyond. I felt myself being pulled as far beyond as I could get.

Kundrel offered to take us to meet the Karmapa's Regent, a renowned monk called Tai Situpa, to ask if he knew any suitably beyond places for our retreat. En route to his monastery we got wind of the passing of a great Tibetan Master who it was alleged had attained the state of Rainbow Body, a name for one of the highest levels of spiritual realisation. Apparently his body had left precious jewels behind after it was cremated and this was considered to be a sign of his high degree of attainment.

His relics were being held at a small monastery called Tashi Jong in the Himachal Province and so we took transport there to investigate. The day we arrived was a special day. All the regular monks had been given holidays and the place was all but deserted. Like most Tibetan monasteries in the area Tashi Jong was a whitewashed collection of buildings built on dry, almost barren land. We walked around for some time before being approached by an old Tibetan who clearly took care of the place. Kundrel spoke to him briefly and he opened a large wooden door for us. It gave entrance to the main shrine room in which the relics of the great Saint were held. Although they weren't actually on display we were invited to sit and meditate and receive the blessing of simply being in their presence. We complied cordially and offered incense. There was energy in the place, but nothing exceptional. Kundrel chanted some mantras and George and I sat. Some time later the gate keeper returned and spoke to Kundrel in Tibetan. She turned to us excitedly,

"Ah we are in luck," she said. "The Abbot is still here. It seems the monks were sent away because today is the day that the young Dzogchen Yogis come down from their six year retreat in the mountains. There are six of them. When they were only seventeen they were picked out for special training. They have all had one teacher each and have been with him since that time practising the secret yogic techniques in the mountains. The Abbot has agreed to meet us. Let us go and pay respect."

We were taken to the Rinpoche's quarters and led in to his room. Butter tea was brought and we were warmly greeted by a solid but radiant man in his late sixties who was the Abbot to Tashi Jong.

"Welcome," he said.

It is the tradition to offer a white silk scarf to the teacher who may or may not thereafter offer it back as a blessing. Kundrel had provided us with such scarves and after bowing and offering them to the Rinpoche he draped them over our heads.

"So I am told you have come to these parts looking for a place to do retreat. Might I ask what your practice is?" he enquired.

I hesitated. I realised that I was not practising according to his tradition and that Kundrel had requested instructions. I wondered if this was a violation of any code. I explained that my friend had wanted to learn from me and that since the basis of my practice had a potent healing application Kundrel had asked if it might be of benefit with her hepatitis. I explained about the old scriptures from Bali and how my teacher Merta Ada was reviving these practices throughout Indonesia.

He seemed genuinely interested.

"So how exactly are you healing the body with this practice? Are you sending Loving Kindness?"

"No," I replied. "We are trying to remove the misinformation that the body has accumulated from the uncontrolled energy of the mind. We see all sickness as misinformation at one level or another. It is basically the body doing something it is not programmed to do, or if you like, something it has become re-programmed to do. From experience we can see that it is not until this misinformation is removed from the system that the body completely recovers."

"Often we see people being treated for conditions with medical drugs that merely work to counter the imbalance from the misinformation but don't go as far as to remove the tendency towards imbalance. That is like having a computer with a virus that causes it to work erratically, and then adding a patch so that it can work around the virus. Obviously it is preferable that the virus is completely removed and the operating system re-booted. Then there is no need for the patch, and likewise with sickness, there is no need to keep taking the medicine."

"So the first thing we have to do is identify where the cause of the sickness lies. This is key. Some sicknesses are caused by imbalances that can simply be addressed with nutrient or medicines. But there are others that are working at a deeper energetic or informational level within the body, producing anomalies of behaviour. Until these are removed the body will not truly recover. This is the case where you see conditions that require ongoing medicinal support. The drugs are not healing the body but keeping a level of balance that allows the body to continue to function. And then there are other sicknesses which no drugs can really turn around. These are the ones where the misinformation is largely coming from the consciousness. There are many people with such diseases that we have successfully helped where drugs could only offer a management regime. Parkinson's, Alzheimer's, Multiple Sclerosis and even some cancers fall into this bracket."

"What is it about these sicknesses that mean meditation can often produce results that medication cannot?" Asked the Abbot.

" Well, you will know from your meditations and investigations upon the body that there are effectively four causes for the different material bases of the body, both gross physical and subtle energetic. These are temperature, nutriment, consciousness and action energy of mind or what we call karma. In order to heal the karmic component of a sickness or disease we need to feel the charge that we are holding in the body around past experiences, i.e. how we have reacted to them. It is our reaction to our experiences that we carry forward with us, not the experiences themselves. These unconscious signatures of anger or craving are playing in the background of our mind incessantly until they are overcome. It has a tremendously debilitating effect upon the body over time.

If we can hold firm the mind and not waver or react when we feel the impression of the old karmic force, be it aversion, craving or ignorance etc, gradually we start to dig out and release the energy of that karma which is causing the disease."

"Very interesting," said the Rinpoche. "This feels like an extension of the practice that we call Vipassana*. It is a part of our practice to purify the mind of its negative states. But it is very interesting how you use it to heal the body. Have you had much success? Can you give me an example of this process at work?"

"Well, take cancer for example," I said. "Many people with cancer come for instruction. Cancer is wild or uncontrolled energy. Now there are hot cancers and cold cancers but always there is uncontrolled energy that causes the cells eventually to divide in an uncontrolled way. Much of the time this uncontrolled energy is coming from our own mind as restlessness, intolerance, agitation etc. The hot energy comes from our anger and aversion and the cold from our greed and attachment. When these factors become excessive we are at a higher risk of developing conditions such as cancer as the subtle energetic base of the body becomes unstable. It works in the same way that a virus does when it corrupts the correct functioning of a computer. If you remove the virus the software will run correctly again. If you take out the interference of the mind the body will start to correct itself."

"Yes I follow," said the Abbot. He sat and reflected on what I had just said. "So simple, and we are already doing it with our mindfulness practices. We just have to direct the energy of the mind more specifically to the sickness. This light that appears in the body is the key. It is a sign produced by the mind when the concentration, mindfulness and wisdom are strong. Once the light appears the mind will have the power to heal the body. But before that there is a danger that the wild energy in the body will actually cause the mind to shake and then there will be no healing and no purification."

"Indeed," I said. "That is why our equanimity is key. It is actually our ability to feel the full force of our sickness with just equanimity and without any attachment or aversion to it that cuts off that force itself. If we care too much, are too attached to our sickness or are too afraid of it, we will not succeed. Equanimity and mindfulness are the keys."

"Very good." He smiled at me. "But you must make sure you train your students in concentration first before they attempt to heal themselves. If they go directly to their sickness before the mind is strong they can do more harm than good."

I reflected on what he was saying. I could see that any wavering in the mind in the place of the sickness was only adding energy to it. He had prompted me to reconsider the preparatory work that was necessary before I taught the main healing practice. It was a theme that I pursued throughout my time in India with George and Kundrel. I had sat Vipassana retreats a few times and even managed them on occasion. There I had felt how the intensity of the practice and effort required to maintain it was often excessive to the point that the heart base of the yogi would shake much of the time.

In this practice we were discouraged from developing deep samadhi for fear we might become intoxicated with the states of serenity it produces, and yet I had felt how the dry approach of going straight into the feeling that arises, however gross it may be, would often be counter-productive if we did not have sufficient mental composure and stability. I had never had the courage to raise this point but the Rinpoche was here echoing a sentiment I had felt myself.

We continued our discussion and became quite involved in the subject. He explained how, in his tradition, complex visualisations of mandalas and Deities were used to stabilise the concentration and help the mind to begin to fathom deep spiritual principles as preparation for the main practice of purification.

We discussed the illusionary nature of the mind, and how the visualisation of mandalas and deities is in truth for the purpose of showing us how the mind is actually almost always lost in illusion and how the fantasy of our individual inner world can bear little resemblance to what is actually going on around us in the manifest world. He explained how we spend our entire lives creating an elaborate idea of ourselves, which in truth serves only to compensate for our inability to apprehend the true nature of things.

I raised the issue that since we are already lost in the elaborations of our inner world, perhaps we are better served learning to develop our concentration and mindfulness on the body to keep us present and connected and avoid the dangers of getting lost in abstract states of consciousness. I made the point that the powerful potential of our mind in meditation to help us maintain a balance in our physical health is amplified considerably if we are applying that mind directly to the body itself rather than an abstract mental object like a mandala or a mantra. It was a stimulating debate and no doubt we could have gone on for hours, but then suddenly there was a knock at the door.

"Excuse me, this will be one of the young yogis who have just finished their retreat. I have asked him to visit me."

The door opened and in walked the young monk. He was only twenty-three years old. His hair hadn't been cut for six years. He looked wild but his eyes shone like diamonds and his skin glowed lustrously. He was a youth in the heat of his prime who had retained his sexual energy since it first reared its head. I stared at him in awe. I felt George doing the same. All the masters I had met had exceeded me in years quite considerably but here before me was a youth who I could feel immediately had taken his practice to levels I had thus far only dreamed of. He was the real deal. I knew it. I could just feel the energy coming off him. It was electric. Yet there was a coolness and poise in him, an aura that filled the room entirely. He came in with a scroll of some kind and knelt before his master. He bowed gracefully three times and spoke softly a few words.

I sensed a kind of pride in the Abbot, such that a father might feel when his son comes home victorious from a great battle. There was a deep unstated understanding between them and much love.

"I haven't seen him since he was seventeen," said the Abbot. "He is one of the most talented young monks, chosen for this intense training. He foregoes all the academic studies that the others go through for the direct experiential approach. He hasn't seen his family or friends or even come down from the mountain for six years."

"His face looks amazing. I can feel the depth of his concentration," I exclaimed. He looked at me and smiled somewhat sheepishly. I felt an instant camaraderie with him. The quest that George and I were on was nothing like his but it was a step in

85

that direction.

As it happened George was also wearing a full head of dreadlocks, and though they were the designer kind and nothing like the matted clumps of hair the young yogi sported, he saw it as a sign. He looked at George, nodded and smiled. His gesture hinted at their common ground and I wondered if perhaps he thought that George had also just returned from six years on the mountain.

The appearance in the room at that time, on that day, of this amazing young man, struck a deep chord in me, and I think George too. We were young, upon the quest for deep meaning and insight. Until now I had had the sense that real wisdom was something that came at the end of a long life's hard work. But now I knew otherwise. There was quite another field of endeavour to be engaged in.

In my naïveté I had felt that my time on Gili Nanggu was real yogic endeavour. For me at that time it had been, but now I knew the score. The mountain this young man had just descended, pulled me like nothing I had ever felt before. It was the pull of seclusion; to ardent and profoundly deep practice. I felt as if I had been practising with a veil in front of me until now. However far I thought I had come, I knew in that moment that there was a depth to this path that I had only ever dreamed of. Once more the fire was lit. We set off from Tashi Jong with a real sense of purpose. We both saw a vision of ourselves in that boy with his diamond eyes and wild face that called to the very depths of our hearts. It was the tamed untamed in him that seemed to embody everything the path had symbolised to me thus far.

So we left Tashi Jong in search of Tai Situpa and

somewhere to do our own austerities and practice.

Sherab Ling is a much bigger monastery by far than Tashi Jong. It is approached by a hair-raising dirt track along one side of a ravine that drops away sheer, to the rocks and riverbed below. There are no rails on the road and it is gravelled and slippery. Our small transport seemed destined to pitch into the abyss a number of times as the driver tore round the corners skidding and sliding as if he were competing in some kind of rally.

I merely gazed into the ravine telling myself. "It is all impermanent. If it's your time it's your time. Just let go."

In truth I had done enough time, travelling around Java in Kamikaze buses, to be able to surrender. We were either going to end up in the mother of all ditches or we were going to meet the Tai Situpa. There was nothing I could do about it. It was written, one way or another. So I made my reflections and left it at that.

The road did appear to go on for ever but in time we arrived at the huge and imposing structure that was home to the venerable teacher and the many young monks who were schooled by him.

There was a far greater sense of ceremony about the place than the monastery we had just left. I noticed this as soon as we arrived by the way we were greeted and escorted, and the way we were introduced to the Master. It was clear this was a bigger deal and yet I had felt an intimacy and connection in our chatting with the Abbot of Tashi Jong that had left a warm glow in me.

The Tai Situpa was a younger man, late fifties, immaculately presented with none of the rugged immediacy of the Rinpoche from Tashi Jong. He was actually a highly revered teacher and his main duty was as regent to the young Karmapa who, at that time, was still in custody within China. He was the holder of many of the teachings that would need to be handed down by transmission to the young Master when eventually he was freed and brought to India. Despite his position, he was most approachable and he discussed with great interest the meditation and healing work I was involved in.

He talked of emptiness and not impermanence as had the Rinpoche, and I began to see that their door to liberation was through the deep understanding of the insubstantial selfless nature of things rather than their inherent transience or impermanence. It was a subtle but hugely significant difference that nuanced the whole of the Tibetan approach to liberation quite differently from the Burmese or Sri Lankan.

The Buddha realised that there are three doors that open to the knowledge of Nibbana*. They are the knowledge of impermanence, suffering, and the selfless - or inherently empty - nature of all things. The Tibetans had hinged their approach on the third of these doors to liberation. From the Buddha's affirmation "Sabbe Dharma Anatta ti" - which means "all conditioned things are void of an inherent self", the Tibetans had developed the insight that sees all things inherently empty and conditionally arisen, and based their approach to the Dharma and meditation on the premise of this emptiness.

Now in essence, these two statements might be construed to be the same but the difference that they would make to the way of approach to the path of knowledge and vision was immense. It was in my discussions with these two great men that I came to see how significant these differences were. It wasn't until some years later when I approached the end of my Vipassana practice that I came to see the point at which these two paths meet.

The meditative experience of emptiness brings us to the direct perception of the clear light essence of pure awareness as the basis of mind. Sometimes called the basic space of phenomena, and elsewhere referred to as Dharmakaya. This is the unmanifest field of pure potentiality from which all conditioned states arise. Knowing this fundamental state of awareness is not the same as coming to know the unconditioned or deathless state of Nibbana. The Tibetan view is not to seek the final attainment of Nibbana as the Buddha had, but urges its followers to remain in the conditioned round of existence for the benefit of others. It is the holding on to the aspiration to serve others and lead them out of suffering that sustains the desire to come to renewed existence, the last desire that is finally relinquished by the Arahant* when he enters the deathless state of Parinibbana*. For as long as there is clinging to any idea of self we will not enter entirely into the unconditioned state, known as Nibbana.

While to forego our own deliverance, that we might serve others, is indeed the highest of all aspirations, it must be known that in doing so we remain bound to the cyclic round of existence with all its inherent perils. I began to sense how we would need to arrive at a very high level of discernment and purification if we were to make such a commitment. Normally this is not a commitment we would make until we had reached the end of the path of purification and the stage of equanimity to all states. As the door to liberation opens to us it is the reflection on the desire to remain for the benefit of others that prompts the aspiration to commit to the path of enlightened service, or the Bodhisattva way.

Our discussions went right into the heart of this profound debate, but beyond this Tai Situpa also had a priceless tip for us:

"Well, if you are looking for a good place to practise I suggest you go to Rewalsar. It is a pilgrimage site for the Sikhs and Hindus, on a lake north of Mandi. But above the town is a mountain on the top of which you will find a special cave. This is where our great Master Padmasambhava* sat in meditation for six years en route to Tibet. It is said that he sat and formulated the way of teaching that has become the foundation of our living system of Dharma today. I feel you and your friend should go there to meditate. Perhaps there is something for you there. There are other caves on the top of the mountain inhabited by a small community of monks and nuns who have lived there since they left Tibet thirty years ago. They are real yogis. Maybe they will have a cave for you. Normally visitors can only stay in the town for a day. Access to the top of the mountain is restricted, but if you have karma you will find a way. You should first go to see the Abbot at the monastery in Isa. Tell him I sent you."

Wow. Now that was a proper tip. I knew immediately that this was our place.

We stayed the night and left after breakfast. I had learned something of real value from Tai Situpa that would serve me well as a teacher in years to come. I saw how the timely giving of the slightest of prompts, if done in the right way, could open the student up to vast and previously untapped territory. The suggestion to go to Rewalsar had come from a deep place of insight and vision in him. I knew he knew why he was sending us there even if we didn't yet. Tai Situpa didn't have time to reignite in me the flame of ancient knowledge that had lain buried behind the fog of my youth and the mistakes I had made in recent past lives. But he did know that this process was just waiting to happen. He merely pointed me in the right direction.

And in doing so he served me far more than if he had invited me to stay and learn from him. He passed me on down the line to the source to find out for myself if I had the key to the treasure trove.

There was a stirring in me that had begun when I first arrived in India. It began with a sense of connection and a knowing that we were just being led along the line of our destiny. I had never doubted that we would end up where we needed to be even if I had no idea where that was. I had simply come to India asking to be shown what it meant to me. Over the days that followed, I felt energy moving in me in new and extraordinary ways. Physically I felt charged, electric. I had been to receive initiations in Chi Kung from a Shaolin Master a few years back. It had left my body buzzing with energy, but this new charge was just rising up from my core and rushing and fizzing through me day and night. New knowledge was coming to me constantly, an ever deeper understanding of things that I could not even express. The way of energy, consciousness, and karma, hinting at an order of things that governed our world and everything in it at the profoundest level. I even began to sense how these laws affected its unfolding at an even deeper way than the scriptures and teachings may suggest.

I began to feel myself being plugged into that deeper place and given direct access. It was like a drip feed that never stopped. I was in meditation almost all day long. I remember discussing emptiness with Kundrel as we drove from Sherab Ling to Rewalsar. As I gazed out of the window of our car suddenly I could see it in everything around me. The solid trunks of trees breaking down into nothing but tiny particles, fizzing and popping into being and always and everywhere arising from and passing away, back into emptiness. And I was empty too. Yes, finally I was really getting it.

That was the heart's longing; to enter into that emptiness. What an extraordinary paradox; that what we think we are looking for is to fill our lives with all kinds of conditioned things, becoming bound up with clinging to them and the fear of their loss, when what we really yearn for is to be free of that very bondage and the weight of carrying all that we cling to. It is the longing to just rest within that emptiness while allowing things to come into being naturally from within it. I really could see what my mind had told me a thousand times. It was through clinging to things that can't be held onto that we suffer. When we allow them to just come into being without grasping, and relinquish all need to label things as belonging to us, then they are no longer a cause of affliction. We are all going to be separated from everything that is dear to us in time. If we could utterly accept that from the outset then it wouldn't be such a cause for dismay and misery. Our sense of loss with the parting of things becomes a deep sense of gratitude and appreciation for the fact that they came into being at all.

The flavour of my meditation began to change too. From the intensity of seeing the impermanence of all things, to the effortless abiding in their inherent emptiness. It was a deep shift in awareness that in stages began to melt away the perception that there was actually anything to be done. Instead of the feeling of needing to strive through strong effort there was emerging a simple recognition of the need to surrender to the way of things and reach a point of acceptance. I knew that the peace I sought would be born of this deep acceptance.

I began to glimpse intelligence at work in the life process that was way beyond the grasp of our concrete mind. Through reviewing the transience of things in my previous practice of Vipassana, and from it the reflection that clinging to anything in the face of such impermanence was the sure way to suffering, a degree of equanimity had arisen that left me much less attached to outcome and ideas. It had stilled my mind tremendously from the wild days of my youth, but it had still left it active and searching for meaning beyond that. And so knowledge had come to me by way of enquiry, reflection and intuition, through meditation and discussion with my Masters. But now my mind began to still itself completely and out of the stillness a deeper current of knowledge began to emerge. Beyond the mind-produced states which I had investigated thus far in my meditation, this was a complete and direct knowledge that seemed to be being downloaded directly into the mainframe of my being.

When finally we arrived in Isa I was already in a deep state of samadhi. I was quite unable to emerge from it and so suggested to George that we check directly into the nearest guest house. Kundrel went off to seek lodgings at the monastery and make enquiries on our behalf about access to the mountain top.

The next day she appeared at our guest house with news. The Abbot of the local monastery had said that no one was allowed on top of the mountain but when she told him that Tai Situpa himself had sent us he became interested enough to request me to visit him. I left George and went with Kundrel to meet him.

"Do you know why Tai Situpa has sent you to this place?" he asked.

"I have no idea except that I told him we were seeking a secluded and remote spot to do our retreat. He told me of the community of hermits on top of the mountain and suggested we look there for a suitable place."

"Those yogis have been there for many, many years, even we from the monastery down here rarely visit or disturb them."

But he continued to quiz me all the time looking deeply into me as if trying to figure just why we had come.

He ordered tea for us and sat in meditation for some minutes while we drank. Eventually he stirred.

"Far be it for me to question the wisdom of Tai Situpa. Perhaps he has seen something I have missed. You will need to get special permission from the Chief of Police in Mandi if you are going to stay here for some time. If he grants you such permission then I will offer you a retreat space half way up the mountain. There are four rooms there which are used for long retreats. Right now there are just two monks up there on a year-long retreat, leaving two spare rooms. You will have to cook for yourselves and carry up water unless you wish to come down daily for food. But if this place is to your liking I will offer it to you. Tenzing Kundrel will have to lodge down here at the monastery as it is not appropriate for her to stay with men. But first you must get a letter from the Police in Mandi. That I cannot help you with."

Again, I could not fully understand why we were being helped so much. I assumed it was largely on Kundrel's account, but it remained a fact that here I was practising and teaching meditation from a tradition quite separate from theirs and yet we were being helped in our quest in every way.

I thanked the Abbot deeply, and assured him we would make every effort to get the permission we needed.

That afternoon George and I took a bus to Mandi some two hours away and made our way to the police station.

When eventually we did gain access to the Chief we were not greeted with the warmth we had grown accustomed to.

"You cannot stay up there," he said. "It is out of bounds to tourists. I can't help you. The best I can do is give you a permit to stay in the town by the lake for two weeks."

I looked at George. It was our first disappointment so far.

"What do you reckon?" he asked me.

"Well we could start that way and see if in time we can't sneak up the mountain."

"But what will we tell the Abbot? He will need to see a letter of approval before he lets us use his retreat rooms."

Whilst we pondered our options the Chief began to discuss other things with us.

"My brother is trying to set up a parapente school in the mountains up north. Do you know anything about parapenting? I know it is very popular in Europe. We are trying to find a way to get the parachutes here from abroad. Do you have any suggestions?"

George looked at me excitedly.

"You know Jim Mallinson?"

"Of course I do."

He was a close friend of ours who had studied Sanskrit at Oxford and now lived half the year amongst the Sadhus* researching various esoteric practices for a PhD he was working on. He also happened to be a very talented parapenter and a member of the British team.

"Genius!" I said. "Of course. He is probably out here now."

"No, he is back home in England but I bet he can help. He spends months out here parapenting every year," said George.

George recounted the story of our friend and his parapenting escapades in the Himalayas.

"Wonderful," interrupted the Chief of Police, "do you think you might ask him if he can help my brother?"

"Better than that," replied George "Why don't I call him right now?"

"Excellent idea" said the Chief. "You can use my phone."

And so we called Jim right there and then and put him onto the Chief who brokered a deal to bring his chutes into India. With this the parapenting branch of India's tour

ist industry was born and the way to the

mountain top was opened for us.

The Chief put down the phone with a huge grin.

"So tell me. How long were you planning to stay?"

"We wanted to do our retreat for six weeks."

"I can't see that being a problem."

He called in his secretary and dictated a letter requesting the local police in Rewalsar to grant us permission to stay for the duration of our retreat.

That evening we stood before a surprised Abbot back at the monastery:

"Well it does indeed seem you have friends in high places. Either that or the gods are on your side. Whichever one it is, who am I to stand in your way? Your motive is good and I must support anyone who seeks to develop their practice and understanding of Dharma. If you come back in the morning I will have you escorted to where you can stay."

Friends in high places, I mused. I was beginning to wonder just how high those places might be.

We dined well that night on curry and dhal and indulged ourselves one last time before beginning our austerities.

CHAPTER EIGHT

Amongst Hermits and Gods

In the cool of the morning just after dawn we carried our few possessions the three miles or so up the mountain to the site we had been offered for retreat. On a ledge half way up were four concrete rooms built into the rock. It was as simple as it could be. No glass in the windows and no doors, with dry dirt for a floor, it was perfect. The view to the lake down below and across to the plains beyond was spellbinding and the sense of expansiveness that opened out before us breathtaking. Finally we had arrived.

We spent the day sweeping and cleaning and walking back to the village to buy the few things we would need: a small stove, drapes for the windows and doors, and bedrolls and blankets for sleeping. We built a small shrine and lit incense as I chanted the Paritta and invited the surrounding devas* to join us and watch over us.

As the sun began to set our two companions and fellow retreatants returned from the forest where they had spent the day in meditation. They were both Tibetan and in their early thirties. They had been on the hill for six months and were half way through their sojourn. They greeted us warmly with gestures and smiles, unable to communicate in tongues, and we immediately developed an understanding and camaraderie rooted in our common goals. That night they offered us meat momos, which we accepted for the first and last time. Their meat was old and tough and quickly reaffirmed our determination to keep a vegetarian diet.

We lit a fire and they smoked cheroots before we each retired in silence to our rooms.

That night I slept deeply and dreamed of ancient times spent in places such as this on similar quests for knowledge and vision.

At four o'clock I was awoken to the sound of music wafting in from the Sikh temple across the valley. My first response was one of joy; to be awoken in this way to the sounds of the devotional practices of others. I sat and began my meditation with the music as accompaniment. But by midday when we stopped to prepare food the music still played. By now it no longer appeared so blissfully devotional but had begun to sound like a blaring racket pumping out from the most primitive of sound systems. It was the beginning of a festival that would go on for days. And all day long we observed car and bus-loads of pilgrims coming and going, each with their own tunes to play. It was like karaoke. By the end of the second day we had started to recognise many of the songs despite the wet tissue paper plugging our ears. Though we laughed I began to suspect that we would need more silence than this if George was to get established in concentration.

The Tibetans seemed immune to the music, which was clearly a testimony to their own samadhi, but George was having trouble. It seemed we hadn't yet found our Shangri-La.

"What do you reckon?" I asked him

"Well it's a bit of a racket, I have to say," he replied.

We persevered for two more days with Kundrel joining us after breakfast and returning to the village at sunset. Then, as we sat in the evening of the fourth day, I had an idea.

"Listen," I said, "We have our permission now. What say we hike to the top and see if we can't find somewhere to stay amongst the hermits?"

So we agreed. The next morning we left most of our stuff behind and followed the trail to the top.

It was another world entirely up there. Huge outcrops of rock with hundreds of prayer flags strung between them blowing gently and mysteriously in the wind. Though there was no one to be seen there were signs of life here and there. Pots left on wood fires, wooden doors marking the entrances to numerous caves and a single Chai shop a hundred metres away back down the track that had led us there.

We sat on stools at a table outside and rested, taking in the scene around us. After some time a wiry Indian man appeared and smiled at us.

"Good morning gentlemen," he said. "Can I get you some tea?"

He went inside and presently returned with a large iron teapot steaming with hot Chai. It was spicy and sweet and we drank it gladly.

"I am Channa," he said. "So what brings you two up here? We don't see many tourists you know."

His English, like so many Indians was quite refined and his grammar good. It seemed that our colonial legacy still held its influence on the land, even in parts as remote as this.

"We have come here to meditate," I said.

"Have you indeed?" he replied. "Well it's a good spot for it from what I hear. Apparently a great saint came here many centuries ago. I think that is why there are so many Tibetans living in these caves. But how did you come to find this place?"

"Let's just say that providence has its way," I replied.

"Well then," he said, "where do you think you will sleep?"

"We haven't got that far," said George. "Just prospecting at this stage."

"I know all the caves are occupied. These people have been here for many years and whenever one dies another is always in line to take his place. But there might be one chance for you. Do you see that building down there?"

He pointed down the valley in the opposite direction to the one we had come from.

"That is a cowshed. It was built last spring by a farmer from these parts, but his cow died before he finished it. That might do you. Would you like me to enquire about it?"

A cowshed. How wonderful. We really were going to be ascetics. I smiled at the thought.

"That would be kind of you."

"Don't mention it," he replied. "Besides, you will need feeding and that can only be good for me, right?"

We all laughed.

We ate pakoras and rice pudding and he took us down to inspect the building that was to become our home. It was basic indeed. It was not yet finished and the floor was little more than rubble.

But it had a flat roof that would be ideal for morning yoga and the view down the back side of the mountain was spectacular.

Channa pointed to a small building on a ridge a mile or so away.

"Those are your neighbours. Goatherds. They come this way now and again but they won't bother you. The water comes from a well half way towards their place. You will need to ask them permission to draw water for bathing. I can see to that too if you like."

And so the stage was set. The farmer agreed to lend us his shed for a month for the equivalent of ten pounds and Channa provided the meals we requested. We brought our things up from the mid-station and finally our retreat began in earnest.

George and I would rise at dawn and sit for an hour or so before doing yoga on the roof in the first heat of the day. Kundrel engaged the services of a local tractor driver who brought her half way up each day. She walked the rest.

There was little to disturb us, but whatever internal distractions we could dig up, and pretty soon our practice was steady and rhythmic.

I began by teaching George anapana*, a meditation practice that observes the rising and passing of the in- and out-breath as a means to establish concentration and mindfulness. It is particularly suited to those of a restless temperament and it eased him into the rigours of sustained practice.

Our bodies became tempered and supple and our complexions glowed more each day. We were happy and had few wants. I explained to him the workings of the mind and how our body arises dependent on karma, consciousness, nutriment and temperature. He worked hard and within two weeks the three of us were sitting long hours every day.

I also checked Kundrel for the cause of her hepatitis and explained that there was a risk of cirrhosis developing. She was a kind and compassionate woman but she worried much and was prone to overexertion. It was born of a fear that she might not be able to reach her goal of Nibbana and so I had to explain that her fear was the biggest obstacle in her way. Her mind was made stiff by her sense of duty and it was this stiffness that was hardening her liver. She understood, but it was a real battle for her to let go and relax despite her long years of training. She could sit for hours with apparent ease, but, whenever I checked her meditation, her mindfulness and concentration were held up by determination and effort and not the energy that comes effortlessly from real tranquillity.

So I began to teach her samatha* meditation and the serenity practices, and asked her not to push herself so hard. While laziness is a hindrance in many, the tendency to overexertion is the main obstacle for others. She needed to dissolve her blockages, not smash them with a hammer.

After a few days of following the instructions I had given her to heal her hepatitis, she presented me one morning with a photocopied manuscript.

"I think you should read this," she said. "I came here from Burma where I spent six months at this Master's monastery. Listening to what you say, your explanations of the Dharma and how we should meditate are so similar to his. His technique is very hard. You have to meditate inside the body of all the other monks or nuns until you can see clearly internally and externally with the light of your mind. He calls this the light of wisdom. But the problem is that it only appears when you attain jhana* concentration. It was too hard for me. I didn't have paramis* enough to get my jhana so I left after six months."

Jhana is the Pali word denoting the deep state of absorption samadhi* where the mind finally becomes one pointed and enters completely into the experience of its object. It is a unique state of consciousness, unlike any we previously experience in our waking or even sleeping life. It causes the mind to function in a totally new way and as such the first time a yogi attains jhana is called the 'change of lineage consciousness'. This is because the karmic seed of this jhana consciousness is potent enough to launch one into renewed existence in the Brahma realms at the end of the life.

In Indian yoga the jhanas had been the milestone by which attainment was measured for centuries and all efforts were put forth to attain higher and higher plane existence in the next life. This was one of the key factors that the Buddha had recognised to be unsatisfactory because even the most exalted life comes to an end and the one following will be unsure. Many were the woeful tales of those who had fallen from grace on account of complacency having attained these dizzy spiritual heights. I came, over time, to realise that mine was also such a tale.

I read Sayadaw's* text avidly.

"Hey," I naively said when I had finished. "Where does he get all this from?" He was teaching the detailed way of meditation as expounded in the

Visuddhimagga. The Visuddhimagga is the magnum opus of meditation manuals. It was composed in the third century by an extraordinary monk called Buddhaghosa, and it is a detailed explanation of the entire path and practice taught by the Buddha. From the first steps in establishing the conditions for success to the final attainment of Nibbana, it meticulously explains every step. Nothing comparable has ever been written and the best that modern scholars have managed is to commentate on it.

However, it has been argued in recent times that the actual practice described was beyond the scope of most monks and certainly most lay yogis. In particular it was considered that attaining the absorption samadhi prior to beginning what is now popularly called Vipassana, or insight meditation, and the depth to which one is expected to meditate on material and mental forms would to be too challenging for most yogis.

The argument for the development of samadhi prior to Vipassana is that until we have developed deep and stable states of concentration we will not be able to clearly discern reality as it is, leaving us to unravel it at a conceptual level.

The argument for beginning directly the practice of Vipassana without developing samadhi is that it may be more important to purify the mind than establish deep states of concentration and serenity. It was on this account that in the 1950s a famous Burmese monk called Ledi Sayadaw first started to teach the modern practice of Dry Vipassana. In this practice the yogi attains what concentration he can and then proceeds directly to the analysis of mind and matter, reviewing these formations as impermanent without going so far as to break them down into their ultimate basis. The debate continues.

Dry Vipassana is the basis of the now popular practice of S. N. Goenka, a former businessman who was forced to retire on account of severe headaches. He became a lay yogi and learned meditation from a Burmese teacher called U Ba Khin. So impressed by the way in which his previously unbearable headaches had been cured by meditation, he travelled back to India to teach. But not for 500 years had there been in Burma a teacher who had mastered and could teach the detailed and exhaustive path to Nibbana according to the Visuddhimagga. So the appearance of Pa Auk Sayadaw created quite a stir.

In his text Sayadaw explained the process to train the mind to view phenomena internally and externally, and how to develop the jhanas on subtle material and mental objects. Until now I had assumed that the healing meditation practice I had learned from Ada had been an ancient Indonesian practice. The basis for the practice had come from an ancient text written on banana leaf and kept in a museum in Bali. The key was this:

"Meditate on your body until the light appears. When the light appears go through the light and feel there with concentration, mindfulness and wisdom. If you continue to meditate through the light, all sickness will disappear."

Most of what I was currently teaching was to elucidate this point by explaining what was the source of the light referred to and the way it arises within our meditation practice. On my retreats I initially focused on teaching the practice that led to such healing.

Merta Ada had told me the story of Anku Puturan, the famous ascetic who had brought the Hindu/Buddhist fusion Dharma to Bali a thousand years ago. We had always considered him to be our teacher, for he had first taught healing meditation to win the hearts of the people of Bali ten centuries ago. The inspiration they had got from being able to heal their ailments through mind training was the hook that allowed Anku Puturan to persuade them to transform their shamanic and animist religious practices into an approach that encompassed the wider scope of the Buddha's teachings on dependent origination and Karma.

I had never stopped to think beyond that, but of course this was all Dharma. Dharma after all means 'the way of things' and this deep process that governed our lives at unseen levels was of course the very fabric of the way of things. These teachings originally all come from the Buddha himself. Sayadaw was teaching the practice to purify the mind of its attachment and clinging but not to heal the body. By growing tired of clinging to the conditioned experiences of the world in which we live, eventually our mind comes to incline towards the unconditioned state that lies beyond. Through seeing the unconditioned state of Nibbana one finally turns away from clinging to forms and is no longer bound by them. This is the final attainment and the liberation the Buddha taught, beyond which there is no higher attainment. Of course, Sayadaw had no interest in healing but as I read his manuscript I could see clearly how the slightest of reapplications of his technique would heal all the sickness in the body.

In Bali we had not taught such deep concentration and our students had had extraordinary results. Imagine if we taught them deep samadhi as well. I began to see how Ada and I were able to feel and see so clearly internally and externally. Even though I had never practised this technique in this life I felt that this was the way I was doing it. As I read Sayadaw's book I knew that I had done these practices before. I knew I could do it again if I went to him. I knew Burma would be my next destination.

As the days passed Kundrel's furrowed brow grew smooth and her eyes began to shine. She was feeling better and the pain in her liver was receding. After a couple of weeks she told me that she would have to return to Dharamsala for a few days to report to her teacher who was due back from a tour of duty. It was her intention to return as soon as she could.

She took her leave with a polite bow and George and I were left to continue alone for a while.

CHAPTER NINE

The Shaman's Fire

There was a brotherhood between George and I that had been there since our meeting in Verbier. It could not have been easy for him to get beyond our familiar relationship and accept me as a teacher, but that he was able to do so with such ease was a testimony to his character. He was humble and gracious when seeking advice and his mind was thirsty for knowledge. He must often have wondered where I was digging it all up from, since for years he had known me as his partner in crime and revelry. We shared our sense of mischief and adventure and it brought colour and joy to our time together in India. We spent nights out on the mountain around fires and often wandered far and wide in search of shady groves and power spots at which to meditate.

During this time I reflected upon how Anku Puturan had taught healing to inspire people to practice meditation and restrain their conduct. George was a healthy young man, he didn't need healing at a physical level. I came to realise that what he yearned for as much as anything was a glimpse of the world that lay beyond the appearance of things. I could see that the lack of knowledge and understanding of this world that lies beyond the veil of appearances was part of the cause for the growing thirst for Shamanic teachings in recent times. In particular there was a growing interest in the visionary plant medicine Ayahuasca.

The processes by which we may gain access to the subtle fields of experience are many, and I had spent much time investigating shamanism in my early days as a yogi. In the end I personally felt that the gradual and systematic access to subtler fields of perception that meditation brought, although perhaps taking more patience and time to develop, led to a more integrated experience of these fields and a clearer understanding of their inter-connectedness with our own physical reality and our perception of it.

But equally I had great respect for what I had learned during my time living with the Ojibawa Shaman who had mentored me in my early days. I felt that the timely sharing of some of these experiences may help some to find a conviction in the benefits of practising meditation.

George had always been drawn to the more shamanic way, and during our time on the mountain I taught him many of the things I had learned along my way, including some of those shamanic practices.

I remember one night of a full moon; we walked to the ridge on the far side of our valley to camp out. He had asked me many times about the vision questing I had done with my shaman friend and early mentor. We spent the evening collecting wood and settled down around our fire as the sun set. I told him of the energies of the four directions and the four great elements and I invited them in through the fire one by one.

He sat beside me as I meditated on them in turn and we watched the flames turn with each new arrival. After some hours he asked if he could sit in my place.

"How come you get to sit there all the time? All the energy is coming in through you. Can I sit there for a while?"

"OK, sure. As long as you collect more wood first. You have a proper sleeping bag and mine is little more than a sheet. I will get cold as soon as I move away unless the fire is good and strong."

He disappeared into the darkness and left me alone to meditate. There was much energy around that night and some of it needed taming on its way in. I chanted Metta and gave a discourse on dependent origination to calm the more restless spirits around.

Suddenly George reappeared in something of a fluster.

"I am sure there is something out there," he said. "I felt as if it was following me around and I could hear something moving in the bushes."

I teased him as he restocked the fire and then made way for him to take my place.

I left him to sit in silence and make his own connection. I lay down close to the fire and slept for a while. I awoke before dawn with the first traces of pink in the sky. I was freezing. The fire was almost out and George was clearly in some kind of a trance. Fire can be quite hypnotic. I added some more wood and blew it back into life. Then as I did so there was a sudden and strange rushing of wind right through the heart of the fire. It came in from the South and left to the North in the direction

George was sitting in. I felt the energy of it pass right through him. The flames lay flat for a few seconds as the air passed swiftly over them, and as suddenly as it had arrived, it was gone.

"Wow!" I said, "Did you feel that?" That was a powerful earthbound spirit passing through."

"What? Is that a problem?" he said, rather startled by what had just happened.

"No. It has been happening all night. That's why I was sitting where you are now. But since you asked, I thought I'd let you hold the energy for a while. How do you feel?"

"I don't know. I feel a bit strange but OK. I got really deep earlier. I think I was out there for a while."

"You were indeed. You can't let your mindfulness go when you are holding the space," I said.

"Oh no," he said. "Do you think I picked up something?"

"You will find out soon enough."

I could feel the being around him but it wasn't troublesome so I left him with it. It would give him an insight into the nature of the subtle realms and their inhabitants.

We sat on the ridge and watched the sunrise before walking back to our shed for a wash. That morning we sat in our room and meditated together as usual.

After an hour or so I took rest and expected George to do so too. When I checked in to see how his meditation was going I could feel the being from the fire standing behind him and stooping over him. It seemed to be holding him in some kind of altered state.

George was breathing very deeply and after a while began to moan very quietly as if his voice was coming through from a distant place. I checked his mind and heart and they were quite in order so I let him be for a while longer to see what would happen. As it turned out he remained in that state for over an hour before quite suddenly I felt the being leave him. He took a deep breath and gasped and in an instant he emerged from his trance.

"How was that?" I asked.

He sat with his head in his hands.

"Wow, what was that all about?" he exclaimed.

"Well I think you had a friend come and show you a thing or two. Anything interesting?"

"Interesting? That was madder than any acid trip I have ever been on."

I left him to gather himself and went out to cut some mangoes. When I came in he was still sitting there. He wasn't in shock for I could feel his body rhythm was quite calm, but he was clearly moved by what had happened.

"It was amazing. I have never experienced anything like that before," he said. "This meditation is powerful stuff."

"What did you see?"

"It was so awesome. I felt this being like a giant bird standing behind me. It wrapped its wing feathers around my face and covered my eyes and then just started to show me things. Like I was watching a movie about myself. My family one by one, who they really were, how I knew them, and what was the real nature of our relationship in this life. It was amazing. I could see why my sister got cancer, and why I fight with my Dad. Like all the parts of a jigsaw put into place for me so I could see the picture they portrayed. It was amazing."

"Well it sounds like you got the cookies in the end last night. This was one of the beings that came in through the fire."

"That's so mad. I always thought that stuff was just rubbish, just a New Age fad. I assumed that if people had visions they were just imagination."

"Well, perhaps now you will reconsider your opinion. Besides these are not New Age practices. The Shamans of old have done it since the beginning of time. That was their way of connecting to a higher intelligence. Things like the fire work we did last night were the bridge they used instead of meditation. But you have to understand that it is not the ritual itself that produces the results but the concentration and mindfulness we do it with."

Once George had gathered himself again we walked up to Channa's Chai shop for breakfast. We were starving and devoured his offerings with relish while recounting to him our adventures.

"Oh my dear," he exclaimed. "You crazy, crazy fellows. You could have been eaten alive. Did you not know there are leopards on that hill? It is so dangerous. A few of the farmers have been killed over the years. You are lucky to be alive."

We both burst out laughing.

"So that's what you thought was following you around while you collected the wood."

"Phew. I knew there was something out there."

"I reckon the spirit and the fire would always keep wild beasts at bay. Some of what came in through the fire was far fiercer than any leopard." I said.

"Maybe, but they aren't going to eat you are they?" he scoffed.

"Anyway. You are still alive," said Channa. "And a good thing too. You will be needing my services for a while longer it seems."

CHAPTER TEN

Maha Guru; Maha Shaman

Padmasambhava was an extraordinary being at every level. To the Tibetans he was the second Buddha, the Great Sage who brought the Dharma to the snow plains and taught it to the wild people who had for centuries worshipped spirits and followed a more animist religion. Around the same time that Anku Puturan had travelled south east from India to Sumatra and Java, Padmasambhava had travelled north. Although they encountered similarly animist and shamanic cultures full of occult practices and magic they approached them very differently. While Anku Puturan taught healing through meditation as a way to inspire the people he encountered, Padmasambhava showed his hand as the Master Shaman. He tamed the wild lands of Tibet, with its pantheon of troublesome spirits and magicians and inspired its people by teaching them the Dharma within the context of their more animist vision of life.

It is hard for us to understand fully the significance of this extraordinary man, as so many of the tales of his life are written in the kind of epic language that might lead us to believe he was a purely mythical being. But behind the fables and folklore he lived the life of a yogi as many others had. He practised deeply and in solitude for many years in India before travelling to Tibet with the teachings.

George and I explored many things during our time on the mountain while practising our meditation but the greatest adventure of all was the giant underground cave that had been the spot where Padmasambhava had sat in long retreat a thousand years ago, before his epic journey that would change forever the people of Tibet.

His cave was the reason that the community of Tibetans that lived up on the mountain now had originally congregated there. Its entrance was through a temple that they had built in his honour.

The energy around the cave was very powerful. The first time we walked up to it I remember George having to come back because he found it made him dizzy. Over the time we spent there we ventured into the cave on a number of occasions. I knew that George was sensitive so we never actually sat for a long time there, but a few days after he left to go back to England I went there alone. I wanted to investigate for myself and see if I could connect with this famous master.

I went in just before dark one evening and crawled through the low passageway that opened onto the main chamber. Inside, the ceiling rose to a height of some forty feet or so and the whole space was dominated by an imposing statue of Padmasambhava. I had been drawn towards him from the first time I had seen his picture on a postcard that Kundrel had shown me, and now felt a strong desire to tune in to him.

I put my blanket on the stone floor, sat down and began my meditation.

The cave was cool and utterly still. The stillness sucked me in and within a matter of minutes I was gone. Gone was the cave, the statue, and any sense of time or where I was. There was just this total stillness. Even the coolness was gone. I entered into my meditation through loving kindness, not knowing what other way to approach. But after a while I surrendered even the loving kindness to the stillness.

And then after some time the stillness became a totally clear transparency of pure light, but a light that appeared to have no essence to it. Always before in my meditation there had been light, and I had come to know that this light was produced by the mind as it approached samadhi. Yet this light appeared now to just simply be there, as if it had been there all the time without me recognising it. Now as I recognised it, it held me totally. My mind was aware but resting on nothing. It appeared almost to be breaking the rules of consciousness for I was aware without taking anything as the object of my awareness. There was just an empty awareness beyond any sense of me. I was just suspended in this transparent luminosity.

Then slowly I felt myself expand upwards. I felt elevated but still immersed in the light. Then suddenly he began to appear, emerging from the very heart of the clarity before me. I knew immediately it was him, as if I had been expecting him to appear all along. Yet I hadn't at any point had the idea to actually meditate on him. I had simply begun my meditation by tuning into the stillness of the cave.

His eyes emerged from the formlessness before

me, deep, staring and hypnotising, and around them his face began to form. I was staring face to face with him as his huge body materialised. He held me with his mind, right between my eyes, and shot a beam straight through my brain. I felt a click and a pop inside my head as if he had just performed some kind of operation. And I suddenly felt a familiarity with this Padmasambhava. I could see him sitting in this cave a thousand years before. I felt his mind as he reviewed his meditation and the task before him. I felt him formulate his way and come to his conclusions. It was like a holographic download. Not linear in nature but multi-dimensional. And it came in at such a deep level that it almost felt like a genetic implant. It resonated through all aspects of my being from the deepest states of my meditation to my very flesh and bone. I was held by him, dismantled by him and poured into his being, merged with him and completely reconfigured by him. I felt the qualities of his mind, even his temperament, and saw why he did what he did and how he did it. I watched as he reviewed the minds of those to be taught and I saw their minds too, and he showed me how he tamed them and how he would teach them Dharma.

Then suddenly he shot three beams of light into me with three symbols and syllables connected to them. Through these three beams he rewired me, opening channels and adjusting my energy. The three syllables came to life as living expressions of truth at a level so far beyond concrete understanding; deep reflections of universal principles governing the way of things at the most fundamental level. And in doing so it brought perspective and clarity and understanding to all of the knowledge I had received so far. It filed itself within me in perfect order, referenced and cross-referenced, completing a picture that finally revealed to me the way of things, their coming into being and their passing away. The creative process itself, revealed in all its simplicity and all its wonder in these three symbols alone.

Om Ah Hum

There was nothing else, nothing beyond this, nothing apart from this, except the final cessation of all things.

I have no idea how long he held me in this suspended state. Gradually and systematically he withdrew the lines of energy between him and me, and the same way he had appeared, he began to fade, until I was left only with his blazing eyes and then the clear, transparent stillness and then eventually the coolness and again my body sitting in the cave in front of his statue.

I just sat there in a stunned silence trying to grasp what had just happened to me. This was something so far beyond a visitation from another being. Such things had happened almost from the onset of my meditation career, but this being was clearly something far beyond any of them. I knew that in Tibet, Padmasambhava had been revered by many as the second Buddha who had come to teach the direct way of the Vajrayana* path. As such he would have been a very remarkable being, but this transmission I had just received from him had come in at a level way beyond any of the concrete principles or mechanisms explained in any texts or scriptures I had read. It felt as if hidden behind even the most secret of teachings was an even more hidden knowledge that wasn't even expressed or made explicit, yet carried in the spaces and gaps between their words, hinting at an order of things that we have barely even grasped.

Even now I am incapable of expressing even the taste or flavour of what happened that evening or how it affected me. I just wasn't who I thought I was any more, whatever that may have been. That is all I can say. I was well aware that I had been through some rapid and startling shifts in perspective the past few years but I had always had a sense of what was happening to me, or what I thought I was becoming. All of that was now gone. There were no reference points to relate back to.

Dharma Brother

I sat in the cave as the cold of the night came on, deeply immersed in the effects of this experience. Then quite unexpectedly someone spoke to me. It was a male voice and it was very close.
I opened my eyes slowly and looked to my left. There was someone sitting beside me.

"Hello" he said. "I am Darius. Are you OK?"
He was Persian looking, with a full beard, and spoke with a soft voice.

"You must have been sitting for a long time. Are you cold?"

I was. I hadn't noticed the temperature drop while I had been in meditation.
He took off his shawl and offered it to me with a smile.

"I came in about two hours ago and you were deep in meditation. So I left you. When I came back you were still here. I could feel something extraordinary was happening by the vibration in here."

"Extraordinary? You could say that!"
"Would you like some tea?"
I nodded. We stood and walked out of the cave.

It was dark.

We walked silently to the Chai shop and sat down outside. Channa was closing up.

"Hello Darius," he said. "Hello Burgs."

"You know Channa?" I asked.

"Yes. I have been staying in his small room in the back of the Chai shop."

"But how come we have never met? I have been on this mountain for three weeks."

"I have been away in the south for a while. I got back this afternoon. Channa told me that you and your friend were staying in the ox shed"

"So how long have you been up here?"

"I was here for a month before I went away. Come to my room and I will make you some tea. Mine is better than Channa's."

"Is that so?" said our chai man with a smile. "Well, be my guests."

We walked behind the shop to a small door, that until now I had always assumed was the store room. Darius opened it and we entered. He lit candles and invited me to sit on one of the two mattresses on the floor.

"I thought we were the only ones up here apart from the Tibetans," I said. "How did you come to this place?"

"I have been studying Tibetan Buddhism for some years now. I heard about the cave and decided I should come. It's quite a special place."

"It certainly is that," I said. "I realise it now more than ever."

"So what was happening to you in the cave?"

I recounted my experience to him. He listened silently as he made tea and then sat on the bed opposite me.

"Ah. You have received a very special blessing.

To receive such a transmission from the Master himself is most rare. I have never heard anyone tell of quite such an encounter as you have just had."

He questioned me for a long time, stopping to reflect deeply on what he was hearing.

"This is very special. I have been to see many masters who take Lord Padmasambhava as their root guru but none have told me a story such as this. You have had the direct mind transmission from Guru Rinpoche himself. Just listening to your story has given me much new insight into his wisdom. Thank you for sharing with me. I am most fortunate to have arrived when I did."

"Guru Rinpoche? That is how many Tibetans refer to Padmasambhava, is it not?" I asked.

"Yes indeed. Do you know his Mantra?"

"I was shown it by a Tibetan nun who was here recently," I replied.

"Well we could meditate on it if you would like to."

"I would,' I said.

I was physically tired from the long hours of sitting on the cold stone floor of the cave, but my mind was clear and bright. The energy of the transmission was still with me. I closed my eyes and saw again the piercing eyes of this extraordinary being.

We began to chant very softly and rhythmically:

"Om Ah Hum Vajra Guru Padma Siddhi Hum."
I tuned in and reconnected to what had happened in the cave.

The mantra rolled around my mind and began to unfold. The three syllables came to life once more and began to draw me deeply into the mantra.
Again I reconnected to the transition from one syllable to another and the relationship between

them as I saw again the creative process unfolding before me at the profoundest level.

I knew the Mantra. It was ancient indeed and my memory of it felt equally so.

Just who was this Padmasambhava and what was my relationship to him?

Gradually as we chanted I felt the connection arising within me again. It was beyond concrete understanding. It was an imprint at an energetic level and it was reorganising me again, as if awakening a sleeping piece of software in the wiring of my mainframe. I felt my mind and its way of functioning reconfiguring, as if I was reloading my settings.

All that had started to happen since I arrived in India began to come into focus and I realised this process had been happening steadily and inexorably ever since. My sense of who I was was being profoundly changed. The world I lived in was no longer the same, and nor was I.

I began to cry, silently at first and then deeply.
Darius stopped his chanting and sat beside me.

"You have had a very deep and powerful experience. I have practised for many years but have learned more from what you have told me this evening than in all that time put together. You must have a special Parami for this to have happened."

"I don't know," I said. "I just sat down to do my meditation as normal and suddenly it was as if my meditation was just happening to me. I had no idea of what I was doing. But there was a wisdom emerging that was so deep and inexpressible. Do you understand what I mean?"

"Certainly I understand much of what you have told me but it is quite beyond any experience I have had myself. Yet I could feel the energy of Guru

Rinpoche here in the room more strongly than ever while I chanted just now. Maybe he was still close to you."

"But he is gone now though," I said. "I felt him leave me just now."

His presence had passed but the impression he left on me stayed, and has done to this day. It changed forever both my meditation and my life. Before, it had always felt as if meditation was something I was doing. Even from the deepest of states I would emerge with a sense that I had been engaging myself in the process. But now it was just a current that never stopped, going on endlessly. Meditation was now just a process of becoming attuned to this current, this deep, innate wisdom. It was impersonal. There was no longer anything to be created, nothing to produce with my mind, just something to abide in, to rest in, to enter into. It was an effortless abiding that defied the understanding of the concrete mind, but which opened the way to a higher knowledge of the way of things. It just was what it was, quite simply and obviously. Just a recognition that previously had only been alluded to or reflected upon but never totally entered into.

I understood it like this. You either know or you don't know. There is nothing to explain or describe. No point in trying to think it through. I knew it was a truth the concrete mind just couldn't fathom or grasp; like trying to use a dictionary to understand maths; the wrong program, wrong settings, and wrong equipment.

This rational mind that we looked through to experience life, the tool we used to try to get to our understanding of what this life means and what it actually is, was fundamentally flawed at its most basic level. We are locked into our way of seeing and being by the way we are configured. I could see now that only with the total dismantling of this mind and its views would we ever come to understand. And yet things are what they are whether we understand or not. Acceptance of this becomes far more important than the understanding.

It was late when I laid my head on Darius's pillow. I felt very old indeed. The process of life turned effortlessly around me and through me as it had done forever. All the friction of it was gone. Its roughness and grossness, dissolved completely into an endlessly clear, even current. I surrendered to it utterly and sank deeply into its embrace as it took me beyond, into the deepest sleep of my life.

Through The Veil

When I awoke it was late into the day. I had slept for more than twelve hours. I had dreamed of worlds both within and beyond our own that lay hidden. A way of things that runs on behind what is apparent. It was an order of things that I had begun to glimpse in the cave the night before.

I lay on my cot looking at the dirty ceiling of Darius's dusty digs. The memory of him from the night before gradually returned but he was nowhere in sight.

I lay alone for some time reviewing what had happened. Now what should I do? As I reflected on all that it implied I sensed in me for the first time ever the complete absence of any need to do anything. Just what was there to do? Although I was deeply at peace, that thought left me slightly confused. To lie here staring at the ceiling was no more or no less meaningful than to go off and try to heal every sick person in the world. To sit and drink tea or to teach meditation: it was all the same thing. I spent the next few days mulling with this thought. Since everything we do was a projection that was essentially empty, what was the point of doing anything?

The peace and ease I felt within me seemed bottomless and yet it was encroached upon by that one notion. What now was the point of doing anything? It was a question I grappled with for some years. Even though I would continue teaching meditation in a systematic way, even though I would travel far to further deepen my practice, I would carry with me forever now the deeper knowledge that there was no real practice to deepen. My life became a paradox and one that I just chose to surrender to until finally some years later I resolved this issue.

So eventually I did get up, and I did go looking for Darius. In time I did leave India and go back to teach in England, but whatever idea I had previously had of what it was I thought I had to do was gone. Teaching meditation, giving healing to someone who was dying of cancer, or watching football on a Saturday afternoon, they were all empty actions and essentially the same, however we may come to label them as worthy or otherwise. I saw for myself that the roles we play in our lives are essentially pantomimes and in truth it doesn't matter what you do: tinker, tailor, soldier, sailor; whatever. It isn't what we do that defines us, but the way in which we engage in it. And the paradox is that to not engage is the only real way to engage.

I left it at that and got back on the wheel one more time.

Darius was in front of the Chai shop eating kheer, a delicious rice pudding with coconut and dates. It was a great treat for us up there and Channa only made it on the rare occasions when he was brought milk by one of the local farmers.

"Ah! Good afternoon," said Darius.

I knew I hadn't been dreaming. It was the same rich smile and soft voice that had greeted me in the cave.

"You must be hungry."

"Starving," I said.

He passed me a bowl. I devoured it with relish.

"So I see you didn't lose your delight in sensual pleasures last night," he said wryly.

"Most certainly not." I replied. "In fact, I would go as far as to say they have become all the more delightful on account of it. Is there any more?"

We sat and talked and I tried to express some of what I was feeling.

"Well they say there comes a time when we have to choose," said Darius.

"Choose between what?" I asked.

"Between our own liberation and the service to others."

I remembered many years ago reading a book given to me by my father. It was a guide to meditation written by Christmas Humphreys. Though not in great depth it was a clear and lucid account of the path of meditation and it had been the catalyst that had first spurred me on in that direction. It ended with a sentiment such as this:

Imagine we were to strive earnestly to work out our own liberation from suffering, and find ourselves standing at the door to that very deliverance. If, for a moment, we were to take a look back at those who were left in the throes of confusion and suffering, would we be then able to pass through that door and leave them to their plight?

It was a sentiment that had touched me deeply then, and I knew now it was moving me once more.

There was nothing else to do but serve; to do my bit to be of assistance to others. I had all along believed that I was doing my best to this end in my efforts to teach meditation and heal the sick. But I realised now that actually until this moment it had all been to heal myself and find my own way. I was mistaken to think that it was really a selfless endeavour. For who was to reap the benefits of my good deeds? Why me, of course.

Now things felt profoundly different. I knew now I could begin to work with a real sense of commitment, knowing that I needed less to be coming back my way. I felt safe. I no longer felt in peril. And rightly or wrongly I felt I could now commit myself to service without regard to my own personal needs.

Although I was somewhat premature in taking for granted my own safety I knew that this was the answer.

I had drunk of my cup and I had a choice. I could simply say enough is enough and stay there in India and enjoy my bliss, or I could return to where I had come from and engage in the battle. I knew then, as I guess I had always known, that it wasn't yet time to lay down arms.

Over the coming days we walked far and wide over those hills. At night I would sit long hours in the cave but Padmasambhava didn't return. But then I knew he didn't need to.

I might have been inclined to think that after the encounter with Padmasambhava I had got what I had come to India for and in many ways I had. It wasn't what I had expected for sure, but I felt I could not take in much more. I needed time to let it all filter through, and settle into me. My world had changed so much and so many times in just a few years. I needed to sit and just be with it all.

George had had to return to England a week before my meeting in the cave, to be best man at his best friend's wedding. I had anticipated spending the last two weeks of my retreat alone. But as it was, I enjoyed immensely the time I spent with Darius and after the night in the cave, I was glad to have him around. We talked much in that time and meditated most nights together, but never hard. I was taking it easy now. Just being with it. Finding my feet and enjoying the enormous sense of expansiveness I felt within and around me.

It was during this time that I first glimpsed at the way by which the old school Theravadan* tradition that I would return to in Burma might be unified with the vision of this new Dharma that had emerged in India and China in the centuries that followed the Buddha's final Nibbana. Now that I was in India I could begin to sense, almost taste, how the Brahmanical traditions and their ideas of the absolute essence of things had been fused with the Buddha's vision. As these views had integrated and mixed further with the tantric traditions, over time they birthed the Mahayana view that the transmission from Padmasambhava had crystallised so completely within me. I knew instinctively that my way was to bring these two threads together within my own path and walk them both together. It would make for a lonely way, for it cast me as something of a maverick on both sides, but I kept my faith in the years to come, held by a deep sense that my real Masters watched over me and guided me from other realms.

In many ways I felt alone. Things had already happened to me that didn't fit the mould, even within the context within which most of these teachings and practices lie, it was not clear to what ground I should return and it wasn't always easy to relate back to my teachers when seeking their advice. Darius had been a lonesome seeker, working his way through the Hindu traditions in his own search for answers, before coming to the teachings of the Buddha. So he sympathised with my position. In the end we spent a very magical time together on the mountain as we both imbibed the essence of that majestic place. It was my home, and my back yard looked out on the snow mountains of the Himalayas. I felt as if I could stay forever. I lived off rice dhal and mangoes, and twenty-four hours a day I breathed air so fresh I could almost drink it.

But if there was any danger of me falling into complacency it didn't last long. I was to be dismantled one more time before the mountains let me leave.

One day Darius and I walked the pilgrimage trail to the next mountain on top of which was a famous Hindu shrine. It was the time of a special puja* and many sadhus and yogis had been making the journey over the preceding days. We had left at sunrise and it was late into the afternoon when we got back to Channa's chai shop.

As we approached I saw that there were two old yogis sitting at the table where we often took our tea. They shone out from some distance away and I was drawn towards then.

"Hey Darius. Look at those two Bubbas. They look amazing," I said.

They did indeed. They were both dressed all in white and heavily bearded with head dresses held in place by jewelled broaches. As we approached I had a strong urge to talk to them. I had felt for some days as if I was waiting to meet someone special to put some context on what had happened and in that moment I believed it was these two that I may have been waiting for.

"Let's go and talk to them," I said to Darius.

They looked like the real deal, shining and serene. I was sure they had the cookies.

As we approached I glanced over to my right down the track that led to the cowshed that had become my home. Walking along the path in our direction was an Indian man dressed as a goatherd with a crooked stick. Outwardly he looked quite unremarkable, like every other farmer on the hill and I didn't initially pay much attention to him. But somehow I knew there was something special about him.

We approached the Chai shop and ordered tea before sitting down near the two men in white. Intuitively we felt not to invade their space so we sat quietly speaking only in pleasantries.

Some minutes later the goatherd arrived and sat at a bench opposite us. He said nothing and seemed merely to be resting. But I felt something strange going on in my mind, as if he was deeply aware of what I was thinking and even trying to communicate with me in some silent way. There were no grounds for approaching him and I knew he wouldn't speak English but I equally felt at a very deep level that this was no ordinary man.

It was as if this ragged little man had called me to him. I don't know how I knew, but in that instant I lost all interest in the shining mystics in white. This man was something else altogether. There was nothing overt to draw me to him, just a knowing. It was as if the movie had suddenly paused to say

"Wait a second. Are you sure you have got it right? Look again."

I had been convinced that the two men in white were the real thing but in that split second I saw something more...much more. This little old goatherd, he was the wizard. I just knew it. And in that instant the two men at the Chai shop had paled into insignificance alongside him.

As I sat there he looked up at me for an instant and held me in his gaze. Something in his eyes burned deep into my soul. There was timelessness about him. I felt he could have been living up in the mountains for a thousand years without anyone knowing he was there. I certainly hadn't seen him before, but I knew immediately he had been there the whole time. Unseen.

Darius and I drank our tea and exchanged pleasantries with the two yogis, and then we stood up and left. I don't even know if Darius had noticed the goatherd. Outwardly he just looked like another local farmer. As we walked away, I felt as if he was looking deeply into me. I knew he knew my mind.

Once I got back to my hut I thought nothing more of him. But that evening as the sun set I sat outside meditating. Suddenly he was standing before me, his eyes burning deep into me as if he was looking into my very soul. What happened next took only a few seconds.

Again it was a direct exchange, a transmission. In just a few brief seconds the whole thing was over.

"You do not know who I am," he said

"No. Who are you?"

He did not reply. He wasn't talking, his voice just appeared directly in my mind. I knew if he spoke it would not be in English, but it was in English that I heard him now.

His stare burned deep into my forehead and there was a blinding flash of light. And in that flash my world was turned upside down again.

Suddenly I was in an ancient building that felt almost like a church.

"This is our world," he said. "It looks quite like yours does it not?"

It did indeed. And yet I knew it was not the same.

"We live here behind the veil watching, taking care, and looking over your world. We are guardians. It's not always easy. Look. See your world…"

Suddenly he gestured at the wall in the building and it opened up to reveal a scene beyond. It was our world I was now looking at, but from the other side.

"This is your world. Can you see how it is?"

I was looking out at in industrial scene that could have been anywhere in Europe. There was a tall factory with a chimney and industry everywhere. Up in the mountains it was the power of nature that ruled supreme. In the world I was looking at it had no quarter. I could only sense the complete absence of its power. As if it had been completely cut off. Short circuited. I felt as if I could see everything at once. See what everyone was doing and what they were thinking and how they were all behaving simultaneously. And none of them had any idea of what they were doing or how disconnected they were. I was in a deeply altered state and my mind was functioning in a way quite unlike anything I was used to. It was as if I was plugged into all the channels at the same time. I could hear his voice but I didn't know where he was any more.

"Yes," I said. "I can see."

"What do you see?"

"It's all gone so wrong," I said. "So terribly wrong. That's not how it's meant to be."

It had all gone so wrong. It was shocking. I was looking straight into the heart of our very world. I watched it turning and felt the force that was propelling it along. And it wasn't right. It wasn't turning under the effortless power of nature that should have been at work. It was turning under the power of the will of man. And it had gone so very wrong. I could see at once both how it should have been and how it actually was, as if it was spinning in two directions at once, the spin to perfection and the spin to chaos. It was unbearable. I felt I was going to explode. I felt the pull of the chaos upon me, sucking me into its spin. I thought I was going to pass out.

Then he reached out and put his hand on my shoulder.

Once again I was staring into the vastness of his eyes. I felt the energy from his hand surge through me like a warm liquid. Everything became bright and all I could feel was love. It was a love like I had never known before, a silent unstated, bottomless love. There was no sense of despair in him, just a deep knowing of how it was and only compassion in the face of it.

"You are right," he said. "It has all gone wrong. But you must not despair. That is the way of things. We watch from here, we do what we can to bring it back in line, but we cannot interfere. We can only encourage those is search of encouragement. You must never expect it to end, for it never will. You must just hold the light and never give up. We are here and we will always be here and from now on you will always know that you are never alone."

He let go of my arm. The veil closed on the scene

I had looked over, and I saw how he was amongst others who I had not noticed before. They were all silently engaged with an endless process that I knew was holding things in place for us in our world. Holding the light so that we might not get utterly lost in the darkness.

Then the building faded and then the light dimmed and I was back again sitting outside the front of my shed. I was completely alone. There was no sign of him anywhere. I looked back up the track but it was empty.

"Don't worry. You are safe."

I heard his voice in my head. I felt him around me, but not present. I sensed the veil that he had shown me and the work that his kind carried on behind it.

I stood up and walked down to the ridge that looked out over the high mountains of the Himalayas. I sat looking out at the endless sky. I breathed out with a sigh. I felt very old, very old indeed. And though I could sense that I was looked over, I felt so alone.

I had known this, the day I threw my harmonica into the crowd and jumped off the stage.

I knew it had all gone wrong, but until now I had thought it was just me deciding to change course. My life had become meaningless but it hadn't led me to judge the way of things. It just wasn't for me anymore. I knew things were out of whack. I walked away because I felt we were all off course, but I had assumed I would be able to leave it at that. I had never wanted to look too deeply into the predicament our world was coming to. But now I had done. It was as if this old mystic had forced me to see what I was trying to ignore. Up there in the mountains it was all in order. It always had been and always would be. But I couldn't stay there forever and I knew it. However much I flirted with the idea of staying in India and living as a yogi, I knew I would go back. I had no choice.

So in the space of only a few days I had seen deeply into two things that sat in direct opposition to each other. Padmasambhava had shown me that there is no need to do anything, while the old mystic had shown me just how much there was to do. I wasn't under the illusion that I could change the way things were but I equally didn't feel able just to step back and live a life of ease in seclusion. I knew eventually I would have to return to England, and continue the work I had begun. But in some strange way there was no longer a sense of urgency, even though I had come to understand more deeply how off-track things had got. I knew I could not do anything about the way things were – the will of man had pitted itself against the power of Nature. It was a battle that would resolve itself without my intervention. Seeing how great was the predicament we had brought ourselves to as a race had allowed me to let go any sense that I might be able to make a difference. All I hoped for was that in some small way I might help others make their peace with it. I knew now that I would have to surrender to the rhythm of things and let everything unfold in a timely way.

It was a relief, however challenged I was by what I saw. I think there is a part of every young man that fantasises about maybe one day being the one to save the world. It is a classic adolescent fixation that doesn't properly get relinquished until we make the ascent into mature adulthood. In many ways, however noble the notion might be, it is quite possibly also the greatest act of self-flattery that we could imagine. I could see in myself as the path worked upon me, how my naïve ideas about having something important to do, gradually yielded into a much more realistic attitude of simple willingness to do. As I learned to remove my own personal will from the equation I began to see more clearly the deeper truth revealed by the wise old goatherd.

Though it took me some years to extract my own egotistic fantasies of myself from the work at hand, I was under no illusion from that point on that the only real teaching was to find and show a way to live in accordance with the natural order, rather than seeking to bend it to our will. It was all too easy to point the finger of blame at those who plundered our earth for selfish means, but even my mistaken belief that I could personally heal another's illness failed to recognise that sickness was nothing more than an expression of an interference or separation from the natural order, and that healing was nothing more than re-establishing it within each individual. I saw many striving with great effort to heal themselves. Some succeeded, others failed, and always it was the same thing that governed success. Those who could surrender their personal will and allow their world to be free of their wilful control of it, healed if they had the karma to do so. Those who were unable to surrender, instead pitting their very will against the sickness invariably failed.

This truth wasn't just expressed in the dismal state of disrespect for nature, but in every level of our lives, from the massive number of people dissatisfied and depressed, to the prolific rise in degenerative illness. All of it was a symptom of an excessive application of our egoic will and a refusal to live in accordance with natural laws. By pitting my own energy against the sickness of another I was as guilty as anyone of interfering with the natural order. It wasn't until I realised that the only role of the healer was to facilitate the natural flow of life, that I stopped making myself sick on behalf of others.

Although my encounter with the goatherd had been only fleeting, the experience was as axiomatic in the maturing of my understanding of the Path as any of the many teachings I received along the way.

A few days later Darius had to go back to Europe to see his wife and child. He had been in India for over eight years, much of it with them, but during the time of his long retreat they had been in Switzerland.

We bade our farewells and I waved him goodbye as he headed out of Rewalsar on the local bus. I went back to the Mountain for a few days to gather my thoughts and plan what I was to do next.

So finally I was left alone there. I didn't practise hard in the last few days. I just enjoyed the time I had left. The cricket world cup was on and Channa had the only TV in the area. Indians love cricket. As Channa said to me, "It is the king of all games."

All kinds of male folk began to converge on his Chai shop to watch their country take part on the world stage. Wonderful and colourful individuals about whose life I knew nothing.

We huddled together around his old TV cheering and sighing, clapping and huffing as the action unfolded.

I remember in particular one tiny man they called the mechanic. Apparently he took care of all the maintenance needs of the few homes in the valley. He carried everywhere the only tool he possessed. It was a large monkey wrench that he hooked into his trousers. Each day when he arrived in the Chai shop he unhooked it from his belt and hung it from a beam in the ceiling. I could only imagine the variety of ways he had learned to apply his lone tool to the tasks set for him. It made me smile every time I saw him. It was the kind of quirkiness that one can see all over India in the imaginative way its people find to get life's jobs done. It typified the part of India I had seen. I remember the mechanic who had come to try to fix Singh's taxi on our ride up from Delhi. He also had only one tool to work with and it too was a monkey wrench. Oh, how I love India.

Two days before I was planning to leave I met a young Tibetan lad who had come up from Delhi to see his mother who was a long-term resident in the caves. He was studying at a university there. He was well versed in the Tibetan way of Buddhism and we spent much time talking. He invited me for tea at his mother's cave one afternoon.

I entered into a scene that could have come straight out of Tolkien's tales. Rough and uneven stone walls and handmade furniture of unfinished wood from the forests around about. There was a single charcoal stove on which everything was cooked and heated, with a vent made of corrugated iron, a few vegetables in a basket and strips of meat hanging from the ceiling.

The tea I was offered was made from buttermilk. It was heavily stewed, strong and creamy.

"So how long will you still be studying?" I asked.

"I have another year if I can afford it. I work in a

sweet shop to pay my way, but my mother has been sick and I have had to provide for her. I may need to miss a year while I save up again."

"How much are your fees?" I enquired.

"I need around a hundred dollars more to cover it."

I was planning to leave in two days' time. I had twenty dollars for food and my bus trip to Delhi. Beyond that I had kept a one hundred dollar bill for emergencies.

On the morning of my departure the young lad helped me carry my things back to town. I gave the bed rolls and crockery we had accumulated to his mother.

As I climbed up onto the roof of the bus I turned to him. I pulled an envelope from my pocket and put it in his hand. Inside was a hundred dollars.

"Here is a little something to help you with your studies."

He was embarrassed and tried to refuse. I stuffed the envelope into his jacket.

"Please," I said," I insist."

The bus turned around to head out of town.

When we drove past him again he was holding the bill in his hand.

"Thank you, thank you so much."

As I left I waved. "You just make sure you pass," I shouted. "And when I come back maybe you can find a cave for me."

"Of course. Whatever you need. Take care. I will never forget you."

I knew he wouldn't, and as the bus drove off I pondered if ever again I would get the chance to give so much with so little.

At Mandi I changed to the express bus to Delhi. I was wedged in between two dreadlocked boys on their way back to their final year at university in England. They had spent their summer in the ganja fields of Manali. They were stoned and slept most of the way. Apart from the fact that my hair was shaved there wasn't much to tell us apart. They too had been out on their quest. I wondered if they had found what they were looking for.

Back in Delhi I went looking for Singh. I found him at the Intercontinental. I had taken the overnight bus and my flight was that evening. I asked him if he wanted to eat with me. I didn't know my way around the city so was glad to have company.

We spent the morning in a sweet shop eating ras mali and gulab jamun. I told him my story and he told me of his epic journey back to Delhi with his sick car. As he drove me around town that afternoon, showing me the sights, it seemed to be no worse for wear. It seemed the Indian monkey wrench was a wonderful tool indeed. I wondered if it would be as highly valued in England were I to get back into the import business? Somehow I doubted it.

CHAPTER THIRTEEN

Temples In The Mist

From India I flew back to Bali to see Merta Ada.
I presented him with the text Kundrel had given
me. He looked at it and smiled.

"Ah how interesting," he said. "Take a look at
this."
He reached into a drawer in his desk and pulled out
a manuscript of his own.
It too was called "The Light of Wisdom".

"Well isn't that a coincidence," he said. "One of
my students gave me this while I was teaching in
Jakarta last week."
We took it as a sure sign. There was no doubt about
it, we would certainly have to go to meet Pa Auk
Sayadaw.

It took me six months to get in contact with
anyone connected to him. His monastery is in a
remote forest area of Southern Burma. There was no
internet link or website. Eventually I got hold of a
number for a retired army major who took care of
practical matters at the monastery. I asked him if I
could come to practice there.

"You could come sir, if you so wished, but I am

afraid our dear Sayadaw is quite unwell and he is not able to teach for now."

"What's wrong?" I asked. How could a master as great as this become sick?

"He has very bad body pain and very severe headaches."

I enquired further as to the conditions, and the Major agreed to send me a sponsor letter so that I might acquire a meditation visa for long stay in Burma. He also gave me the name and number of a liaison in Rangoon who would help me when I arrived.

No sooner had I put down the phone than my mind started hatching its plan. I had read Sayadaw's great work on meditation. He was clearly a highly attained master. Would it be too precocious to go to him and suggest he try our method of healing? Perhaps he simply hadn't thought of it. It would be so easy for him with his level of samadhi. I felt it my duty to do what I could to heal him.

Ada and I took a month out to travel together to some of Asia's ancient Buddhist sites, on a trip that would eventually take us to Burma and Sayadaw. In Bangkok we applied for Burmese visas and finally flew to Rangoon. By the time we got to Burma however, Sayadaw had been sent to Taiwan for medical treatment.

We had two weeks left for our trip and so we took the chance to see something of the country while we were there. We had met up with Sayadaw's liaison officer in Rangoon. He was an elderly man called U Thet Tin and a gentleman in every way. He was delighted that we had shown so much interest in his Master and took it upon himself

148

to ensure our trip was not entirely in vain. He had an old minibus and agreed to take us on a tour of the country. He was in his seventies and had a heart condition but his enthusiasm was limitless. We spent two weeks travelling with him and our journey finally brought us to the ancient city of Bagan.

We drove into Bagan at dawn, everything was pink. After eighteen hours of driving on broken roads from Rangoon it was a magical sight indeed. Bagan is an extraordinary place in the heart of an extraordinary country. It is a one hundred square mile plain on the banks of the majestic Irrawaddy River, and sits today as a monument to a golden age in the history of Burma. An age in which the Buddha's Dharma flourished and spread like a bushfire through the hearts of the people.

There is something otherworldly about Bagan that sets it apart from all of Asia's other ancient sites. Because of the troubles that Burma has faced with its military government over the last twenty years, it is little visited by tourists. Many stay away as a protest, and those that do go, have to deal with an almost non-existent infrastructure. Travelling in India is a breeze compared to Burma. Our route north had taken us mostly along the famous road to Mandalay. It is called in Burma, Highway Number One. U Thet Tin had told us it would take eighteen hours in his old Toyota minibus. I was surprised since the distance was only six hundred miles. But then I was a rookie and had no idea about Burmese roads. Highway number one turned out to be a single track road built by the British in the days of the empire. They had lined it with Tamarind trees much of the way which provided welcome shade, but it has not been serviced since. It is potholed and broken and the ride was a real bone shaker.

At one point we came upon a river that intersected the road. There was no bridge across it. Like every other vehicle travelling that route we were at the mercy of the waters. We were lucky. When we arrived the sandy river bed was dry and apart from the occasional push from the gang of locals who took it upon themselves to ensure safe passage for travellers, we were not held up. U Thet Tin however told us that there had been many times when the waters rose so suddenly that cars and trucks had been washed away downstream. During the wet season the road was often impassable for days or weeks on end.

That is Burma through and through. Somehow it has struggled along till now and unlike the rest of South Asia, which has been industrialising at exponential rates, it is completely undeveloped. Most roads are still ox tracks and people meet up to trade at the crossroads. I had come to learn Dharma in Burma and all around me I saw life going on as it would have done twenty-five centuries ago when the Buddha wandered and taught through northern India. In the end it is possible that for all the hardships its people have endured under the Junta, there may yet be some advantage to be had. Most of South-East Asia has done in forty years what took two hundred in Europe and America, and because of it, most of its infrastructure is poorly planned and held together by threads. Burma may yet get to learn from the mistakes of its neighbours and in time come again to be the Jewel of Asia that it once was. It is all just waiting to happen.

U Thet Tin of course was right. It had taken eighteen hours to get there but although we were tired we felt that the trip had fully immersed us in the country.

It was early morning when we arrived and the sun was not yet up so our guide and friend had suggested we climbed a hill on the edge of the plain to watch sunrise and take in the view over Bagan's countless ancient temples.

We climbed the hill, on the top of which was a beautiful golden pagoda. Even as we climbed I had felt something stirring in me, but it wasn't the sight of the Pagoda or the view over the plain of Bagan that ignited the flame. As I stood up after offering incense at the stupa* and turned to look behind me it struck me like a lightning flash. Our Pagoda marked the end of a ridge of hills that ran away into the distance before me. It was these hills that snatched the breath from me. I knew these hills, I knew this place. I gasped. The world span around me and I could hardly stand.

I felt a rush shoot up my spine and through my whole body. "Oh My God!" I cried. "I have been here before." In a flash of light my head exploded. I knew this place. I knew it well.

I ran over to Ada and U Thet Tin. "I know this place. I have been here before. In another life I lived up on this hill. There is a cave underneath. I sat there and meditated often. I meditated in a monastery on this side of the hill as well." I pointed out over Bagan as we stood on the hilltop overlooking the vast plain that housed its thousands of ancient pagodas and temples. "And when I died I was cremated here on this hill and my ashes enshrined on the other side of the hill over there."

151

I was blathering. Ada looked at me curiously. But I knew what I said was true. All my life I had known this place. Seen it in my dreams. This was the place I had seen when the Shaman had sent me journeying years before. It wasn't just a vague sense. I knew it well, in detail.

"There is a monastery down there. I can draw it for you. I know how the monks walked and sat in meditation, and where they exercised. I know its shape, how it looks. I can draw it. Do you have some paper?"

U Thet Tin was wriggling with excitement as he fumbled for paper in his bag. As I drew, I described the place I was drawing:

"It was a meditation temple. I sat in here and the young monks sat in the middle. And there was a corridor all round and outside a courtyard where the novices did their exercises daily. Here!"

I passed the drawing to U Thet Tin. "Tell me is there a temple like this down there?"

"Oh. There are many. Many like this. Oh this is wonderful, and there really is a cave beneath this hill. An old monk used to sit here in the time of Anawrahta, the first King of Bagan. He was a wandering monk who travelled up here from the south. It was a very important time in our history. I will tell you all about it."

He paused and turned around to look out over the other side of the hill and away from Bagan. He pointed.

"You see that white stone building down there?" I could just see it amongst the trees in the distance.

"That is the Shrine of the wandering monk. Oh this is wonderful." This tired and frail old man suddenly looked like a little boy despite our long night on the road.

"Come!" he said. "We must find this temple of yours."

Less than ten years ago the exquisite temple complex of Angkor Wat in Cambodia was opened up to tourists. An airport was built and package hotels swiftly followed. What was once one of the most hauntingly beautiful spiritual sites in the world today is a circus and what vibration from its ancient times might have survived, has now gone completely. Not so in Bagan.

There are over three thousand temples on the plain and there could not have been more than fifty tourists in the whole place. What few we saw were only in the most famous of pagodas. We were able to sit and meditate in countless shrines and temples knowing that not another soul would bother us. The energy of meditation was everywhere and it was powerful. Unspoiled in the thousand years since Bagan's golden era.

We did indeed find the old Indian monk's cave and meditated there. We visited his shrine and scoured Bagan's countless pagodas for three days looking for the temple I had drawn. Many of the ancient red brick buildings closely resembled my picture. But always there was something not right. I had such a clear picture in my mind. I knew every detail of the building we sought. Most of the pagodas in Bagan had a central chamber which served as a shrine at which to worship and put respect to the Buddha, often with four statues facing the four directions symbolising the Buddhas of the four ages past. But my temple had not been like this. The central Chamber had been empty. It was a meditation hall with raised alcoves for the senior monks to sit in all around the main room. Outside there had been a courtyard. I had such a clear vision of me standing in the doorway looking over the courtyard and watching the junior monks exercise in the mornings. It was these two features that set my drawing apart from all the temples we found. They were all so similar but not the same. After three days we decided to give up our search. We were intoxicated with the splendours of the place, but the golden nugget we sought, which was to verify my testimony, had eluded us. The cave had been there and the shrine, but not the monastic temple. It was exciting but nothing conclusive. Time had run out and we had to head on.

We drove out of Bagan at first light, leaving by its dusty tracks in the same pink light that had greeted us. We had seen many marvels and I had dreamed much of an ancient time here. Even Ada had said that this place felt familiar to him. At this time I was yet to ordain and had not the means to review my past lives to see if my visions had been true or not. And so we left it as an open book, but certainly a place to come back to.

But then as we drove across the plain I suddenly felt that rush shooting through me again.

"Stop!" I cried "It's in here on the right." I pointed down a narrow track leading through a grove of trees.

"What do you think Ada?" asked U Thet Tin.

"OK," he replied. "One last look."

We took the track, at the end of which was indeed a fine looking Pagoda.

"Ah." cried U Thet Tin. "This looks promising." His enthusiasm over the past few days had exceeded even mine as he had sought to prove that I might indeed have been here in the past. He had introduced me to the Abbot of the local monastery and must have recounted our story a hundred times in those few days.

We approached the pagoda. I knew immediately that it wasn't the one. Even if I had wanted it to be, inside I knew. It had the courtyard but not the empty central chamber. A huge Buddha dominated. It was a shrine, a place of worship and not of meditation.

"Oh well." said Ada. "It was worth a try."

A young boy of about ten stood beside us. He had tried and failed to sell us paintings.

"Do you want to climb onto the roof?"

We accepted his invitation.

"Let's climb up and sit for a while before we leave," said Ada. And so we sat and chanted the Paritta one last time.

It took a while for the headiness of the past few days to clear but our meditation was clear and deep. Suddenly we were disturbed by U Thet Tin's shouting.

"Burgs, Burgs! Come quick."

We stirred from our sitting and climbed down to the ground.

"I have just been talking with these locals about your temple."

He pointed to a ruin about a hundred yards away. "That there is the original monastery, built by the Indian monk. It was destroyed in an earthquake and never restored. Go! Go and take a look. See if that is it."

I looked at Ada.

"Go on," he encouraged me. "We will wait here. You never know, that could be it."

I felt a cool stillness in me. It had overcome the excitement as I walked slowly across the dry land to the ruin.

There was indeed a courtyard and the raised entrance as I had seen in my vision. As I stood in the entrance and looked out at the courtyard the perspective was as I had remembered.

I went inside. There was a corridor leading around a central chamber and even alcoves raised up in the walls. But the door to the central chamber was boarded up. The building was partially collapsed and unstable, but I had to know. How could I leave with this stone unturned?

I prised the wooden boards that sealed the chamber. There was not much light. It was dank and shadowy inside, but I could see that it was empty. I fumbled in my bag for a torch to light the room, but I already knew. I could feel it in my bones. I knew this place. This was it. Days, weeks, months, years I had sat here, teaching Dharma and meditation. I had no idea yet how or why I had come to this place and why I should be so connected to Bagan. It would be another two years before I finally came to see dependent origination and review the pathway of my previous lives. Only then would I understand the journey that would lead me from India to Burma and later Bali, thence on over time to the life I had now, born in England.

For now my samadhi was not yet matured enough to see these things clearly. I had only the vision that came to me years before, the vision that I had forgotten until three days ago on the hill here in Bagan. Here I was standing in this ancient ruin in the ancient capital of this ancient land, and it felt like home. More so than anywhere I had ever been before.

I went outside and sat in the entrance, and I cried. I don't know why I cried. It came from so deep inside me and they were very old tears. I cried for myself. I cried for how far I had come, how long was the road and how far from the path I knew I had wandered. I knew then more than anything else that this moment marked the beginning of the end of a long journey home. I felt in my belly that feeling that had first stirred in me and set me out on my adventure years before. It was the same feeling I got when I first heard the Pali chants and realised I already knew them. It was the feeling of being re-connected to something that is so much a part of you that it seems incomprehensible that you could have been separated for so long without even knowing it. I knew now that the long road I had travelled since I left my old life behind had largely been to reconnect to this place and what it meant to me. I knew that all my seeking had been to bring me back here. I knew the answers lay here. It was for this that I cried, and for the long age of separation and darkness that was now drawing to a close. For the first time in my life I felt safe, for I knew I was back in the hands of a power that would hold me and carry me. I knew I was home.

I don't know how long I had been there when I felt a hand on my shoulder. I looked up.

There was Ada, smiling down at me; my teacher, my best friend and elder brother.

"You know what Burgs. I really feel you were here. I feel it very clearly in my meditation. I was here with you too. We travelled up from India. You were my friend and I visited you here. You stayed here and I went on to Sumatra. You must stay here and meditate. Then you will see clearly."

He was right, it was a choiceless decision. Ada returned to Bali alone and I began my time in Burma. It was the beginning of my coming home.

157

CHAPTER FOURTEEN

Stay Here And Meditate

"Stay here and meditate, and then you will see clearly." That is what Ada had said to me when we were in Bagan. They were wise words indeed. In fact the only guidance a teacher ever need give a student. Our challenge will always be to stick to the task until the fruit ripens, until we do learn to see clearly. Indeed isn't that what all of us long for? To understand what we don't understand, to see what we cannot see? I know I did. It was all I wanted.

And so I did indeed stay in Burma.

Ada returned to Bali and I went directly to Tanlyn monastery. It was the second centre of Pa Auk Sayadaw and since he was not even in the country I decided to go here first rather than trek all the way down to the south where his forest monastery was. Besides, I had heard that while Sayadaw himself was away the next best teacher was the Abbot of Tanlyn. I spent a day in the city with U Thet Tin buying the few things I would need, and off I went.

I had no idea where I was going, only that I wanted to meditate long and deep. I was pulled like a magnet and longed for the simplicity that monastic life offered.

U Thet Tin drove me out to Tanlyn and presented me to the gate keeper. I felt rather like a foreign student arriving for his first day at boarding school.

I was greeted warmly. U Thet Tin had called ahead and asked permission for me to join the monastery as a lay yogi. There was quite a stir with my arrival as I was the only foreigner apart from a Japanese man about my own age who most people there thought was crazy.

I was given a mug and a steel plate and shown to a simple hut twelve foot by nine that was to be my new home. I had five sarongs and five white tee shirts, a gas heater and some Burmese tea, a copy of the Visuddhimagga and a book of Pali chants, a toothbrush, toothpaste and a brick of red soap that smelled of naphthalene, one pair of sandals and an umbrella. That was it.

U Thet Tin helped me move in. We swept the room thoroughly and then sat and drank tea together. He told me how much faith he had in me, and that he prayed I would be successful and attain Nibbana so that he may earn great merits from supporting me. Then, quite unexpectedly, he got up from his chair and knelt before me and bowed three times.

"You are to be part of the Sangha* and you are striving for liberation. I must bow to you now. I am old and have not the strength to sit long hours now, so please try hard for me too. I know you will be successful. Good luck."

Then he stood, held my hand briefly and left me alone. He was the last familiar face I would see in Burma and I had only known him for a week or so. Yet I felt not a trace of loneliness as he left me to the work ahead.

I will never forget the feeling of sheer relief when I shut the door on my kuti that day. It was the bliss of seclusion. I am well aware that to many, such a predicament would have been horrifying. Waking at three-thirty, sitting in meditation for an hour and a half six times a day. Taking food only once. But at that time in my life there was nothing else in the world that I wanted.

I literally dropped straight into deep samadhi the day I began. It was as if a switch inside me had just been waiting to be turned on.

I was to report to the Abbot daily. Being the only foreigner there he was particularly interested in my progress. U Thet Tin had unfortunately briefed him on our adventures in Bagan and I sensed there were high expectations of me. Yet strangely I never once had the feeling that I had something to achieve or prove. My progress was seamless. I reported daily to the teacher for instructions and spent the rest of the day practicing until I had accomplished whatever was asked of me. My mind became clear and bright and extremely supple. I would wake at three-thirty and sit as long as I could. In all the time I was there I never once made it to breakfast as I was so deeply immersed in my meditation. When I did first stir, usually around seven or eight, I would shower outside before reporting to the abbot. He would review my practice and check my meditation before instructing me for the day. I would then return to my kuti till lunch at eleven thirty. Most of my hard work was done by noon and quite often I had completed what was asked of me by then. So the afternoons were spent reviewing my practice and going over it again, and once I was satisfied I would spend an hour or so reading the

Visuddhimagga. I never sat in the main meditation hall with all the other monks as I was sitting for long spells and I found the formal schedule disruptive. During the last sit of the day, while all the monks were in the hall I would go outside to practice Chi Kung for an hour or so to keep myself physically fit and strong. And that was my life. Every day it was the same. No variety and no longing for variety. I felt just a sublime simplicity and a serenity that comes with the absence of restlessness and the knowledge that there is enough time to do what you have to do.

I was, however, not entirely alone in my quest. There was, as I said, one other foreigner at the Monastery. He was a Japanese ex-Zen Monk, thirty years old, who had disrobed and come to Burma. He spoke only the simplest of English but we established a camaraderie that I came to value greatly during my time at Tanlyn.

I had been there maybe a week and had not yet really introduced myself to anyone but the teacher. The Burmese Monks always smiled and checked I was OK while we took our showers together daily. It was the closest we came to social time. A series of huge barrels from which we scooped ladles of cold water served as our showers. The first I knew of Zen, as I called him, was when he slipped a bar of half decent smelling soap into my hand at bathing time one day. He said nothing, just nodded and walked on.

Then a few days later he just walked into my kuti one afternoon and sat down on the floor in front of me. At first I rather resented the intrusion. He made no effort at conversation but started boiling water on my gas stove. It was clear he intended to stay for tea. He put the water on to boil and then exited as suddenly as he had appeared. A few moments later he returned with a foil package containing what turned out to be quite the most delicious tea I had ever tasted. He brewed and served and we became friends from that moment on.

"You and me. We have to push hard," he said in his clipped staccato accent. "Push hard every day. Non-stop. Pain is illusion. Pain is illusion."

He managed to convince me that we should be extending our capacity for sitting long periods. In Pali this is called the practice of Adhitthana* and it means strong determination. He wanted us to increase the period in which we sat without moving by half an hour every day. At that stage I was up for any challenge, and so began our efforts to see how long we could sit.

We started with three hours, then three and a half and so on until we were sitting six-hour stints. It got to the point where we would just sit straight through from wake-up bell till lunch. By now I had reached the first level of absorption samadhi called the first jhana and sitting had become almost effortless. The abbot was visibly pleased with my progress and U Thet Tin had been back to visit and told me how happy my teacher was. I was the first yogi to get this level of concentration in such a short time.

Then one morning, Zen walked in and shook me from my meditation.

"I have new plan. Stop doing 'Pain is illusion'. I do 'Who Am I? Who Am I?' I want to do twelve hours. Tomorrow you tell them I no food. No knock my door. I start five o'clock morning. You come my room five o clock evening. I finish. OK?"

163

Twelve hours! Now I know he hadn't yet attained to jhana and so his body would not be without pain. And so this could only be an extraordinary effort of determination. For most people the body begins to burn with aches and pains of all kinds after two hours or so. It varies depending on our concentration and equanimity but until the mind enters into absorption and all awareness of gross physicality ceases there will come a time where the body simply objects to remaining still for too long. I know from my own efforts that if I was doing any kind of meditation other than abiding in deep samadhi the body objected to sitting more than three hours. Just ask yourself how long you think you could sit still and remain concentrated without fidgeting and becoming restless and agitated. How long can you even lie still in bed at night without having to move? One hour maybe two? But sitting without moving for twelve hours simply repeating to yourself the question, "Who Am I?" Even I was impressed by his gesture.

Sure enough the next day he sat in his room without moving for twelve hours and at five o'clock he emerged from his endeavour looking exhausted but with his tireless enthusiasm still intact.

"Ah this is good. I like this Who Am I?" he said.

And then the next day he left.

He came into my room around eight o'clock in the morning and announced that he was going to go on a walking meditation retreat. He wanted to walk to the Shan state in Northern Burma and meditate in the mountains. It was a distance of many hundreds of miles. He shook my hand and kissed my forehead and walked out of my room and out of the monastery carrying no bag, with only the clothes on his back and no money in his pocket. And that was the last I or any of us at Tanlyn ever heard of him.

But the brief period I spent with him as my companion motivated me and spurred me on. If I might have had any tendency to complacency he instilled in me an ethic of sustained effort, yet he taught me to meditate with a smile. I shall forever be in debt to him for that. For there are many who never find joy in their meditation. I have no idea what happened to him but I have little doubt that it didn't matter to him in the slightest where he ended up. He was an utterly spontaneous being living completely in the moment with no regard for anything other than that.

I continued my retreat in Tanlyn. The Teacher wanted me to practice the Kasina* meditations before Pa Auk Sayadaw returned. He had been in contact with Sayadaw and told him of my progress and Sayadaw had requested that I be taught all of the samatha meditation practices. These together make up a complete set of some forty meditations which can be developed to various levels of concentration. I had started meditating on the internal parts of the body. I began by reviewing my own body and once my concentration developed I had to meditate on the inner body parts of other monks as they sat in meditation. To do this I had to sit and meditate in the main hall for the first time.

I had read of this practice from Sayadaw's book 'The Light of Wisdom' given to me by Kundrel in India. The process by which we train the faculty of remote viewing to see internally and externally with the power of concentration is very similar to the way in which the ability to feel inside the body of others is developed. It is just a slight adjustment of the application of our focus with intent upon viewing rather than feeling.

I had already developed the feeling aspect in my time in Bali with Merta Ada and so the seeing came easily once I adjusted the focus of my concentration. Both these practices are what we call direct perception. Our awareness arises directly inside the object to be reviewed and is known directly in the base of the mind rather than through the sense doors of eye or body as is the normal way our mind functions. In this capacity we are able to know objects that are not apparent to our senses of eye, ear or body etc. Every time our mind appears it produces subtle matter which has light. The colour of this light depends upon the qualities within the mind in that moment. As the mind becomes more concentrated and mindful and as our wisdom faculty develops this light over time becomes white and eventually extremely bright and clear. It is the light of the mind that is produced in deep samadhi meditation that illuminates the object to be known directly. So the power of our samadhi is the key to success. There is no visualisation involved. The mind simply sees directly without the use of the physical eye itself.

Any of you who may have read Roald Dahl's book 'The Amazing Story of Henry Sugar' may remember the tale of the man who could see without eyes. He was a circus performer who could ride his bicycle around the busy streets of India blindfolded. Well if such a feat were to be performed in real life it would be through the power of this light of samadhi that it was done.

Anyway, this light appears once our mind reaches a certain level of concentration and how bright it becomes thereafter depends largely on the ability of the yogi. In truth it is something that takes many years to develop fully but does arise swiftly in some yogis on account of their previous practice in past lives. It seemed I had this ability for I achieved my samadhi in the first ten days at Tanlyn.

"Ah, you have tremendous Parami," my teacher would say. For it was rare amongst the monks for this faculty to appear so swiftly.

One morning while concentrating particularly deeply on the middle bone of my thumb, the light that was illuminating it literally exploded in all directions. I had been reviewing the bone as white in colour and suddenly all I could perceive everywhere was this vast even field of brilliant white light. Gone was the bone of my thumb or any awareness of my body for that matter. I was quite simply lost in this white light. I had no idea what was happening. I had no reference point at that time. I simply sunk my attention into this field of whiteness and everything stopped. When I emerged from my meditation I had no idea of how long I had been sitting. I had been beyond any sense of time or space, just deeply absorbed in this infinite whiteness.

When I reported to the Abbot he smiled. He said something to the assistant monk who was translating for me. He quizzed me at length about the nature of my experience and asked me to review it in my mind as he checked for himself. It seemed I had entered deeply into the jhanic state of absorption. Normally this is a state that the yogi develops gradually through sustained practice, day-by-day, week-by-week, month-by-month. Often the first experience of jhana is rather fleeting as it is hard to maintain and the mind slips easily back into the un-unified state of concentration. Yet I had entered so suddenly and so deeply into jhana that not only did I not understand fully what had happened, but I found it quite hard to emerge from it. Pa Auk Sayadaw told me himself some time later when I was practicing under his guidance in Pa Auk that while working to establish first jhana I had actually entered deeply into the third jhana. The Abbot told me it was on account of my previous practice and that I should continue now to develop and stabilise further my absorption.

Most of my time in Tanlyn thereafter was spent in this deep state of samadhi. Then one evening it came to my mind that I should phone my father to see how he was. I had been out of contact for some time and while deeply immersed in my practice I had neglected to keep in touch with my family.

I called Dad from the phone at the lodge. He had always been extremely supportive of my spiritual endeavours and I was lucky not to have to tap dance around when explaining what I was up to. I told him I was at a monastery in Burma and he congratulated me on my courage. I had started to teach him meditation soon after I myself had begun with Ada and he was one of my most committed students. But his health was not good. He faced many challenges.

Before coming to Burma I had effectively walked away from my clothing business. I had left it in the hands of someone who had persuaded me that they could take it on. In truth I wasn't that worried what happened to it. I had had a good run with it and it had brought me to where I was now. I was well aware that it could have been very successful indeed but my heart had been pulled inexorably into nobler pursuits and I could not turn back. I had managed to find an Italian fashion brand to take over my factory in Bandung so the future of the workers there was secure. I had agreed to design one more range of clothes after which the brand was to be wound down or someone else would have to take over. All I had asked from the agreement was a small cash sum for the residual stock that I was passing on at cost. During the heady days of 'Making Madness A Way of Life' we had spent every penny of the vast sums that had come through the business. I had saved nothing and this small settlement would be all I walked away with. It amounted to less than fifteen thousand pounds but it would give me the cushion to start teaching.

I was determined to teach in England on a donation basis. It is the tradition with spiritual teachings that they are offered up freely to anyone who wants to learn. The student is simply asked to make a donation to the teacher according to his means. Although donation of this kind is not the normal way of doing things in our culture I felt that if I received enough to support myself by donation then it was a sure sign that it was my karma to be teaching in the country of my birth. The small capital that I would be left with when I passed on my business was enough to get me set up.

Dad told me that evening that the chap who was taking over my business had reneged on his deal and not paid me the money he owed for the gear I had given him. At that particular time I wasn't too fussed about it but it was clear that my Dad had a real bee in his bonnet about it. He had loved my business dearly and played a huge part in it over the years. He was very bitter at the thought that someone else was going to take it off my hands for free. I told him not to worry and that if this guy wanted to pay he would. If not there wasn't much to be done about it without a messy legal claim, and that was something I had no inclination to get into.

We discussed things briefly. He said he did think I should be at home to take care of my affairs. I told him that I was ready to move on and was happy to take my chance with it.

Dad wasn't really satisfied with my attitude and made it clear.

I hung up the phone and walked back through the monastery to my kuti and sat back down on my cushion to meditate.

Now it is stated in the Visuddhimagga that one who wants to strive for these jhanic states of samadhi needs to go far away from all worldly distractions to a remote place. Upon receiving instructions from his teacher he must strive ardently day and night not flinching from his quest. I was lucky in the ease with which samadhi had come to me and until now hadn't really appreciated the importance so many other monks and yogis attached to seclusion. But as soon as I sat down on my cushion that evening I knew. I had instinctively known that there is a time for spiritual practice and a time when the worldly affairs would take precedence. I would often implore my students not to expect progress if they had not attended to their duties, for at the subtlest levels of the mind this unfinished business will relentlessly pull the awareness away from the object of concentration and exclude us from any entry into any real samadhi or serenity. The entry into jhana is marked initially by the overwhelming sense of utter surrender and letting go. It is the complete disinterest in anything but the object of meditation that opens the way to absorption and unification.

I sat on my cushion to continue my meditation. But I was unable to pick up as I had left off. Where before my mind had been clear, stable and still, I now felt the subtlest vibration in my heart that disturbed the stability of my concentration. For some days I had been able to drop into samadhi almost immediately, taking only the time it took for my breath and body rhythms to calm down. My mind was drawn towards nothing except its object and I was undistracted, both externally and internally.

While I had discussed the situation with my Dad I had felt quite at ease with my decision to let go my business and not get into a contest over it, but I knew as soon as I sat that my equanimity was not as complete as I might have thought.

The basis for samadhi is the stillness and stability of the heart base. This is the subtle energy base that is the support for the arising of our awareness and active consciousness. It is like the runway from which our mind launches out to grasp at external objects. It is also where we land the impression of those objects, giving rise to our direct experience of them. Our ability to land the objects of our experience is governed by the condition of the runway, or heart base.

If your heart base is not stable then you are easily shaken by the experience of life. If the heart base is strong and steady and thick then we can land challenging experiences without losing our balance. A weak heart base is like having only a rural landing strip to bring home all of life's challenges. Such a person will live in fear of encountering things they know will land too heavily and shatter their balance. It is like landing a Boeing 747 on a local airfield. It is a recipe for disaster. A strong heart base is like Heathrow Airport, able to land 747s all day long. And the condition of our heart base is determined by how reactive or equanimous our mind is in the face of the experiences we encounter.

I reviewed my mind for the cause of this vibration I felt in my heart and realised, of course, that it lay in the unresolved business at home.
I knew immediately my time in Burma was over for now. I would progress no further until I had sorted out my affairs. I packed there and then and in the morning went to the teacher to ask permission to leave.
He was dumbfounded that I should break my practice now when I was clearly on a roll. For me there was no choice; to have pushed on at that point would have meant stiffening my mind with the desire for progress and suppressing the call to attend to my duties. I realised later when I joined Pa Auk Sayadaw in the forest just how attached most people get to their practice; how badly they want success. I always saw this as a hindrance. We need to be utterly committed to our practice but this degree of attachment will keep the mind gross and cloud the way to higher states. Deep samadhi is an effortless abiding, one that the mind will either enter into blissfully and with ease or not at all. It is in effect a by-product of the conditions we set up within ourselves. It is borne of the ease and serenity of our heart and as such nothing can be of any real

importance to us in the moment of entry. In the end the highest state of samadhi is still a state that will last only for a while and in that sense it is the same as any other state, in its impermanence. It is our equanimity to it and our acceptance of its transience that is the key to our heart's release, not our absorption itself. I was happy with my practice. I knew I would be back. But for now I had to return to England and attend to things there.

The Abbot implored me to stay. He told me how rare it was for someone to have the talent I had, and that I should stop at nothing until I had finished. He dearly wanted me to wait for Sayadaw's return. He even told me that Sayadaw had been waiting years for the chance to teach someone who might take these Dharmas to the West.

In some way I felt surprised that he couldn't see that there was little point in my staying. I felt from the outset, that progress would come when the mind was undistracted by worldly affairs. I saw later, in the forest, so many who were working relentlessly day and night to achieve these levels of samadhi. Many of them came to me after alms round at midday to ask my advice about their practice. It was well known that I had been successful with the jhanas and they would come hoping I might impart some special piece of knowledge that would open the door for them. But always I came to the same conclusion. Whenever I checked the minds of those who asked me for advice, I could feel clearly the reason they were unable to achieve samadhi. There was still too much they clung to or too many things that troubled them. The Buddha implored the serious aspirant to renounce the world and live a simple life for the purposes of achieving Nibbana. The renunciation is to seclude us from things that lead to bondage, but no guarantee that the mind is free from attachment or aversion. Renunciation as a suppression of desire is not the same as its non-arising. Attachment is a state of our mind and as such one who clings will cling to anything. Take away most of our distractions and we will still find some small thing to cling to. Be it our status within the community of monks, our position in the alms round cue, where we sit in the meditation hall. Even the robes and begging bowl may become an object of pride for some. When we are free of this clinging we hardly need such seclusion. I had always felt we needed to extinguish our desires by seeing them through and resolving them into disinterest and eventually renunciation. I could see no way in which suppressing them would end them. It is a hazardous approach I know for we are easily intoxicated with sensual desire. But I have come to know over the years that suppression of desire means it often does not rear its head for purification.

Nibbana is easy to achieve for one who clings to nothing, but it is impossible for one who clings to anything. So how do we get to the point of clinging to nothing?

Through the systematic refinement of our character through virtue and the wisdom that comes to know that there is in truth nothing that CAN be clung to. By living virtuously and experiencing life's rich fruits with discernment and restraint we turn our greed and attachment into gratitude and appreciation. In this way we might come to a point of feeling satisfied that what we wanted and needed to do has been done and so come to a sense that we have entered into life and drunk of it fully before we finally let go.

We need to refine our aspirations through the experience of living life. This experience reveals to us in stages the transience of any satisfaction we achieve from ego gratification. Until such a time we will continue to deeply define ourselves by our ego view. Be it "I am a Fashion Designer", "I am a Blues Harmonica Player", "I am a Monk", "I Am a Yogi", "I have reached first, second, third, fourth jhana," or "I am a Meditation Teacher": it is always a pantomime we are playing out, just an idea of ourselves to which we cling. When our point has been made and our existence justified at a mundane level it is easier by far to turn away from worldly pursuits, towards nobler goals. If our renunciation is rooted in the sense that life is just hard and unpleasant or even unfair then that renunciation is rooted in aversion and aversion is not one of the doors to liberation. Our renunciation must be a joyful turning away from that which has been lived and experienced fully within us so that we can let go blissfully. Though I hadn't realised it at the time, I had already seen first-hand an almost perfect example of this way of renunciation in the way in which my Grandfather approached the end of his life.

CHAPTER FIFTEEN

Granddad

I had observed my grandfather preparing for his death some years before. It was a beautiful lesson in letting go. He had retired at the end of his working life from West London to a small village in Dorset. He had bought a small cottage with a large garden, with the single intent of pursuing his two great loves; woodwork and gardening.

My brother Grant and I had learned so much craft from him in the years of our childhood. He showed us how to carve wood, fish for perch and pike, grow soft fruits and how to roll our own cigarettes.

We adored him. He was our mentor and a source of what seemed like infinite wisdom.

He was born in Fort William in the highlands of Scotland, to devoutly Christian parents. His father was a church minister who had instilled in him both an unwavering faith in God and a deeply loving and caring nature.

His was the last generation to be raised on true Christian principles, and also the generation who had fought and died in the Great War. His was a time immediately preceding the surge of materialism that brought England's modern middle class truly into being and so he was unspoiled by the complex of aspirations that we have inherited.

There was within him a genuine love of simplicity and a deep, unstated wisdom. His heart was uncluttered by the mass of desires we have latched on to. He found his bliss with ease at the end of an honest and hardworking life, as a decent man, who had upheld his sense of duty and executed it to the end.

He worked from the age of fifteen till his retirement in the distribution business, first as road hand to a lorry driver, then a driver himself before graduating to depot manager of SPD and later middle management in Unilever.

My mother was his only child and he was utterly devoted both to her and to his equally devoted wife. His sole desire throughout his working life was to provide for them with diligence and honesty, and seeing my Mother's life unfold before him was enough to justify the life he had been given.

He was truly unspoiled by selfish desires and personal needs. His joy came exclusively from the happiness of his daughter and later her family, which meant of course that Grant and I were the world to him.

We spent so much of our childhood in his garden. Grant and I had grown up outside. All of my earliest memories were of being covered in dirt, living in trees and playing endlessly in the adventure playground of the big outdoors.

Granddad's garden was the adventure to end all adventures, and from the moment we arrived all we saw of the inside of the house was mealtimes and bedtime. Occasionally in the depths of winter we would be driven in before bedtime by the cold and on those rare evenings we would play cards round the fire with Dad and Granddad and on occasion Mum and Nana. But for the most part the garden consumed us totally.

Closest to the house, in clear view from the conservatory were Granddad's prizewinning flowerbeds. In truth these were the least interesting part to Grant and I, as being the most fragile they were the most out of bounds. Couple that with the fact that whatever entertainment they might afford was clearly within view of the adults who resided predominantly in the conservatory, and there was little on offer to us boys by way of adventure. Our world began beyond the flower beds in the more hidden reaches.

The exception to this, however, was the coal bunker. Around the back of the house and just out of sight of the conservatory, it was a source of endless pleasure. It was a large concrete structure with two round entrances in the top like manholes and two doors at the front from which coal was extracted.

Our game was to climb in through the top and make our way down through the coal and out the doors in the front. It was a race. We would climb over the garage and jump down onto the bunker, entering through the manholes and out the front.

Needless to say the adults derived nothing like the pleasure from our antics that we did and we were scolded severely for the atrocious state in which we emerged. Yet it was strange that we were never banned from the bunker, rather strongly discouraged. The danger was pointed out to us in no uncertain terms along with such exclamations as: "Just look at the state of you two boys."

I realise now though that the freedom to explore such things was granted us out of a certain pride that our elders seemed to gain from observing our fearlessness and wild abandon. Perhaps it was for this that our game was tolerated as it was.

The bunker race aside however, it was in the world beyond the flower beds that we learned our art. It was the art of creating worlds within worlds. This was a time when parents did not live in fear of stalkers and child molesters and so we were free to roam as we pleased.

Granddad had two sheds, the potting shed and his woodworking shed and each of them became the location of countless camps and hideouts over the years. Nana would often refer to us as "You little monkeys" and upon reflection this may well have been a response to the time we would spend suspended in any way possible above the ground, in the rafters of the sheds, the roof tops themselves and any tree we could find. We slung hammocks in the rafters and built tree houses from anything and everything that would bear our weight.

Our magnum opus was the conquering of two particularly tall poplar trees that soared high above the house. Again it was a race; how high and how fast. When we first learned to climb it was an overwhelming challenge. Our small bodies were well tolerated by its supple branches but we were no more than four and five when we first launched our campaign to reach the summit. Fear and our limited reach determined how high we got but as the years progressed there came a time when we finally achieved our goal.

I was nine and Grant eight. We had grown somewhat since our efforts had begun. We had the reach now and had found the courage, but we were no longer the wee things we had been. The branches became thinner the higher we got and so it was a delicate balance that afforded us final access to the canopy top.

I will remember till I die the view of the world when I first poked my head up above the foliage and looked out over the rooftops below. Poplars are tall and sway considerably in the wind and with the extra weight they now bore this swaying was amplified.

I think perhaps it was the first and only time I can remember actually being red carded by Mum and Nana. They came down the garden that afternoon rounding us up for tea. Every other time we had climbed the poplars the foliage had provided cover and it is possible that they had never before actually seen us scaling these dizzy heights. But now my head poked above the top of the tree and came into clear view. "Hi Mum," I shouted, immensely proud of my achievement.

"What do you think you're doing?" she screamed. "Just GET down from there immediately. Where's your brother? He's not up there too is he?"

"Hi Mum," he cried from the tree next door. He was as yet concealed and so not initially in view.

"You two boys get down from those trees right now!" cried Nana. "You'll give your poor mother a heart attack."

In hindsight I can only imagine the horror Mum must have felt to see her two cherubs dangling so precariously and at such height.

Even Dad scolded us that day. But Granddad held his peace as he always did, winking at us in the background while we got our dressing down.

It was the following morning while we worked to cut wood with him in the shed that he made his only reference to our recklessness:

"You know, you two boys should be more careful. You nearly gave your mother apoplexy yesterday. Next time try to get down before teatime, hey?"

That was Granddad through and through, ever an ally and staunch supporter. He tolerated anything that stood for a hearty sense of adventure. It was rudeness and disrespect that he wouldn't stand for. If ever we answered our mother back impolitely he would have something to say, but climbing the Everest of all trees even at risk to life and limb? Well, this was to be highly commended.

Four years later Mum caught Grant and me leaving the newsagent at home with two packs of cigarettes. We were off to the golf course to play havoc and smoke ourselves stupid.

She busted us good and proper that day. There was no escape.

As punishment she made us write to Granddad and confess our sin. She insisted he cut off the "fruit" allowance he had been sending us for school each month. It had been this money that had funded our new found nicotine habits.

When we went to visit him over half term Mum told us in the car that we could expect stern words from Granddad when we arrived.

He would always take us to his woodwork shed whenever he needed to talk man to man with us and sure enough he asked us to join him there after lunch that day. Sheepishly, Grant and I traipsed down the garden in his wake and followed him into the shed.

"Now you know your Mother is most disappointed in you. She has asked me to stop your allowance. Have you got anything to say for yourselves?"

"Sorry Granddad."

"Sorry Granddad."

We muttered our apologies with heads bowed.

He reached into his back pocket and pulled out his wallet and his tobacco pouch.

"OK. Now don't you ever tell her," he said, "but here is your allowance. I will send it to you directly at school from now, but if ever she finds out we will all be in trouble."

He handed us our money and rolled himself a cigarette. He smoked St Bruno ready rubbed pipe tobacco in roll ups - something my Mother could never quite get her head around. He finished rolling and then made another, and handed us one apiece.

"There you go," he said. "If you are going to smoke, then at least smoke a real cigarette. Try that for size."

It was strong and pungent but neither of us was going to choke. We smoked the roll ups with infinite pride and joy. It was the day we became men.

Now I have always maintained that there is a part of every boy that doesn't become a man until he has earned the respect and acceptance of his elders and mentors. Being granted this is a fundamental rite of passage that tells us we are ready to stand on our own two feet and begin our stepping out into the world of adulthood.

I know so many men who feel incomplete in a way they cannot express and I am convinced it is on account of not being granted this acceptance or rite of passage by the elder men in their lives. Some part of them feels emasculated or inadequate because no one they admired ever said to them: "Hey, you are all right son."

Well Granddad was doing it now as Dad would do himself the day he picked me up when I had been suspended from Wellington.

Though I did not fully understand the full implication of these moments they were axiomatic in granting me the courage and freedom to enter completely and fearlessly into life. Of all the gifts both these two men ever gave me as I grew up, this acceptance and respect was the most precious of all. I wouldn't have traded it for all the miles of Scalextric or all the model airplanes on the planet.

Grant and I knew the score; Granddad was telling us that he did too. It was a special day.

And so it was with Granddad. He was a man of few wants and easily satisfied. He had his garden and it was his world. It was immaculate in every way. He kept his composts at the very end and his vegetable plot in front of that. Then rows of soft fruits leading up to his apple trees that shaded his two sheds, and in front of them his lawn and flowerbeds.

Grant and I would work hours with him in the holidays, digging, weeding, pruning and picking. The work changed with the seasons and always there was a deep sense of order and rhythm. There was a time of planting, a time of growth and a time of fruition and of decay; and each stage, an integral part of the grand scheme of things.

As he grew older an injury from a fishing accident that had broken his knee years before began to take its toll. Finally, one year, the time came for him to dig up his vegetables, one last time, and sow grass seeds instead. He lawned the farthest part of the garden and left it to rest. Two years later he conceded the soft fruits and likewise turned their domain to grass.

In time he decommissioned his tool shed and transformed the woodwork shed into a potting shed and turned his hand to perfecting his chrysanthemums. There was never a sense of loss just a steady reapplication of his energy in tune with his resources. Eventually he left everything beyond the sheds to rest and worked only the flowerbeds closest to the house.

Grant and I had grown and we no longer needed the hideouts that we ruled in our childhood. Visits now were spent sitting in the conservatory chewing the fat and discussing life.

Granddad's one regret was that he hadn't been allowed to go to the war with his brothers. He worked in the distribution business and so was commissioned to stay behind and play his part in the supply line that kept the country going. It was important work, but not enough so in his eyes, to make up for the fact that so many of his friends had given their lives to earn the freedom that Grant and I grew up with.

He had never had the chance to give his all and so failed to find the hero in himself. It was quite sad really, to think that we should all have to fight and die at war to be a hero. Both Grant and I knew he was a hero in every way.

The last time I ever spoke to him was from Bandung in Java. I had finished the last season with Mad Rags and was negotiating the deal with the Italian label to take over my factory. Mum had told me he had been taken ill and was in Dorchester Hospital.

Nana had been ill the previous year and spent some months in the same hospital. Granddad had driven daily the hour from home to be at her bed side. She was terrified of dying and couldn't let go. Granddad wasn't ready to either, and he had asked me to visit to see if there was anything I could do. I was working with Ada and my meditation had already begun to mature.

I went to visit her in hospital the day her kidneys began to fail. Mum and Dad took Granddad home and I stayed on with her. Many people hallucinate when death approaches – some of them see blissful visions, others fearful ones. Nana was an angel and had been all her life, but her absolute refusal to accept the fact that one day she would die had filled her with fear. She didn't have faith like Granddad did and had never taken time to contemplate life after death.

And so, as her body failed, she became both scared and confused. I was quite unsettled by her distress. The doctor came and told me she may not make it till the morning. It was midnight. I sat with her through the night occasionally comforting her and talking of the good old days when Grant and I were just kids.

"We had some wonderful times, didn't we?" She said at one point as I sat stroking her forehead.

But most of the time I spent deep in meditation with my mind in her body, supporting her life with my mindfulness. I was determined to stop her kidneys from failing, if nothing else, so she could see Granddad one last time. By the morning her delirium was over and her kidneys started to function normally again. The doctor couldn't understand it and said she was a very lucky lady.

186

She began to recover and two weeks later she was back at home. But that length of time in hospital had left her very frail and she could hardly stand. Granddad took up his duties and walked daily to the shops on his lame leg. He cooked for her and washed her and held her hand at night.

He gave his all to care for the woman he had loved all his life but it took its toll on him and he was worn out. A few months later it was he who was in the hospital, but Nana was in no shape to visit daily. Neither was she emotionally able to give the support he had given her. She was simply too afraid of losing him and cried most times she visited. Mum and Dad moved down to Dorset for a while to take care of them both.

Mum had told me that I should finish what I was doing in Asia before coming home and I had agreed to do so, but then one evening she phoned telling me Granddad was dying.

I called him in the hospital.

"Granddad. How are you? I hear you've been causing trouble again."

"Oh it's you Guy. How lovely to hear from you. Aren't you in Asia?"

"Yes I am but I am going to come home immediately."

"You shouldn't be calling me from way over there. It must be costing a fortune."

"Oh don't you worry about that," I said, "How are you feeling?"

"Oh, I'm alright old boy. Can't complain. It's a wonderful hospital and they are taking such good care of me. These nurses are amazing you know. I don't know how they do it, day in, day out, looking after old codgers like me."

"Listen, you soak it up Granddad, you deserve all the attention you can get. I'm trying to get a flight home tomorrow. I'll be straight down to see you."

"Don't you put yourself out for me mate," he said. "I'll be fine."

I did fly back the next day and Mum picked me up at Heathrow. I was thinking to go straight down to see him but Mum suggested I stopped in at home for a shower and some breakfast. By nine that morning we were on our way to Dorset.

"I'm not sure we will make it," said Mum. "The nurse called while you were in the shower and said his heart was fading fast."

I meditated on Granddad all the way willing him to hang on. I remember so clearly the moment I felt his heart stop. We were on the A303 driving past Stonehenge and Mum was listening to Faure's 'In Paradisum'.

"I think he's gone you know," I said to Mum. "I can't feel his heart all of a sudden."

"Oh Guy. I'm so sorry. It's my fault we stopped off. Perhaps we should have come straight down."

I was right. We arrived at the hospital just too late. He had died at ten thirty just as we passed Stonehenge. The nurse told us but we both knew already. We could tell from the look on her face as she greeted us.

He was in a ward with a curtain around his bed. She led us in. He lay on his side with his mouth slightly open. I held Mum in my arms and we both cried deeply, unable to speak. She had lost her Dad and I my mentor.

I could still feel him in the room around us. He was so present I could almost hear his voice. I knew he was telling us not to worry. He was alright. He hated to see us cry. I think we both sensed this and we pulled ourselves together. We sat on his bed and held his hand. I stroked his forehead. We told him how much we loved him, and thanked him for all the joy he had given us. And then we sat silently and rested in the space he was leaving. After about half an hour I could no longer feel him in the room.

Nana was staying at Mum's house as she couldn't take care of herself, but I knew that Granddad would go to his home. I suggested to Mum that we drove there and spend the night so that we could take care of all the practicalities the next day.

The house was empty but spotless. Everything as it had been since my childhood.

We made tea and sat holding hands, taking in all that was left of him around us.

"Let's take a walk up his garden," said Mum. "I could do with some fresh air."

It was quite extraordinary. I hadn't been to the house since Nana had come out of hospital. There wasn't a blade of grass out of place. But there was lawn where all his vegetables and fruits had been. Even the flowerbeds had been cut back. We went into his shed and everything was packed away tidily in boxes. He knew he was on his way. He had gradually said his goodbyes over the last few years and had obviously decided he wasn't going to be a bother to anyone when he went.

His old garden was a labour of love and took daily care and attention. The garden he left behind would need no tending in his absence. He had tidied up his affairs and gone on his way leaving nothing unattended to.

I saw in that moment the depth of the wisdom he had kept in his heart. He understood impermanence as much as any of the monks I had meditated with. His life was an exquisite expression of that understanding. He had sowed seeds and brought forth fruits. He had delighted in them daily but when it was time, he let them go without a trace of regret.

His last words to me: "Oh, I'm alright old boy. Don't you worry about me."

He was right. We wouldn't have to worry about him. All that was left was to sit and send him love and let him go with gratitude.

I think it was in that moment that Mum finally came to understand the extraordinary being who had been her father. She just squeezed my hand to say she had understood.

Later I sat up through the night. He did indeed come to the house. He sat in his old chair and I sat in Nana's opposite him. They were the two chairs they had spent every evening of their retired lives in. Nana knitting or doing puzzles while Granddad read Churchill's 'A History of the English-Speaking Peoples', or sketched with charcoal.

Mum was asleep upstairs. We just sat together resting in the space. He was taking it in one last time. Then at two a.m. he went. He just faded into emptiness and was gone.

Dad told me the next day that he had come to say goodbye to him in the family house where he was with Nana. In the early hours of the morning he had woken to see Granddad standing at the end of his bed. He thanked Dad for taking care of his beloved daughter and asked him to look after his wife. Then having made sure that all was as it should be, he finally took his leave.

We played Faure's 'In Paradisum' at his cremation and we honoured his noble but simple life, but I knew already that he had gone. I knew too that this world would not see the likes of his generation again. His was a generation who really did appreciate what they had, who took hardship in their stride and had none of the sense of entitlement that so easily spoils many of us.

The Buddha implored his monks to be of few wants and easy to serve. Granddad would have set a fine example to them in both respects. Mum always reckoned that from the time of his retirement till he died he and Nana lived and ran their home on ten pounds a day. Most of his life savings were still intact when he died with a request that no expense be spared taking care of Nana.

Though perhaps her karma would normally have taken her from us before Granddad, had I not interfered, she outlived him by five years. But those years were quite empty without him and I am sure that the only reason she was left behind was because she couldn't let go. I often wonder if in fact I had done her an injustice by fighting for her life that night in the hospital and perhaps it might have been Granddad who would have spent those extra years with us had I let things be.

It was a big lesson to me. What actually constitutes a compassionate act? It is not always the case that we should give our all to save someone who is dying. It's life, or the certain end to it at least.

I remember reflecting on this when the doctor first told us that Dad was terminally ill. His heart was already weak, and I wondered what quality of life he would have had, if I had dug deep enough to get him through his cancer. It's funny how one lesson in life, often over time, shows itself to be a preparation for another.

When Dad's time did come, I didn't interfere, however much at times I wish I had done. But then everything in life is impermanent. It is a fact that in time all of us will be separated from everything that is dear to us. It is only by coming to accept this to be an absolute truth that we are protected from the deepest suffering that loss can bring.

I learned early to appreciate the gifts life had brought me and the wonderful beings who had loved me so much. But it was never going to be early enough. I can remember clearly having no idea of the sacrifices Mum and Dad made to keep me safe as I grew up. The sacrifice of a parent that no child ever understands until they become one themselves.

Now only my Mum remains. She is fit as a fiddle and will probably live till she's a hundred. And I truly hope she does.

CHAPTER SIXTEEN

Sayadaw

My first stay at Tanlyn monastery had been brought to an abrupt end by the news from home regarding my clothing business.

I had a choice to make.

I had made an agreement to sign over production rights to a Hong Kong businessman who wished to carry on the production of my label. I had accepted a royalty agreement which, if the new business was successful, would have provided me with the income that would allow me to follow my wish to offer the teachings in my own country on a donation only basis. I was determined to honour the tradition of not charging people to learn meditation but I knew I would need to support myself in some way.

However, what my father had told me over the phone that day had rather rocked my plans. In short I had been duped. I had had a friend who had agreed to help me broker my exit strategy, but when the crunch came it was clear that neither my partner nor the Hong Kong businessman had any intention of honouring our agreement. My choice was whether to fight for it or let it go.

I had been following my way for some time and the cut and thrust of hard business was not something my mind was inclined towards. I knew that a legal battle would be messy and I didn't feel that the Hong Kong guy would even be able to keep the vibe of the label going. My gut feeling was that he would fail to sustain the interest in the brand that my gang had generated and so I decided not to contest what was happening.

I saw it all as karma. If this new guy didn't have the understanding of where it had all come from I doubted that his version of the label would succeed once I and my gang withdrew our energy. So in the end I accepted some cash for the residual stock that I signed over to them and made my way back to Asia to pick up where I had left off.

In truth I was smarting from the way I had been treated, but equally I knew that if I wasn't prepared to put up a fight there was no one else out there going to fight on my behalf.

So I let it go. Mad Rags had served me and many others well over the years. It had bonded a group of young warrior spirits that would stay connected for life. We had asked a few questions and dined out well. I never thought for a moment that it was something I would still be doing in old age. So I took my money and caught the first plane out I could.

On the flight back to Asia I mulled over where I was at and where it all might be heading.

The extraordinary events in India had left a profound impression on me and my first spell in Burma had started to put some structure to my practice, but I needed to complete the picture and get some perspective on what had actually happened. I knew that Pa Auk Sayadaw's thorough and systematic approach to meditation would eventually help me fill in the gaps.

However did I come to have such a profound connection to both this great master of the Tibetan tradition and the ancient civilisation of Bagan? They represented the opposite ends of the spectrum as far as approach to the Buddha's path is concerned.

I had had clear memories of a past life in Burma but until now had no recollection of any previous connection to Tibet. I was, however, beginning to glimpse more deeply the role karma played in everything. It was time to look into this.

I had read Pa Auk Sayadaw's manuscript and his explanation of the way of reviewing past lives. I had already looked into regression as a means to uncovering this most tantalising of mysteries. My meditation had taught me that memory and imagination appear in the mind by exactly the same process and through the same mind door. I would need a very discerning tool to review this field with integrity.

I understood that I would have to try to make sense of why this was all happening to me. I needed to understand the role my past had played in it all, but I knew equally it was easy to get carried away. I had read the New Age accounts of past life experiences and realised that if they were to be believed then Cleopatra and Joan of Arc must have split into many fragments at death to appear in time as numerous housewives in middle England.

Dependent origination was the key to understanding it all, for there is nothing that comes into being without due cause.

My intention was to return to Bali and touch base with Ada and see if he wanted to come again with me to try to meet Sayadaw. I was sure he could train me and help me develop my meditation to the point where I could see more clearly into these things. He taught the entire path of meditation in all its intricacy – the development of the jhanas as the basis for investigation, and the exhaustive analysis of material and mental states that lead eventually to the knowledge of dependent origination and the causal chain that brings things into being.

It was through following this causal chain that we could retrace the pathways of our past actions beyond this existence into the lifetimes that had gone before. His was the path of detailed and exhaustive investigation, and not of inspiration and intuition. The Light of Wisdom is the way of direct perception that simply sees things as they are and finally takes us beyond speculation.

Much of the knowledge that had come to me had done so through transmission. Now I felt the need to ground this understanding in direct experience through diligent and disciplined practice. Besides, I could not expect my students to learn the way I had. I would have to teach them a systematic approach to the development of insight and wisdom.

I had read the Visuddhimagga and knew it to be the manual of practice I needed to follow. I wanted to develop all the techniques the Buddha had taught so I could offer them to my students according to their needs. I could see now that we could not rely on one technique alone and that we needed a wide-ranging skillset to turn our mind into a tool of real discernment and understanding, by which to navigate out of our confusion to clarity and vision.

My flight to Bali went via Malaysia and so I decided to go briefly to Penang and look in on a talented young Chi Kung Sifu named Yap who I had learned from a few years previously. Since my initial stay with him we had become good friends.

I took a taxi to his house. It was a Saturday afternoon.

"Ah, hi Burgs!" he said with a beaming smile. "How are you doing?"

"I am doing well," I replied. "I am on my way back to Bali from England. I thought I would take the time to catch up. Have you been well?"

"Very well indeed," he smiled. "Actually, I have to go to give healing to a famous monk who is staying here in Penang this afternoon. I will be away for only an hour or so. Make yourself at home and later we can go and eat durian. I will know how well you have learned from how much you can eat."

It was a man thing. A challenge we played whenever I visited, to see who could eat the most durian. It is a pungent and potent fruit that is very heaty. You either love it or hate it. Sifu loved it and it was a gauntlet he often threw down.

"OK. I am up for that," I said. "So who is this monk you are treating?"

"He is a famous master from Burma. He has been suffering with terrible headaches and body pain. I have been asked to see if I can help. His name is Pa Auk Sayadaw."

My jaw dropped. Surely not?

"I don't believe it!" I said. "Pa Auk Sayadaw is here? Why only recently I went to Burma with Merta Ada to see if we could help him. We were told he was in Taiwan."

"He was, but he has come here to stay at one of our temples and take further rest. So you know of him then?"

"I certainly do. I spent a few weeks at one of his monasteries in Burma once we realised we couldn't meet with him."

"Well in that case I think you had better come with me."

I couldn't believe it. I had decided to come to Penang on a whim. I had no idea Sayadaw was here. Just who was pulling my strings? Perhaps the old goat herder from Rewalsar was still watching over me, or maybe Padmasambhava himself? I gave up even trying to figure it out. Either way I was about to meet my master and wouldn't have to make the arduous trip to the forest of Southern Burma to do so.

We signed in at the reception to the temple and were taken through the main shrine room to some private quarters in the back. We waited for some minutes while the attendant announced our arrival. A Burmese monk came to greet us. Sifu was led in to see Sayadaw and I waited outside with the Monk.

"So you are Burgs?" he asked.

"Yes." I replied.

I recognised the monk. His name was U Agginna. He was maybe ten years older than me and one of Sayadaw's closest disciples. He had been the first Burmese monk to stay with Sayadaw in the forest and the very first to complete his practice. I had seen a picture of him at the temple on the hill overlooking Bagan the morning I had had my flashback and remembered my past there. From the first time I had seen his picture I felt a deep bond with him, a feeling of brotherhood. I felt a great warmth at seeing him now.

"Ah, we have heard of you from Tanlyn. The Abbot there reported to Sayadaw of your progress.

He was most disappointed that you left. Sayadaw is eager to talk to you. We were not expecting to see you here."

"It is an extraordinary coincidence." I said. "I just came to visit my friend, Sifu Yap. He just told me when I arrived earlier today that Sayadaw was here."

"Ah, sadhu sadhu sadhu," he said. "It is very wonderful. Sayadaw says you have great paramis. He wants to instruct you personally. He will call you to see him when his treatment is over."

I sat silently in the corridor with U Agginna reviewing the practice I had done in Tanlyn.

After half an hour or so Yap emerged.

U Agginna stood and beckoned me to follow him.

I was led into a small room with a simple bed in it. Around it were three monks.

Sayadaw was sitting up in the bed. He smiled at me as I knelt and bowed.

"Please sit," he said.

He looked at me for a few moments. He was a small man with infinitely kind eyes. I could feel immediately the love that he radiated and the profound wisdom it masked.

"Please tell me about your meditation," he asked.

I looked at U Agginna for guidance.

"Sayadaw will assess your progress. He is very interested in you. Please tell him what happened at Tanlyn."

I began to recount my experiences there.

I did not tell of what had happened in Bagan. I simply gave an account of the progress I had made under the Abbot in Tanlyn.

Sayadaw never stopped looking at me as I spoke. When I had finished he closed his eyes for a few moments. I knew he was reviewing what I had said.

"Very good," he responded. "You have great paramis. You must finish your meditation. Whatever you are planning to do I urge you to try to re-arrange your time so that you can come back to Burma with me as soon as I am well. I want to teach you systematically."

I knew it was a great honour that he was so interested in me. Equally I knew I had no choice. Immediately I agreed.

"I have to go to Bali to help my teacher for two weeks. After that I can come."

"Very good," he smiled again and his eyes flashed.

I asked him how I should continue with my practice until I could come to Burma.

"You must carry on developing your body parts meditation. Start to stay in one place for long periods. One hour, two hours, three hours. If your sign comes again, ignore it for now. I will teach you the Jhanas in order when you are in Burma. Please be sure to come as soon as you can."

The sign Sayadaw was referring to was the sign of concentration that begins to appear as we approach jhana. In Pali it is called Nimitta* and it takes different forms depending upon the meditation subject. Usually it is a light of some kind and needs to be clearly differentiated from the many other kinds of light that may appear before the mind when we meditate.

I knew there was nothing more to say. I knew what I had to do. And I knew Sayadaw was tired and needed rest.

I thanked him for his time and bowed before standing to leave.

"We will arrange for you a sponsorship letter so you can get a one year visa from the embassy," U Agginna said once we were outside. "Please be sure to come as soon as you can."

He gave me the number of a contact in Singapore who would keep me posted on Sayadaw's progress and from who I would collect my letter.

My meeting with Sayadaw was quite a contrast to the teachers I had met in India. We spent no time talking of Dharma and the view of it. He was clinical and practical. I learned later that this was his way. He was interested in one thing and one thing only: genuine progress in meditation, and the development of insight that is born of direct perception. He had no time for mulling over philosophy or views.

In his book there was only one view to come to and it didn't need discussing for we would each of us arrive at it in our own time through direct knowledge. There was no part to play for our rational mind. In that respect his approach resonated with what I had learned in the cave from Padmasambhava. You either know, or you don't know; and when you know, you know you know. When you don't know, you don't know you don't know.

I had no issue with this, and I was excited by the prospect of giving myself time to really develop my skill in meditation. I felt that so far most of my progress had come from a talent that I previously did not know I had.

This is what is meant by the Pali word Parami. It refers to any ability that one has on account of previous practice and cultivation, usually in previous lives. It actually means perfection and not talent for it is understood that what appears to be talent is only ever the result of prior work and effort put forth in this or previous lives. It is not something that appears by chance or in an inexplicable way.

The extraordinary thing about the Buddha's Dharma is that, if it is practised diligently enough, the knowledge it leads to in time comes to explain all the phenomena that we in the West have speculated on and turned into philosophy. It appealed to me greatly, for I had left behind any academic aspirations I may have had when I left school.

I did read the scriptures but they were only references to point the way and not a doctrine to be held blindly. It was the knowledge of direct experience that I was in search of and I knew I would find it in Burma.

I returned to Bali determined to honour the agreement I had made with Sayadaw. I called back home to England and cancelled all my plans and when I finished the retreat with Ada I called to Singapore to see how Sayadaw was doing.

He had recovered enough to go home and was due in Burma in a few days.

I flew to Singapore to apply for my visa and followed him back to the country that would finally bring everything into focus for me and allow me to ground the extraordinary events of the past two years. I was ready to be still for a long time. It had been a roller coaster and I now longed to just sit with it all and let it settle.

CHAPTER SEVENTEEN

Into The Forest

The adventure of the past few years had dismantled and reconfigured me with a momentum I had no chance to fight against. I was literally dragged headlong into it, and in Burma I finally found an evenness and rhythm that allowed me to process it all.

My time in Rewalsar had given me a taste for routine that my life previously had never had, but the events there had been so extraordinary that I was left almost breathless. It wasn't until I finally arrived at Sayadaw's monastery in the forest of Southern Burma that I began to catch my breath.

I had lived the life of a monk while I practiced in solitude on Gili Nanggu, but wasn't there long enough to fully decompress. There was then an intensity in my practice that was serving me and keeping me focused. Now I began to find my ease, and began to enjoy the real fruits of my meditation.

A community of two hundred monks and some fifty nuns had grown up around Sayadaw since it became apparent that he had such extraordinary talents. He had never intended to become a great teacher. He was alone in the forest and had been for many years when people in Burma began to get word of him and start coming for instruction.

It is said that there has not been a teacher in Burma for five hundred years who has taught the complete path of meditation in accordance with the Abhidhamma* and the Visuddhimagga. These are two immense bodies of work handed down through the centuries. The first is the detailed analysis of the way things arise and function at a causal level and the second is the manual of the path to this knowledge through meditation and direct experience.

There are many who have made an academic study of the Abhidhamma, believing that the knowledge it expounds is beyond the grasp of our conditioned minds. Only in the Visuddhimagga and its commentaries are we to find the systematic explanation of the meditative attainments that can lead to direct knowledge of these things rather than academic study of them.

There was no record of anyone teaching this path in recent history and Sayadaw had made it his life's work to bring these practices back to life. He had spent ten years alone in his forest with these and other texts, deep in meditation, breathing life into these truths through his direct experience in meditation. It was even widely argued that the jhanic states of concentration that he taught were beyond the reaches of all but the rare few who chose a life of total seclusion.

On this account there had emerged a modern approach to meditation, which is called the Dry Vipassana method, that replaces the incisiveness of powerful concentration (samadhi), with strong effort and determination in the battle to break the wrong views that keep us bound up with ignorance, attachment, and greed.

I had sat these courses and seen yogis white knuckling it for ten or more hours a day asking sheer determination to do the work that their samadhi should have done for them. I had students myself who had tried this way. It was powerful and life changing but left many of them fragmented by the experience and unable to integrate it back into their daily life.

The Buddha had taught us time and time again that serenity is the antidote to our restlessness and agitation and serenity is borne of one thing, deep concentration. It is stated so emphatically in the Suttas, and it seems unthinkable that any serious yogi would even attempt the path out of suffering without first ardently committing to establishing his concentration.

It is our very impatience that cuts off our progress at the first of the many hurdles we come to, so how could we expect to get success without establishing our patience and serenity? The sheer desire to break out of our suffering can often be extremely intense. There is a profound difference between renunciation that is rooted in aversion to the things we face in life, and that which comes because desire has faded and with it the attachment to the idea of still having things that need to be done.

I saw a clear differentiation in my time in the forest, and elsewhere, between those whose minds were still rooted in aversion to the unpleasant, while still holding on to myriad attachments, and those who had truly begun the process of letting go. When such determination to avoid suffering comes without the willingness to let go attachment, it often ends up becoming the very wall we cannot cross. It is necessary to come to a deep level of acceptance and surrender to the way of things if we are going to make any real progress in freeing ourselves from the suffering we face.

The teachers of the dry method, which bypasses the samadhi stage, claim that yogis in the modern age do not have the time to develop such deep concentration. I believe the issue is not time but the fact that we desire the distractions of sensual pleasure more than the peace of serenity. In the end we will always follow the things we desire most. Better we tire of our attachments and come to meditation when we truly seek what it brings us to. Why try to convince yourself to let go when in fact it is the last thing in the world you are ready to do. It is tantamount to mental torture.

I remember giving a discourse in Singapore one time to a group of dedicated and committed Buddhists.

"What do you want? What do you really want?" I asked them.

"Why Nibbana of course," many of them replied.

"Do you? Do you really?"

I reached into my pocket and pulled out a piece of paper.

"I have in my hand here a ticket to Nibbana. It is for anyone who wants it. You can take it now, on one condition. You have to stand up right now and walk out of this room and never come back. Do you want it?"

I offered it to a lady who sat in front with her husband.

"Oh no," she said, "not just now. What of my husband and children?"

"There. You see?" I said. "Now do you understand why you cannot get your concentration? It's because you don't actually want to let go. So don't torture yourself trying to force yourself to. Make first your peace with the life that you do have."

You see, Nibbana is easy to attain for one who clings to nothing, but impossible for one who clings to anything. The basis of serenity is non-distraction and the basis of distraction is desire for variety of forms. Before we try to convince ourselves that we need to let go, we need to look deeply into what it is we are clinging to.

When you desire peace more than anything else in the world, that peace is already right in front of you. The real work of meditation is to find the serenity and acceptance that turns away blissfully, it is not in the hours of sitting cross-legged with smoke coming out of our ears muttering, "It's impermanent, it's impermanent. Let go, let go," that we break free.

The Buddha didn't turn away just because he was oppressed by everything, but because he found a bliss in surrender that surpassed all sensual delight. It was through following his bliss that he came to his final attainment, not through running away looking over his shoulder in fear. He did become disenchanted with things and he tried and failed to cut off his attachment as an act of will.

He drove himself almost to death for six years in his desperate attempt to wilfully break this lingering attachment. It was only through his final surrender to the way things really were, as he finally saw dependent origination, that he realised that letting go was a choiceless and blissful process borne of his deep serenity and the wisdom it had led him to.

I loved the monastery and atmosphere of life in the forest. I was ready for it. I had filled my cup and become intoxicated with life in the heady days of my youth. But for all the highs it took me to, I had never stopped to breathe out. Here finally I really had the time to take that long out-breath and decompress.

Sayadaw was adamant that all his students developed their concentration as far as they could. In truth, his approach to Vipassana depended upon taking the ultimate basis of mind and matter as the field of investigation. Twenty-five centuries have passed since the Buddha lived and science is only now starting to reach down deeply enough into the essence of things to grasp the truths that the Buddha realised with his mind.

He insisted that if we did not break down our perception of compactness, we would never come to perceive things as they truly are. It is through failing to break down this compactness and recognise the continuum of processes that constitutes the life of a human being that we get so lost and wrapped up with our ideas about ourselves and what we think we really are.

It has taken science all this time to break down this compactness and see consciousness and matter as a dance of energy that pops in and out of existence, incessantly giving only the illusion of a concrete structure to things. So for sure, it takes tremendous levels of concentration to see these things with our naked awareness.

All other practices of Vipassana that I had encountered before took the compound concepts of the body and mind and investigated their impermanence and inherent emptiness as the route to the loosening of the grip of attachment.

The principle is simple. If we can truly come to see and accept that absolutely everything in our world and our lives is completely impermanent, then in time, as we come to accept this truth, we will of our own free will stop craving for and clinging to these objects. Being separated from that which we long for and not getting what we want is the cause of our real suffering.

It is the reason we live in fear. For although we might try to convince ourselves that we can endlessly be surrounded by the objects of our desire, we know at a deeper level that we will in the end be separated from everything and everyone that is dear to us. It is a truth, however unpalatable it may sound. We all know it, however hard we pretend not to.

Even if we are able to desperately hold on to all the objects we desire until the very end, we will still be separated from them at our death. We refuse to reflect on these things and prefer to bury our heads in the sand.

This understanding of the truth of impermanence transforms our attitude to every aspect of our life, and in time leads us to the point of non-attachment that finally sets us free. It is so often implied that such non-attachment must be a dry and lifeless existence, but such a view fails totally to recognise the opportunity this brings to truly dance with life joyfully and fearlessly. The hardliners who suggest that we should be marching headlong towards a total renunciation miss this point entirely.

As I said, the Buddha did not turn away just because he was oppressed by life. He turned away because he had drunk of his cup and was full. He had lived the life and satiated himself, so that when he turned away it was with no sense that he had missed something.

The reason we find it so hard to follow his path is because we haven't learned to live harmlessly and constructively enough to recognise the extraordinary opportunity that this coming into being affords us. It is the opportunity to come to a deep understanding of the nature of love and realise that the experience of such love is an unconditional response rooted in appreciative joy.

Once we have begun to recognise and earn for ourselves the real fruits of virtue and blamelessness, we free ourselves of regret. The path doesn't start with renunciation, it ends with it. The renunciation comes only after we have perfected our virtue and gone beyond selfishness, to learn to live life completely, without any detriment to others. This is the real path.

The Buddha himself categorically stated that it was virtue that leads to serenity and concentration, and concentration that leads to the insight and wisdom that finally causes us to let go and free ourselves from suffering. Our first goal is to establish ourselves in virtue, to stop bringing suffering upon ourselves and others through negligence and selfish action.

I entered deep into my practice as soon as I arrived in Burma. I rose at three-thirty and sat right through till lunch, stopping only briefly at nine-thirty to interview daily with Sayadaw. I was so immersed in my practice that I never once felt the urge to stop for breakfast. That first long sit of the day was when all my work was done so that by the time lunch came I went for alms knowing that I had earned a rest. I didn't force myself to sit.

I sat because I longed for it. I longed to enter deeper and deeper into stillness as a resolution to the frenetic pace at which I had lived previously. Yet I knew all along, that it was because of all I had done in my youth and not in spite of it that I was able to let go and surrender so completely to my meditation. I had no axe to grind. I wasn't forcing myself to do it because I was desperate for enlightenment. I did it because I wanted to. There was nothing else I wanted more.

I knew I had lived lifetimes of sensual distraction in my youth. It was out of my system. There was nothing to prove to my ego. I wasn't there because the world had dealt me bum cards. I was there because it was the only thing left to do. I was ready to go unnoticed in this quiet backwater, far removed from all I had grown up with and take up the greatest challenge of all.

It wasn't the challenge to become something, but the one of unbecoming. I was letting go all the structures and conditioning I had lived with. I was formatting the hard drive and reloading a whole new operating system. The old one was way outdated and I knew it. The more I entered into it the more I realised that it wasn't actually a challenge.

Samadhi is the state the true mind longs to rest in, when the ego lets go its grip. Far from being a contrived state that we struggle to maintain, over time I came to realise that it was quite simply just a process of attunement. Just a simplification of the mental structure which in stages leads to deeper and deeper states of stillness and serenity.

Think about it. To know peace is the heart's deepest longing. Where do we find our peace? We find that it is already there, when the mind stops charging around in its madness, seeking gratification externally in all the cul-de-sacs it is capable of dreaming up.

I realised quickly that all I had to do was leave my mind alone and give it permission to do nothing. Samadhi quite simply revealed itself out of the stillness that was left behind once the mind stopped its clattering about.

I became so completely immersed in the moment that I lost all sense of myself. I began to realise that up until now I had related all my experiences back to my subjective sense of me. I am doing this, doing that. It's me that is meditating. Even in my progress with meditation, up to now I had always emerged and related it back to my idea of myself. But now "Me" was out of the way. There was no sense that I was doing anything, just an immense sense of expansiveness and presence.

Mind and thinking simply became bare awareness and all the noise was gone.

Sayadaw was teaching me the 'eight samapati'*, or eight samadhi attainments. These are the eight stages of jhana or absorption, reflecting deeper and deeper levels of concentration and serenity. It was the jhana consciousness that finally erased the sense of subjectivity, for in that state there is nothing but the unification of the mind with its object.

The stream of subconscious awareness that governs our sense that there is actually someone thinking and doing is cut off at this stage. The level of absorption with the object becomes so complete that there is no awareness arising in any of the sense doors and no wavering at the heart base or mind door. There is only direct perception.

It is just an infinitely steady and even stream of awareness unifying itself with its object. It was quite different from the inclusive state of clear light that had come from the transmission of Padmasambhava. In that state the mind rested effortlessly within a state of clear light, and although formations arose naturally out of this clear light, there was no inclination of the mind towards them.

I came to recognise this as a sublime state of equanimity that rested within itself, utterly un-distracted by other objects. Though the heart base became genuinely still in that state it was not initially a state of absorption.

Only later, when I had learned the jhana practices from Sayadaw did I return to the clear light mind, and taking that as the object enter into full absorption upon it. The jhanas were a totally different state. The object of absorption was mind-produced, (i.e. it takes an internal sign that is produced by the mind as a result of sustained concentration on its original object).

Rather than a natural state in which the mind rests when it leaves everything else alone, the jhanas are a contrived state of mind, produced deliberately through right effort and training.

Where, in the clear mind state, other objects were simply left as they were, in jhana the goal is to seclude the mind from all awareness of external, and even internal objects through one pointedness and the total fixation of the mind on its chosen object. It was the total withdrawal from the gross sensory field of awareness that made the jhanas so profoundly still.

The difference between each stage of samadhi is the degree of subtlety and serenity of the mental states which arise from the first to fourth jhana and the increasing subtlety of the object and the deepening withdrawal from gross sensory distraction in the fifth to eighth.

At the eighth jhana the mind is in its most rarefied state of active consciousness, beyond this there is only cessation. When the Buddha first renounced his royal life it was these eight jhanas that his first teachers taught him.

They are extraordinary states and cannot be appreciated until one finally enters into them. I realised once I began to experience them myself in meditation just how dry and flat are all the accounts of them in the various texts and commentaries I had read. For within these states a profound wisdom is also expressed that unravels deep mysteries about the workings of our higher mind.

In all there were ten meditations that Sayadaw taught me by which to develop the jhanas. They were the meditations on the four elements of earth, water, fire, and air, the colour kasinas on white, blue, yellow and red and the space and light objects. Together they are called the ten kasinas.

Sayadaw was not satisfied until I had been successful in all eight jhana's using all ten kasina objects. Each time I returned to him he would ask me if I was satisfied with my meditation. Each time he would ask me if I would like one more.

Although the Buddha found these states to be profound and deeply peaceful, he recognised that we cannot abide in them forever and in time must return to the mundane way of consciousness that is inevitably afflicted and oppressed by the gross and unpleasant.

It was the realisation of this that caused him to shun the traditional approach to enlightenment in India at that time and seek his final deliverance from all suffering for himself. It was the realisation of Nibbana, or the unconditioned state, that became the causal cessation of all suffering and his final release.

However, it needs to be understood that the jhana states of concentration were the very foundation and basis of his meditation and opened the door to the deep and penetrating insight that allowed him to finally break through the veil of ignorance. This jhanic state of concentration is the Right Concentration in the Buddha's Eightfold Noble Path*.

When I had read the Visuddhimagga, I had been in awe at the description of these states, but now I was practicing and entering into them. I saw clearly a deep intelligence at work in the very structure of our consciousness and it was this intelligence that led me naturally from one level to the next. Each jhana was the logical conclusion to the one previously and together they began to draw out an exquisite map of consciousness itself.

I felt something deeply profound at work here. It was almost a telepathic communication with the teacher. He would give me instructions and I would walk back to my kuti and sit. There was no need to review what he had told me. It was almost as if I anticipated the exact flavour and nuance of these states as he gave the instructions.

When I came to sit my mind naturally inclined to them and they opened up to me. It felt almost like a remembering. Each time I entered into the next level there was a familiarity as I recognised the subtle flavours and nuances. The jhana meditations on the four elements yielded profound insight into the function and nature of material states that had not come from my previous practice with Merta Ada.

The only time that I wasn't in meditation was when I was eating, showering or interviewing with Sayadaw. I even found at times I was entering into sleep with full awareness. Somehow I knew I was falling asleep but I was fully awake.

I watched as the dream scenes emerged from the heart base and as they subsided I was left with the exquisite clear state of luminosity that I had entered into in the cave in India. I realised again that this was not a mind-produced state but a natural state that we were left with when our active mind finally stopped.

I smiled at the reflection that we enter into a fully realised state of consciousness every night when we sleep. The only problem is that we never know it. I could see now just why sleep was so important. Once our lower mind was out of the way, our higher mind was free to go to work with all its infinite intelligence, to undo the chaos our ego produced in our waking state.

These deep states of concentration were far from the escapist pursuits they are often accused of being. There was a wisdom and intelligence that was being revealed that I knew now was the driving force behind our very lives. It was our separation from this that was the cause of our pain and despair. It was this that our hearts longed to come back to. Now that I had finally made my way there, it felt as if nothing could undo that peace.

I began to feel an overwhelming love and profound respect for my teacher, for the skill and care with which he was guiding me. He had waited for many years to find a Westerner to whom he could teach at this level and he so dearly hoped that I would push on to the end and bring this Dharma back to the west.

He had been criticised by many schools of Dry Vipassana who claimed it was not possible to develop these deep states of samadhi or to investigate material states at the most fundamental level.

I knew he was grooming me. I had interviews twice daily now and had to report to his kuti at seven each evening when he had his daily meet with his senior monks. I would sit and give him energy for his neck pain and massage him while he talked to them in Burmese. Occasionally they would quiz me about my practice.

My concentration continued to deepen daily as I worked systematically through all eight jhanas on all ten of the meditation subjects that they are developed on.

I was close to completing this stage of the practice when one morning I awoke as usual and started to sit up in my bed to prepare for my meditation. As I did so I realised that I was already deep in samadhi. I just stopped. My mind had stopped, my body stopped. I just stopped where I was. I was still there when the bell went for lunch. I hadn't even gone for interview. I hadn't even made it to my cushion. I could feel everything around me.

Outside I could feel the forest. I let my mind go to the meditation hall where many of the monks sat and I could feel them all, one by one and all together. There was nothing separating anything. I could feel the mind and body of everything I put my attention to, but there was no sense of directing my mind from anywhere to anywhere. It was simply arising wherever I placed it, and everything was arising from that clear, infinitely still space that Padmasambhava himself had arisen from in the cave.

I asked Sayadaw about this state for I knew it wasn't any of the eight jhanas I had been practicing.

He just smiled and said, "It is from your previous practice. I think it is from Tibet."

I tried to draw him out on this statement but he simply changed the subject. I knew he knew but I was willing to accept that he didn't feel it necessary to discuss. He had previously explained how many yogis get hung up on attachment to such states once their samadhi develops, and the real goal of the Buddha's practice was wisdom not serenity. I accepted Sayadaw's wish not to discuss such things.

I did have a strong desire to unify the very direct approach shown to me by Padmasambhava and the systematic path to wisdom that Sayadaw was now teaching. I decided that I would put my experience in India out of my mind to give full attention to the practice at hand, but I equally knew that the transmission I had received in the cave was colouring my whole experience along the way.

I was nearing the end of the serenity session. The hard work of the investigation of mind and matter, that would reveal the true nature of things, lay ahead.

CHAPTER EIGHTEEN

Friends In Hidden Spaces

As I have explained, the jhanic states of samadhi produce extraordinary states of peace and well-being and open the door to higher capacities that previously the mind was incapable of. Such psychic feats as the ability to review our past lives, and direct knowledge, are all by-products of the sublime states of concentration entered into in jhana.

Furthermore, since all the jhanas take fine material objects on which to establish their concentration, they open us up to the awareness and direct experience of the subtle realms of existence that most of us are previously unaware of.

This was something extraordinary. I had already become aware of many other kinds of beings in subtler realms than our own, but as I worked my way up through the jhanas I began to understand more and more about these realms and the kind of beings that inhabited them.

Our folklore is full of stories of all kinds of mythical creatures, of gods and angels, of demons and ghosts, and over time I began to realise that there is more to all of this than just imagination.

219

One of my first encounters had been back in Gili Nanggu in Bali when I encountered a hermit who sat and meditated with me whilst I was practising in the temple. Guru Rinpoche had also presented himself to me from this subtle realm of existence. But now almost daily I was encountering extraordinary things in my meditation.

I remember when Sayadaw was teaching me the jhanas on loving-kindness, at that time we were in Taiwan together on a retreat he was giving at a Mahayana monastery. He told me I should gradually extend the field of my concentration to include the entire compound of the monastery.

The difference between the previous jhanas and Metta, or loving-kindness jhana is that previously we take a mind-produced space into which to extend our samadhi. In the Metta jhana we are literally extending the field of our awareness to include a larger and larger field of external space.

The power of our loving kindness is determined by the strength of our concentration and its ability to hold evenly this extended field of awareness. Once we have established this open field of concentration we pervade it with our previously developed feeling of loving kindness.

As I extended my mind beyond my room into the arena beyond, all kinds of extraordinary things began to appear to me.

The process of remote viewing is one of direct perception and does not involve our physical eyes. It allows us to perceive visual objects that are distant. As I began to take the compound beyond my room into my concentration many previously hidden inhabitants began to reveal themselves to me.

The first I came to know was a miserable wretch of a being with a small lumpy body hanging around the drains outside the kitchens. He was a pitiful looking thing grubbing around for food scraps. Such beings are known as Pretas* or hungry ghosts.

They are born in this state because of their excessive greed in their previous life. The karma of this greed fruits in their mind at death to produce a consciousness in the next life that suffers from insatiable cravings that are never satisfied. It is the destination of many who surrender themselves to addiction and craving in this life or the excessive gratification of sensual desires that are never satisfied.

In the end I became quite familiar with this poor wretch and would regularly save him food from my lunch. Though he was unable to eat the physical essence of the food he could partake its nutritive essence. If I would put out a banana for him, although it would still be there the next day, were I to peel it and take a bite myself it would be quite tasteless for he had relieved it of its nutritional essence.

I learned much from my miserable friend. Certainly he impressed upon me the suffering that being slave to our greed and craving can lead us to.

The next friend I made in these realms, however, was far from living in such misery and gave me a glimpse of the fruits that virtue can bring us to.

It lived in the Bodhi tree in the middle of the main courtyard. The Buddha achieved his Nibbana whilst sitting under such a Bodhi tree and so it is customary for Buddhist temples to plant one somewhere in their grounds as a symbolic recognition of the Buddha's attainment. Many monks and nuns at the monastery would sit in its

221

shade while taking rest, and in the evenings offer candles and incense.

On the day that Sayadaw had given me the instructions on the air kasina meditation he had suggested I take the movement of the leaves in the Bodhi tree as the object by which to attune to the motion aspect produced by the air element. I walked back to my room and stopped off at the Bodhi tree to review my instructions and take up the sign.

On that occasion the sign appeared spontaneously and I entered into jhana almost immediately. I sat for a while working through the first to fourth jhana in stages and emerging each time to review them. Within an hour I was back in front of Sayadaw with a smile on my face for this had been the quickest time it had taken me to succeed in any of the kasina jhanas. He was pleased too and smiled.

"I knew you would be back before lunch. Did you like that one?"

"I did indeed. I think it is my favourite so far," I said.

"Do you know why?" he asked me.

"I just loved the stillness of it. And I was amazed at how quickly my mind entered this jhana. It was as if it already knew what it was going to be like," I replied. Quite unexpectedly the air kasina meditation, which took motion itself as the original object, had resolved itself into the most deeply still samadhi of all the elemental jhanas. This had been because as the sign of concentration developed, it had been the absence of the motion and the feeling of utter stillness that had opened the door to jhana.

"When you practice dependent origination, you will see why it was so easy for you."

"Can't you tell me now?" I pleaded.

As usual he declined my request for further information and sent me on my way with new instructions.

There were in fact a number of reasons that this meditation had been so easy for me.

I saw the first, one day as I was practicing loving-kindness and pervading the space beyond my room to the area around the Bodhi tree. I was taken aback by a brilliant light that seemed to be radiating from the upper branches. As my mind began to perceive this light the blissful feeling of my loving kindness intensified and my samadhi deepened further still.

I concentrated and sent love towards the area at the top of the tree and then stilled my mind there. Gradually from within the centre of the light a vague form began to emerge. It was itself blissful and full of love and at first I took it to be an angel of some kind. I realised that the light I had perceived around the tree was emanating from its heart base and was in fact the aura produced by its very pure and loving mind.

I felt such extraordinary love for this being who quite simply lived in the top of the Bodhi tree, delighting in the energy of nature and the good vibration from all the monks and nuns who daily put respect and made offerings there.

Over time I came to know well this tree deva and understood that its presence there was one of the reasons we all felt so blissful and happy after making offerings to the Buddha.

This deva had been born in this realm on account of both its extraordinary virtue in its previous life and its delight in nature.

Our forests are full of such beings, some great, some small. The karma that produces this kind of existence is the virtue of conduct producing the heavenly realm existence, and the delight in nature producing the appearance in beautiful natural environments.

The folk tales of fairies and angels encountered in enchanted woods all hinge on the subtle perception somewhere down the line of the real presence and existence of beings such as this tree deva.

It wasn't until I began the meditation on dependent origination that I understood fully why I had resonated so deeply with the air kasina meditation and the being that dwelt in the Bodhi tree, or why the jhanas and in particular the air kasina had come so easily to me. The explanation of this process is quite technical and I do not wish to labour the reader with it here. Please see the appendix on rebirth linking consciousness.*

CHAPTER NINETEEN

Strive On Earnestly

In time I finished the serenity session known as Samatha. It was time now to prepare for the insight or wisdom session, which in modern times has become known as Vipassana.

Vipassana is the practice of reviewing the nature of material and mental states until they are perceived by direct perception and understood as they are. The purpose is to come to what is known as Right View as a resolution to whatever concepts we might have developed regarding these states. So the next session was the investigation of mind and matter.

I returned now to the four elements practice and had to review all the matter of my body and those around me until I could perceive clearly that my whole body was in truth nothing more than the arising and passing of the four elements of materiality.

Using the powerful states of concentration that I had just been practicing I spent day after day reviewing the four elements in all material forms until they broke down first into light, and then clear light, and finally into nothing more than a mass of tiny fizzing particles popping in and out of existence.

It was at this stage that I started to understand why Sayadaw had been so insistent his students develop such deep states of concentration. The process we are investigating is so fleeting and transient and happening at such a microscopic level that it appears as nothing more than a blur of fizzing energy; until we can snapshot it precisely enough to catch each moment of arising, standing, and passing away of each particle of matter within us. It is only by capturing these very brief moments that we can begin to fathom what is actually happening within each one.

It is rather like capturing a frame of a movie so that we can review it long enough to absorb all of the information being conveyed. At this point we come to the absolute certainty that nothing material is inherently there. It merely pops into being dependent upon conditioning causes and instantly passes away.

It is interesting that this is a remarkably similar view to how quantum physicists now realise the material universe to be behaving. It inspires me tremendously that the Buddha was able to perceive twenty-five centuries ago with bare attention and focused concentration what today we are managing to witness only with the most advanced technology.

I often wonder where we would all be now if we had invested a fraction of the effort we have put into developing technology into refining and developing our minds.

If we were to try to review the impermanence of a table or a tree or even our bodies, it is not immediately apparent how impermanent they are. We might make the reflection that they will all decay over time but this is not the same as seeing impermanence in every moment of existence.

To see this we must break down the illusionary perception of compactness until we can see all matter to be nothing more than the momentary arising and passing of transient and ultimately insubstantial states.

Of course, today quantum physics has now reached this same understanding that everything is nothing more than a dance of energy that brings things into momentary existence before instantly passing away again. But reading about it is not the same as seeing it. Something profound happens to us when we start to see this process going on endlessly within everything around us.

Sayadaw insisted that we must first resolve matter into this ultimate basis, before reviewing it as impermanent. He argued that it was through failing to do this that our mind fought and battled in its efforts to let go its clinging to forms, because however hard we tried to convince ourselves that all things are impermanent it is not until we have seen this at an ultimate level that the letting go becomes an effortless and frictionless process. This is called in Pali, Bhavana-Maya Panna, or the wisdom that arises from direct experience.

The Buddha argued that it is only this direct knowledge that cuts off our clinging and allows us to glimpse the quantum field that sits timelessly in the background as the real basis of all phenomena. Given wisdom or intellectual wisdom does not produce the same effect.

It amounts basically to this. Only that which has absolutely been seen to be true will be unconditionally accepted as the truth. Anything short of this is just a speculative view. The real goal of meditation is to come to this absolute knowing of things that cuts off all wrong views.

This is the real work that we must do. It is the opposite of retreating into exalted or transcendent states of samadhi for it takes the mundane objects that we cling to in life and looks upon all things with the penetrating insight that knows them to be impermanent and unreliable.

It is through hinging our hopes of happiness and contentment on the acquiring and holding on to these impermanent and transient objects of form that we find ourselves in such bondage to them. We are bound in the end to be let down or disappointed by them if they reveal their impermanence to us without us ever having anticipated their decay.

Only when we have come to the genuine acceptance of this truth of impermanence can we reclaim our lives and dance with it in the absolute knowledge that neither life nor anything that presents itself in life will last indefinitely. Prior to that point we live constantly in the fear of being separated from these things that we cling to.

Once we have totally accepted in the deepest part of our mind that we are going to be separated from everything that comes into our lives, we begin to appreciate them in the moment of their appearance without being dismayed by their passing. This is Vipassana meditation.

It is the hard work of meditation that produces permanent changes within us, that brings us in stages to an ever deepening state of acceptance. It is out of this acceptance that a true state of appreciative joy and unconditioned love are born. Knowing there is nothing to be won or possessed or to call 'mine', we can live fearlessly amidst the ebb and flow of life without clinging to it.

It is said that jhana is the momentary cessation of suffering because for all the bliss we encounter in these states we must all, in time, emerge from them and return to our mundane existence.

Nibbana however is the causal cessation of suffering and it is reached with the complete non-attachment to forms that opens the door beyond our conditioned reality to the realm of the unconditioned. Once we do not cling we are no longer oppressed, and once we are un-oppressed we can truly begin to dance fearlessly in our life, knowing it is a gift that will end in time.

So now it was time for the real hard work. I had loved the concentration practices and been totally drawn into the profound jhanic states of absorption and one-pointed concentration. My mind was sharp and clear and I felt strong and fit.

I began the materiality session with real enthusiasm, for it brought me back to where my meditation had begun in Bali with Ada. We had developed the meditation on the body and its elements for the purpose of healing it and removing the dysfunctional patterns that caused sickness and decay.

It had fascinated me to see how this body really comes into being and what actually was causing it to arise. We come to see in time that all the matter in our body is produced by only four causes – temperature, nutriment, consciousness and action energy, or what we call karma.

While only part of our body is produced by temperature and nutriment, many of the most important bases that account for and govern its functionality are produced by karma and consciousness. This is why there are so many illnesses that cannot be treated by medicines and why so many can be resolved with meditation.

For meditation produces powerful wholesome consciousness and action energy (karma). There are so many examples of people who have come to see me with conditions that their doctors cannot resolve, and yet within a few months or sometimes only weeks of meditation these conditions correct themselves. It is because all sickness is basically misinformation.

Meditation is the process of correcting this information so that the body can reclaim its functionality. I was already deeply fascinated by the extraordinary mechanisms by which our body becomes sick and heals itself at an energetic level.

In the days that followed, I re-connected to the insight that my meditation with Ada had begun to develop, and it opened out with ever more subtlety and depth. In truth, I was even more fascinated with this aspect than I had been with the jhanas.

Many people come to my retreats thinking that meditation is going to heal then. But what allows them to heal is the gradual letting go of the misinformation that has accumulated and produced sickness in the first place. The insight they gain from learning to see is the real Dharma, for it is the process we are living and experiencing 24 hours of every day of our lives, not a dry philosophy or doctrine that a wise man taught us a long time ago.

The Buddha didn't tell us, "this is how the world is", he taught us how to look deeply and honestly into the living processes governing our lives so that we could start to see for ourselves what is actually going on here. This is what changes us: seeing for ourselves what we are really a part of, what this life really is. It is that which prompts changes in attitude and the letting go of negative habit patterns like craving, anger, restlessness, stubbornness and intolerance.

It is always the seeing of the living processes at work within us that opens the door to both letting go and healing, and not the act of sitting cross-legged, watching the breath or paying attention to bodily sensations. As I have always said, there are three aspects to the harmonious mind.

Concentration and mindfulness alone will not bring about the causal cutting off of negative habit patterns. It is only when together they lead to insight knowledge, and with it equanimity, that the process reaches its transformative potential.

Now I was actually watching the dance of life going on at its most fundamental level. I gained undreamed-of insight into the nature of sickness and it was all borne of this exhaustive discipline of bare attention to the way of things. In a little over a month I had finished this session. I wanted to go even further into it but Sayadaw wanted me to push on into the mentality session.

By this time I had two kutis in the forest. One was just at the bottom of the steps up to Sayadaw's abode. He had put me there initially because I had to go so regularly to interviews and he didn't want me wasting time walking through the forest. However while I was there an old Burmese monk who lived on a hillside right at the edge of the forest passed away.

I was offered this kuti so that I could be more removed from the daily traffic that passed my place close to Sayadaw. One day I decided to make a strong determination to stay up and meditate non-stop for twenty-four hours. I was reaching the end of the meditation on mental states and felt I was ready for a breakthrough.

I walked up the hill at first light and spent half an hour airing the place and sweeping. The huts were made entirely of wood and needed regular cleaning and maintenance.

The window opened out over a vast plain that rolled away into the distance. The view it gave was a marvellous sense of expansiveness and I decided to take that sense of spaciousness to set up my samadhi before I began my Vipassana. I sat on the bed so that I could look out of the window and once I had taken the sign I began my meditation.

After about an hour I emerged from my samadhi and turned towards the reviewing of states, first material and then mental. There is a state called Vipassana jhana where the mind becomes deeply absorbed in the impermanent or substanceless aspect of the states it reviews. It is not strictly speaking true jhana because the object is not stable enough to reach full absorption, but it is a strong samadhi that we use to quickly bring our wisdom aspect to maturity.

That day I entered deeply into this state. I was so totally held by it that I lost all sense of time or place. All I could perceive was a mass of impermanence. Everything that arose broke apart instantly, but instead of going directly to the emptiness that lay behind this impermanence as I had learned from Padmasambhava, I held my attention on the forms as they arose and passed. My intention was to reach a state of total dispassion to forms through resting on their impermanence.

The meditations on emptiness had produced in me deep levels of acceptance, which in itself had loosened considerably the grip of attachment, but it had never left me feeling oppressed by the conditioned nature of things, allowing me instead to continue my dance in a detached way. Sayadaw was teaching the path to Nibbana which required us to relinquish all attachment to conditioned states so that the unconditioned would in time reveal itself.

There is a profound and hard to grasp difference between the empty state of awareness that I had already learned to abide in and the knowledge of the cessation of conditioned forms which is the Nibbana object. I knew these things were not the same. Sayadaw had warned me that if I became satisfied with my state of emptiness I would not progress further, so I agreed to continue with the investigation of states.

As the day progressed I continued in this way for hour upon hour, sinking my mind ever deeper into the relentless decay of all that appeared before me. At one point I decided to emerge from this practice and enter into jhana to refresh my mind from the onslaught of this mass of impermanence I was beholding.

But as soon as I developed the sign, which would take me into jhana, that very sign itself would break down into impermanence. There was no longer any refuge. I had to push on. Everything was breaking apart; my body along with the mental states that perceived it. It was all just a sea of energy arising and passing. I was no longer oppressed by it. It simply was what it was. I didn't care about it; I wasn't really interested in it any more. I just sat in it, hour after hour after hour.

And then suddenly, quite unexpectedly, something came over me with absolute certainty.

"Stop. Stop now." I was prompting myself. "If you don't stop now you will never come down from this mountain and you will never leave the forest."

With a jolt I came out of my meditation. It was late afternoon. I lay down on my bed exhausted. I was in some kind of shock. And in that moment I knew my time in the forest had come to an end.

I simply got up and walked back down the hill and through the forest and went to see Sayadaw. I told him I was going to leave. I wasn't making a decision, I was quite simply compelled. I had to go back now because if I didn't stop, I would never return to the work I had committed to do. I would not be able to. It was just something I knew. It was a direct knowledge that appeared without thought.

I sat in front of Sayadaw trying to explain myself. Of course he understood what was happening to me. He tried to dissuade me.

"What has happened? Why do I feel this?" I asked.

"It is on account of your previous aspiration," he said.

"What do you mean?"

"When you reach dependent origination you will see for yourself."

"Can you not tell me?" I begged.

He just smiled. I knew that as a monk he could not give me this kind of information. It was for me to see for myself. But he did his best to convince me that I should stay.

"You should stay here and finish your practice. You are almost at the end. You should take this Dharma back to your country and teach."

"But Sayadaw. I am here in the forest and even here there are only a few who can practice this meditation. If I go back to the West I could wait all my life for anyone to approach me for these instructions. Those with such aspiration will find their way to you. You are the Master. There are countless people in my world who haven't even started on the path that long to find their way. It is these people I must serve. It is my job to sow the seed of Dharma in their hearts. I have to go now or I never will."

He sat effortlessly with no overt sign of emotion, except that I noticed a single tear running down his face.

I knew I was making the biggest move of my life. In so many ways it was lunacy. I knew how rare it was for me to have this chance. But I had no choice. What is more I knew Sayadaw understood too, however disappointed he was. I had sensed the joy he had had at having a young yogi from beyond his country that he could instruct in such a personal and detailed way. He was like a father to me and I knew I had become like a son.

And now I was leaving before he had finished teaching me.

I told him what had happened on the hill, I explained in detail how my meditation had been.

"If you have paramis enough it is possible to see Nibbana from the state of knowledge of arising and passing. The last stage of knowledge before we see Nibbana is usually the knowledge of equanimity to formations. Your clear mind state is a sign of this equanimity. There are yogis who reach this stage and cannot go further even though the door to Nibbana is open. This depends on aspirations they have made in previous lives."

Suddenly it hit me. Nibbana! I had never even stopped to think about it. I had never even made the reflection that it was to attain this state that I had come here. In fact that wasn't why I was here. Here I was, in the forest of a foreign land, practising amongst monks and yogis who were striving for that single goal above all else, yet this aspiration had never arisen in me.

In fact when I thought about it I knew it wasn't why I came. I came to learn the skills by which I could be of service to others. I was brought here by my sense of duty. It was true that I was deeply committed to mastering these practices, but it was never with Nibbana as the goal. Nibbana is the cessation of the aggregates of clinging and their causes.

I realised that my aspiration to serve was the final attachment and that I was unable to break it. And it wasn't a choice. I was bound by that aspiration, and yet it wasn't one I could consciously remember making. I knew it had been made in a previous life for I had never stopped even to think about it in this one.

My mind rolled back over the journey I had been on in the past few years and I could see that I hadn't actually decided consciously to do any of this, it had been a process that had just carried me along. It is true that I was compliant but I wasn't wilfully making these choices. Right back to the evening in Bali where my friends had prompted me to go and listen to Ada speak. I would not have gone if not prompted. I just allowed myself to be carried.

I could begin to see what was happening. I sat with Sayadaw in silence, and I could feel his unwavering love all around me. He was no more able to intervene in the process than I was.

"I will be back. I promise," I said. I knew I would. "But there are things I have to do."

"You must come back as soon as you can. You know death is always unsure."

Phew. I knew what he was saying. It had been five hundred years since a teacher had been able to teach meditation in this depth. I had begun to see my past lives and knew that I had not practised meditation like this since the life I had had as a monk in Bagan.

Since then I had fallen into all kinds of trouble on account of becoming embroiled in life and fought hard to claw myself back to where I was now. How rare was the chance I had now. To leave at this point was the weightiest decision I would ever make. Before I slept that night I did something I had never done before; I prayed for guidance.

CHAPTER TWENTY

Aspiration

I lay on my bed as the sun went down, pondering on the question that had been raised by my unexpected decision to leave.

If my aspiration had never been to attain Nibbana, then what could it possibly be? Everyone else at Sayadaw's monastery was there seeking that one goal. It was the highest of all goals, the final and complete deliverance from the suffering caused by the cyclic round of existence in the conditioned realm. It marks the entry into the 'Deathless State' as it is called, and the remainderless cessation of all suffering.

Sayadaw had explained to me the process by which we review our past lives and I had spent some time trying. Some more recent ones had begun to reveal themselves to me but in none of them could I detect the aspiration that would have opposed my final attainment. I knew that at the end of my life in Bagan, where I had been a teaching monk, I appeared again in the same place but as a lay person who chose not to renounce during that life.

Clearly even back then something had caused me to turn away from the path. I could see by now how this decision had brought me to immeasurable suffering on various occasions in the past. But still, even today in this life, with the full knowledge of the dangers inherent in maintaining our attachment to this conditioned existence I was unable to cross over the threshold

For now, the way was there for me. I could see the mechanism and the Nibbana object was presenting itself clearly to me. But my mind simply refused to grasp it. It was an almost impossible paradox. In principle, for me to have come so far on the path, I must have been working tirelessly to that end for many past lives. Why would I have chosen to put forth such effort if I was not seeking the deliverance that the path opened up to?

Everyone at the monastery was baffled that I should want to just walk away. It wasn't that I had got fed up, or longed to get back to the life of sensual indulgence. I was happier in the forest than I had ever been, but I knew I just couldn't stay.

Since I could not find the cause of this response as I reviewed my lives back to the time in Burma, I decided to look back over my current life to see if I could find any clues.

And the more I looked back over my life the clearer it was to me that I had never once made such an aspiration to reach this goal. In fact I realised quite quickly that this had never been the reason that I had launched myself headlong into my journey of spiritual enquiry. Yet it was equally clear that there was a relentless current pulling me along. I had to have been prompted by something, so what was it?

As I reviewed my life, eventually I came back to my first real spiritual encounter. It was during my days of Mad Rags shortly after I first went to Bali.

During my time running my clothing label I had spent a winter season in Colorado, prospecting for a suitable shop outlet to take my range into the US ski market. That winter I met and befriended an Ojibawa Native Indian Shaman and Medicine Man.

He took me in and I ended up spending most of my time there with him roaming the foothills and learning of his shaman ways of healing. It was during that time that I reclaimed the deep connection to nature that I had always had as a child, and he shared with me many wonderful practices to open and deepen that connection. He taught me how to journey and vision for medicine and included me in his healing ceremonies.

Sometime later he came to England to host retreats on shamanic healing practices and run a sweat lodge ceremony at a retreat centre in Dorset. I decided to take my brother Grant along as a birthday present. I had been out of touch with him since the winter in Verbier and it was a good chance to reconnect.

We turned up in the morning as the last touches were being put on the wooden frame that would support the sweat lodge.

The Native Indians used the sweat lodge as both a purification exercise and a doorway to visioning. Basically it was a domed construction about twelve feet in diameter made of wood and covered with skins. A fire is lit outside the entrance in which a number of large stones are brought to great heat.

Once they are ready, the participants enter the lodge and after due preparation of the space, the stones are brought in one by one. Each time the stones come in water is poured on them producing steam. The confined space quickly becomes intensely hot.

Our master of ceremonies was a bear of a man, six foot four and weighing over a hundred kilos. Jet black, swept back hair cascaded long down his back. He had a large piece of turquoise in his belt buckle and wore a ten gallon hat. He looked every bit the part.

Grant and I introduced ourselves to the group and in turn to our guide. His stare was intense and his energy strong. He had a powerful sense of presence about him.

Over the day we sat and listened to him talk of the ways of his people and how we had come to lose our connection to nature. He referred to its power as Great Spirit and his idea of it was something like a personified notion of the Tao.

Grant and I had both grown up outdoors and nature was our friend, so we both resonated deeply with what he said. The earthiness of him and the work he had us do that day appealed greatly and we both warmed to him. We were part of a group of twelve people to take part in the ceremony.

We sat and smoked tobacco in a huge ceremonial pipe and talked amongst ourselves of whatever issues were raised. Some were there seeking healing, others inspiration. Grant and I were just checking it out.

When the time came we all undressed and entered the lodge one by one. We sat in a circle round a hole in the ground that was to receive the stones. The first stone was brought in and our host poured water. It was mid-September and rather chilly, but the place soon warmed up.

242

As we sat taking in the steam and the aroma of herbs he talked more of the wisdom that Nature holds and of the access to that wisdom that can be gained from reconnecting to it. Then he asked us all to reflect on our aspirations for the ceremony that was about to take place so that, in turn, we might speak of them openly and bring them to life.

With each new stone the space became hotter. A talking stick was passed around as each of us in turn spoke from the heart. I had no idea what I was going to say.

When the stick came to Grant he said quite simply and with complete honesty. "Great spirit. My name is Grant. I am not sick and I came here because it was a birthday present from my brother. I have nothing to ask but I pray that I might learn to love well."

It had been a few years since we had hung out together. It was good to hear him speak. Grant is a wise old soul who has wandered far in search of his way home, and though he has never been on the kind of mission I have been, his life has also been quite a journey. In those few words he spoke his truth perfectly.

Then the stick came to me. I had been mulling over expressing gratitude to my parents and asking for integrity in my business, but when I took the stick, nothing. Just a pause, an emptiness.

Suddenly, and with a voice that seemed hardly my own, I said. "Great Spirit. I pray for your guidance. May the wisdom of the universe flow though me for the benefit of all mankind."

I have no idea where it came from. But there it was. My aspiration. There was a pause as I tried to fathom just what it was that I had asked, as more water was poured on the fire.

Then Grant nudged me and muttered,

"Nice one Burgsy. That's a big one. Where did that come from?"

"No idea," I whispered back.

But in that moment something had happened. I knew deep inside that a door had opened. I felt in the subtlest of ways a shift in energy, although I had no idea then in what direction it would take me.

The ceremony continued and ran its course. There were other rounds in which we spoke more freely of our hopes and dreams. It was indeed quite a moving experience and by the time we had finished there was quite a connection between us all.

In turn we emerged from the heat to the cold of the autumn night. We took our towels and wrapped ourselves in blankets and went inside to drink spiced tea and relive what we had just shared.

The Shaman approached Grant and I and thanked us for our contribution. We thanked him back.

"Your Brother has medicine in him like you," he said. "You should both use it one day."

We were flattered but took it more as a sign of good will than a serious call to arms. Yet as we drove away that night we talked of things that we had shared in our childhood, a belief in energy and a secret way of things.

A flame was lit that would glow slowly inside until it was finally ignited that night in Bali when I first heard Ada speak. I wanted to help people, to end people's sickness and suffering and I knew that evening in Burma when I reviewed all of this that it was the thirst for the knowledge of how to do this that had first shaken me from my slumber.

It was this aspiration, to know and connect to the wisdom of the universe that was driving me on, unconsciously but inexorably. The unstated mission was to find the way to heal all of our sickness, to roll back the rate of decay and bring our life principle to its full potential.

Mine had not been a path of cutting off but one of cultivation, of finding out what we were truly capable of. I wanted to serve, to do my part, to justify my existence before I was ready to hand in my cards and seek my leave. When I saw it, I knew it was that. That was the reason I couldn't cut off.

At a deep unconscious level some part of me believed I was here to serve and I was in search of the knowledge of how to do this. I had no idea where first I had made my vow, but I knew now where I had relit the flame in this life.

Though I hadn't realised it at the time, that night in Dorset in the sweat lodge was the beginning of the search that took me in the end to the Buddha and his wisdom. Finally I realised that there is no healing greater than to come out of ignorance, so we might see clearly and take accountability for our lives and actions, knowing that we and only we will ever be the cause of our own suffering.

Since we, in our ignorance, have brought all of our suffering upon ourselves, then we hold within us the key to the end of that suffering. No one else will deliver us out of suffering but ourselves.

I began my search believing that this power was somewhere out there to be found on the high planes or the farthest reaches of the soul. I set out looking for the miracle cure to our ills, practising Alchemy in India and Bali in search of the Philosopher's Stone, and the mystical elixirs of immortality.

But in the end I came to see that the power is there within. Latent, maybe dormant, even cut off completely, but always waiting to be re-ignited when we are ready to step back and stop interfering with the highest intelligence of all. The intelligence that seeks only to perfect us, if we would just learn to get out of the way and let it.

This was the knowledge I really sought. The full understanding of the function and workings of the life principle itself and through it the knowledge of the way to realise our full potential. I did not believe that life was only a process of suffering with no inherent point to it.

The Buddha was right and will always be right ; suffering is inevitable in our conditioned existence , but it is so only on account of our ignorance of our true state of being. I was not ready to see that life is just a process of suffering. For all the hardship we bring on ourselves, life is also a miracle too. That we have even come into being is the greatest of miracles.

I needed to understand what this meant before I could close the book on the long round of wandering on. I couldn't go where Sayadaw was taking me, not yet. In my naïveté I still thought the world needed saving and that I had an important role to play in it.

It wasn't until two years later that I came to understand the wrong view that bound me to the idea that in order to serve I would need to forego my own enlightenment.

CHAPTER TWENTY-ONE

Dodrupchen

The next day at lunch time I sat for the last time with the small group of foreigners who were living in the forest practicing under Sayadaw. Most of them were from Taiwan, Malaysia or Singapore. They all spoke English and we had developed a companionship over my time there. Many were curious about my success with my practice, and some had introduced themselves to me and became my friends.

Theo had been one of the first people to approach me at the alms round queue and quiz me about my meditation. He was a lay yogi from Singapore, a married man who had taken six months out from family life to follow his heart's desire to penetrate the Dharma and master his meditation.

There is much intrigue surrounding the jhanic states and since Sayadaw did not give much away in interview other than the basic instructions necessary, the fact that there was now an English speaking yogi who had achieved such levels of samadhi and could talk of them in a language other than Burmese created something of a stir, even more so because that yogi was a rogue outsider from England with no apparent background.

Theo and I connected immediately and to this day he remains a dear friend. First he and then others began to discuss their practice with me as we took alms and ate.

Our lunchtime gatherings became an enjoyable break from the solitude of intensive practice and the only time I spent with other people. I think we all enjoyed these times. We came in time to call our gang the Pindapata Club. Pindapata is the Pali word for the monk's daily duty of begging for alms food.

That day was the last time we convened and all of them were shocked that I was leaving.

"How can you leave now?" One said. "We need you to stay and finish so you can teach us."

I knew that they had trouble communicating with Sayadaw. His English was good but not perfect and in truth he only started giving personal guidance and instruction once the student had reached a level of concentration approaching jhana.

For many in the monastery this was the big challenge they faced. Some had been there for many years trying to get their samadhi. I had begun to try to assist them in this by sitting with them after lunch and answering their questions or giving guided meditation to help them navigate their way through. I knew they valued this time.

Although that day I promised to return I did not know when I would and I realised I may never see some of them again.

It was in truth an emotional farewell. I went to say goodbye to Sayadaw one last time and I sensed a disappointment amongst some of his senior monks. To this day I often wonder what would have become of me if I had stayed, but I didn't.

Theo had invited me to Singapore to give a seminar which in time led to me conducting a number of healing and meditation retreats. One of the regular attendants spoke to me of her affiliation with a Tibetan teacher called Dzogchen Rinpoche.

She was responsible for him when he visited Singapore and had said on a number of occasions that she could arrange a private meeting with him if I wished. He was the only Tibetan teacher to whom I had any connection and I knew he was due in Singapore to teach around the time I was leaving Pa Auk. I felt that maybe it was time to seek some guidance on what had happened in the cave in Rewalsar.

I called my friend from Rangoon and she confirmed that Dzogchen Rinpoche was due to arrive in Singapore in a few days, so I flew down to meet with him.

I went first to an evening talk that Rinpoche was giving. He was young, maybe forty-five years old and spoke excellent English. The next day I was taken to the house he was staying at where we sat and talked privately.

I carefully recounted to him my story from India and the meeting with Padmasambhava in the cave.

He listened with great interest until I had finished.

He sat quietly for a minute or so before commenting.

"This is most rare," he said. "You have had a direct mind transmission from the Great Master himself. I am head Rinpoche of my lineage and we do indeed take Padmasambhava to be our master, but your experience is very rare and most precious.

It is not for me to teach you regarding this, for you are receiving teachings directly from the Master.

We have in our tradition some teachers who we call the Light Masters. There are three of them alive now. Only they can give you instruction and teachings about these things. I will give you their names and if someday you have a chance I suggest you try to meet one of them. I am a public figure but they are much more private and you will have to travel far to find them. If you have karma, which I am sure you do, then one day you will meet with one of them."

He wrote three names on a piece of paper together with three places in the world where these Light Masters could be found. There was no address. Just a place name.

He handed it to me together with a beautiful picture of Padmasambhava.

"This is the picture of Guru Rinpoche that I use when I meditate on him. Perhaps it will help you keep your connection. Even for someone within our tradition to have experiences such as you have had is most rare. That you have had them while following a different path entirely suggests you have an extraordinary connection to him. Perhaps one day you will find out why."

He gave me a card with the address of his monastery in Southern India and an invitation to visit him there at any time if I so wished. And then we said goodbye. It was a meeting reminiscent of the ones I had had with the other Tibetan masters I met in India. It was brief, intimate and to the point.

And each one had prompted me in the direction I needed to go at that time. There was no explicit teaching given, just a suggestion in which direction to go to, to come to further understanding for myself. I had no idea who these Light Masters were, but I knew that when the time was right, I would meet with one of them.

I had recently been back in contact with Darius who was now back in India. I had discussed with him my decision to leave the forest and he suggested we meet up. We had had news that the young Karmapa had escaped from house arrest in China and was now in India. I had seen pictures of him when he was a young child and had been moved by his appearance. I had always felt that one day he would become a great master and now he was fifteen and had escaped after years in captivity in China.

His monastery, which had been empty since his predecessor had died fifteen years previously, is in a remote province between Nepal and Bhutan called Sikkim. We assumed that he would be taken there to assume his position of authority within his tradition. It seemed a rare opportunity to try to meet him and so we planned a trip to this mountainous north-eastern region of India and the foothills of the Himalayas.

I agreed to meet Darius in Calcutta from where we would make our way north. It was the first time I had been back to India since my adventures in Rewalsar where Darius and I had met.

Sikkim is a remote province of north eastern India that until recently had been an independent Kingdom. Access is limited and requires a special permit which can only be acquired at the border.

We took a train from Calcutta as far north as we could and from Siliguri we travelled by Land Rover up into the Himalayas. The road was narrow and winding and rose steadily into the mountains. The scenery was spectacular and the road followed a river up through narrow gorges and ravines.

We were amongst eight people crammed into the back of the open Land Rover, and as we gained altitude I was glad to be packed so closely between other bodies. The roads were so winding and steep in places that even the fearless Indian bus drivers dared not venture here, and these four by four vehicles were the only way to reach our destination.

There was a caravan of them heading in both directions, each one loaded to the hilt with bodies and bags. As is often the case the driver is also the mechanic and many times we passed stranded vehicles with the hood up and the driver's head buried deep in the faulty engine.

Luckily our car did not break down and we arrived in the main town of Gangtok late in the afternoon.

We were heading for a small village on the other side of the valley from Gangtok called Rumtek. This was where the Karmapa's monastery was situated, and our final destination after almost twenty-four hours travelling.

We alighted from the jeep and I claimed our bags from the roof as Darius ran off in search of a taxi to take us the hour's ride over to Rumtek. We arrived finally as the sun set and found ourselves a room at the only guest house in town.

It was February and we were high up in the mountains. It was freezing. There was no hot water and I had no warm clothes. It was a fitful night's sleep and I was glad when the sun came up and we were able to get hot butter tea from the Tibetan owner.

Like so many of my trips I had not really made plans and I could begin to see now how ill-equipped I was. I would clearly need a new wardrobe if I was going to spend any time in these mountains.

Rumtek is a tiny hill station with two shops and one guesthouse. We would have to go back to Gangtok to acquire the provisions we would need. But we were tired from the travelling and didn't fancy going straight back over to the other side of the valley so we decided to take a stroll into town in search of the Karmapa's monastery.

It took us only five minutes to realise how poorly planned our trip really was. The Karmapa was not in Rumtek and never had been. He had been taken to Dharamasala upon his escape from China and had been there ever since, being debriefed by the Dalai Lama and his various other preceptors and teachers.

After the Dalai Lama, the Karmapa is one of the most significant figures in Tibetan Buddhism. This young man was the seventeenth in a lineage that pre-dated even the Dalai Lama's. His predecessor had been a highly revered and much loved master and so there was much interest in the emergence of this young man from China after many years in captivity.

I had been quite moved when I saw pictures of him as a young boy in Tai Situpa's quarters. He had an extraordinary presence about him even at the age of eight and back then, as now, I had a strong wish to meet him one day.

In our enthusiasm we had thought that by coming directly to his monastery so soon after his escape, we might be amongst the first to meet with him. It was quite naïve of us, for we hadn't even enquired beforehand if he actually was in Rumtek. And sure enough, he wasn't.

However, it was a beautiful place, much more so than the smoky town of Gangtok across the valley and so we decided to plot up for a while and do our own retreat. It was nice to be able to move freely and keep my own time after the rigours and discipline of monastic life. I felt very relaxed and alive and was quite content to rest up in the mountains for a while. Besides, we felt there was a chance the Karmapa might turn up while we were there.

We spent the next two days setting ourselves up. We rented two rooms on the top floor of a private house with a flat roof on which to exercise and enjoy stunning views over the valley. We made the trip back to Gangtok to buy warm clothes, and various necessities which included a gas stove, a bag of rice and various vegetables.

I had learned in Rewalsar, during the few days that George and I had shared digs with the two monks there, that the Tibetan yogi diet consists mainly of fatty red meat and very few vegetables. It is on account of the high altitude at which they live. The meat and fat heat the body and vegetables are scarce at such altitude. I had not eaten meat since I first went to Burma and so it was clear we would have to provide for ourselves.

We set ourselves up well and settled in to the place. I began to pass on to Darius what I had learned from Sayadaw, explaining to him in stages the practice of meditation from the development of concentration to the investigation into first material states and then mind. We also spent some time investigating the Tibetan way of meditation that

254

Darius had learned over the years from various teachers.

We had been there for about five days and I was on the roof doing Chi Kung when Darius approached me excitedly. He had been out scouting around town and got talking to a couple of monks who spoke some English. I thought perhaps that he might have heard of the arrival of the Karmapa.

"You know what Burgs?" he exclaimed. "I don't know why I didn't think of it before, but I know one great master who lives across the valley in Gangtok. I was just speaking to these monks and they told me about him. I had completely forgotten. I came up here ten years ago and he gave me teachings. I think we should go and visit him while we are here. I can't believe I didn't think of it before."

"Well, why not?" I said. "I don't think the Karmapa is going to show up and it would be nice to meet someone new. What is his name?"

"He is called Dodrupchen Rinpoche."

"Wait a second." I said. The name struck a chord. "If I am not wrong…"

I went down to my room and dug out my wallet. In it was the piece of paper Dzogchen Rinpoche had given me. I opened it up.

"I thought so! Hey, Darius," I called up to him on the roof. "He's one of the teachers Dzogchen Rinpoche told me I should meet."

I ran back upstairs.

"How amazing!" I gasped. "That in all the remote places on earth where we could end up he is just a few miles away. That has to be karma. Maybe that's the real reason we are here."

"Look." Darius was pointing across the valley. "You see that white spire poking above the trees

255

over there? Just above the town. That is his monastery."

I followed his gaze and located the stupa he pointed at.

"Yes! Indeed," I said. "That is exactly where we should go."

The next day we took the school bus across to Gangtok with the kids. Dodrupchen's monastery was on the edge of town and we passed the road leading up to it as we drove in. We jumped off the bus and walked the rest of the way.

As we walked, Darius recounted to me his previous experiences with Dodrupchen ten years ago. He had stayed for a while nearby and visited twice a week for a few months. Sometimes he had an audience with the teacher and sometimes not.

The Rinpoche was now in his early seventies and spent large parts of the year in solitary retreat. We were hoping we would have more luck meeting him than we had with the Karmapa.

We were in luck. As it happened it was mid-February. Not the season for visiting these parts but it was, however, approaching Tibetan New Year. We had passed many more people walking up the hill to the monastery than I would have expected. When we reached the top we understood why.

There was a puja, or ceremony going on. It was the annual festival and Dodrupchen held a puja that ran for ten days leading up to New Year. They were two days into it. As we approached the monastery it was clear where the main focus of activity was.

There was a large hall crammed to overflowing with both monks and lay devotees. Inside we could hear the distinctive sound of chanting, occasionally interrupted by horns, cymbals, bells, and drums. It was a powerful sound and there was an intensely strong energy around the place.

We approached and peeked through a window. Inside there were rows of monks sitting cross-legged on the floor in front of low tables on which were various instruments and scrolls from which they were reciting ancient texts and mantras.

"Look," said Darius. "You see the big throne-like chair at the end of the hall? That is Dodrupchen Rinpoche sitting there. Apparently this is a powerful purification ceremony to clear away and neutralise all the negativity and bad energies that have accumulated around the region. They will go on all day and almost all night for ten days."

Quite unexpectedly a bearded monk approached us and ushered us into the packed hall. He signalled for people to make way for us and led us to the back where he gestured for us to sit down. What could we do? Neither of us had any idea what was going on but we sat down compliantly.

The room was packed and we were wedged in between people totally unable to move. It was not long after nine in the morning. Around one o'clock there was a short break for lunch and we were able to stand up and stretch our legs.

Although I had felt very connected in the room and resonated with what seemed to be going on I felt like something of an impostor. This was clearly a sacred and special time for all those attending and I didn't feel it was appropriate to just join in uninvited. I discussed this with Darius and we agreed that we would head back to Rumtek and come to seek an audience with Dodrupchen Rinpoche when the puja was over.

The bearded monk who had first ushered us in approached us once more. Surprisingly, he spoke some English. His robes were not the same as the other monks and had a white stripe through them. What is more he had long dreadlocked hair and a beard. He looked quite amazing. It turned out that he was a Dzogchen monk from Bhutan and had walked here for over a week to attend the ceremony.

He told us that Dodrupchen would be taking interviews for a couple of days after the puja finished and that we should come back then and request to meet with him.

We thanked him warmly and went our way back to Rumtek. In truth I was torn about going back and was tempted to stay at the monastery and join in the puja even though I didn't know what it was about.

I remembered the time I had attended Bante Giri's cremation ceremony in Bali. I had had no idea what that was about at the time but as I sat there I had remembered the Pali chants and how spontaneously I had been able to join in. Perhaps a similar download was waiting to happen here?

Three years later we did go back to Sikkim and attend the full ten day puja but this time we decided not to impose and went back to Rumtek.

We carried on our retreat and without the restrictions of the monastery I was free to do long hours of yoga and Chi Kung. My body quickly became strong and toned. I felt a strength coming to me that I hadn't had since my youth. I slept little and never seemed to tire. My eyes were blazing and my skin shone. In Burma I had had no mirror and so I was quite taken aback by the noticeable change in my appearance. I felt utterly alive and I was loving every moment of each day.

Eight days later we were back in Gangtok.

There were still many people around the monastery. The pilgrims who had walked from

Bhutan were preparing to leave and there was still a buzz about the place. Everyone seemed to be uplifted by the event they had just taken part in.

The two of us milled about the place trying to work out how and where we might get the chance to meet Dodrupchen. The Bhutanese monk who we had met the week before was still around and we approached him for advice. He was helping to broker a deal for two pilgrims who were trying to sell their blankets to buy food for the journey back home to Bhutan.

In that moment, what pride I might still have been holding on to, was shattered. Perhaps I had come to think that I had shown a special dedication to have travelled so far and wide to meet my teachers. It possibly had been the source of some false spiritual pride, but I knew in that moment how little effort I had really had to make. I had had no real hardship to face. My teachers were there for me whenever I needed them and I had had to make few real sacrifices to get to where I was now.

These pilgrims had walked a week to get here and had another week's journey ahead. They had not even got to speak to their master. They had sat with him for ten days, sleeping little and offering their energy to the group cause. On the last day they had got to hold a string cord that had linked everyone in the room to the Master and in that moment they had received his blessing.

Now, having fulfilled their duty and aspiration, they were preparing to take the long journey home. I passed my Kullu shawl to the monk and gestured him to give it to the couple he was bargaining for.

I sat down beside the stupa and watched as they completed their business, and as I sat there I wondered exactly what I thought I was expecting from Dodrupchen Rinpoche. Did I really think I was worthy of his time? I had had lifetimes of guidance and schooling. What more did I expect? All that remained now was for me to walk the path.

I sat amidst the throng of humanity that buzzed around me and felt their hopes and dreams, their prayers and aspirations. I realised how blessed I was. For mine had been answered and mostly fulfilled. I knew I was ready to go to work.

When he had wrapped up the business he was attending to, the monk came over and joined me beside the stupa. Darius appeared from the crowd.

"So you would like to meet Dodrupchen?" said the monk. "Come with me. I will see what I can do."

He led us through the monastery to some rooms towards the back where there was a queue of people waiting in line to offer respect and ask blessings from their master.

Our friend spoke to a senior looking monk who appeared to be presiding over the proceedings.

He shook his head. I could tell he was saying no.

The monk came back with the bad news.

"Maybe tell him that Dzogchen Rinpoche has sent us here," I said.

He raised his eyebrows in surprise and went back to the monk officiating. The two of them returned shortly.

"Can you explain why Dzogchen Rinpoche has sent you here?" asked our friend.

I very briefly told him of my experience in Rewalsar.

The two of them exchanged words in Tibetan and the official hurried off.

After ten minutes or so he returned and again exchanged words with our interpreter before ushering us to follow him.

"You are in luck. It seems Dodrupchen has requested you to see him."

We were given white scarves and told that we should present them to Rinpoche. The Bhutanese monk had been requested to come in with us and translate along with another young Tibetan called Jigme.

As we waited outside Rinpoche's room Jigme introduced himself to me.

"Is it true that Dzogchen Rinpoche told you to come to see our master? It is quite unusual what you say has happened to you. You are very fortunate to get the chance to meet with Rinpoche but I think he is interested in your story."

In truth I was feeling a little nervous about meeting this great man. I knew so little about him but could sense already that he was someone very special. I felt suddenly an extraordinary feeling that he already knew everything about me. I felt completely transparent, almost exposed.

I had not even had that feeling when I first met Sayadaw. Then I felt I was coming to meet an old and very dear friend. This was something different. I knew there would be no personal connection with Dodrupchen but certainly there was a connection and it was strong indeed.

We were to see him one at a time. I asked Darius to go first. He had met him before and it might break the ice and in some way pave the way for me.

I waited outside as Jigme led the other two in.

I had on my shoulder a cloth monk's bag in which I was carrying a large diamond cut piece of Topaz which I had picked up in Burma. I had held it

261

when I meditated for over a year and suddenly it came to me that I had to give this crystal to Dodrupchen. I knew somehow that this was how he would know if my testimony was real or not. It held the vibration and energy of my meditation and I knew that it would speak more than words of the experiences I had been through.

After a few minutes Jigme came back out and gestured for me to follow him in.

I was surprised. I actually felt nervous. So much so that I forgot to take off my shoes at first. Darius was still in the room and sat to one side. I knelt before Rinpoche and bowed three times. It was the Burmese way but I was unfamiliar with the Tibetan practice of prostration.

I offered my scarf which he took and placed over my head. I gestured to him my gratitude and smiled.

He said nothing. He just looked into my eyes. I sensed an inclusiveness about his awareness that took everything around him in simultaneously. He was just resting effortlessly within himself and I could feel the clear coolness of his mind as he looked at me.

In those few moments I downloaded to him all the information regarding my experience. I cannot explain how I did this, it was similar to the exchange I had with the goat herder in Rewalsar. It was a mind-to-mind exchange and in a few brief moments I knew we came to understand each other. Before he even spoke I became his student and received his teaching and in barely a few seconds I knew I had already received what I had come there for. He simply showed me his mind, I understood and acknowledged, and all of this before we even spoke.

Then he looked towards Jigme and said a few words in Tibetan.

"Please tell Rinpoche what you experienced in Rewalsar," he said.

I spoke for a few minutes telling only the detail of what happened. There was no need for me to explain whatever I thought I had come to understand from the experience.

Rinpoche sat silently for a moment before speaking to me through Jigme.

He gave me instructions which I cannot here recount but I knew so deeply that I was receiving a very high blessing. But also I felt an extraordinary relief to be sitting before someone who understood what I had gone through, who knew without me needing to explain myself, exactly where I was at. If meeting with Sayadaw and connecting to Burma was like coming home for my heart, this was like being plugged in to something equally important to me.

I knew I would never have the intimate relationship with Dodrupchen that I had with Sayadaw, but equally I knew I would from this moment always be connected to him. He knew what I knew, and I did not need to explain anything. It was an extraordinary relief.

When I had finished speaking I reached into my bag and pulled out the topaz crystal.

"I would like to give this to you," I said. "It is a token of my understanding. It has within it both the clear light and the rainbow."

I held it up to the light that shone through the window and it produced a rainbow on the floor between us. I passed it to Rinpoche. He reached out and took it from me with a smile.

He examined it and looked deeply into it and held it in his hand and closed his eyes. I knew there was no hiding anything from him now.

He smiled again and said something to Jigme. "Ah, this is very wonderful," said Jigme. "Rinpoche says he needs this crystal on top of the shrine at which he does his daily puja. He has been waiting for a crystal exactly like this that is shaped like a diamond. He says he did not know where he would find one. He thanks you for your gift."

I was delighted that my gift served not only as a gesture of my understanding but would also be something of use and value to my teacher.

As I made to leave he said one thing more. Jigme again translated.

"Tonight in your meditation connect with Rinpoche and please come back in a few days to tell him of your experience."

As I left I knew I would not often see this great man again. I felt an extraordinary connection to him and yet it was in no way personal. I knew it existed at an unspoken level, as had been the connection with the goat herder.

That night he did indeed come to me. As I sat, the silent transmission I had received in those few moments when he held me with his gaze and his mind, came alive weaving its way deeply into my meditation.

I sat on my bed in the most unfathomable state of peace and ease as I entered into the sublime stillness of the clear light that I had seen in the cave as I sat before Padmasambhava. I knew now that this was the state that I had been entering into in the midst of my practice in Burma. Suddenly I knew there was nothing I had to achieve. There was nowhere to go to, nothing to do.

I sat in that state all night and when Darius came in to see me in the morning I was still there. Not fixed or fixated, just resting in the very essence of my heart and taking the ease. I knew in that moment that I was at peace with myself, the world and everything in it. I honestly felt I could have stayed there forever. There really was no need to move.

To do anything now was merely a choice but not something of any real importance. To have stayed in the mountains or to have gone back to England to serve, it was all the same. And although I knew I would go back, it was no longer something I had to do. I finally felt free to choose.

That night I finally came to a clear understanding of how all these profound states I had been investigating fitted together. The clear light mind that Guru Rinpoche had shown me in Rewalsar was the very basis of Dodrupchen's mind and I knew from that day forth it was the basis of mine too. It was not that I had reached a higher level or entered into something new. It was that I had fully come to recognise something that had always been there.

This was not a mind-produced state like the jhanas but the natural and untainted basis of all awareness. It was like the template upon which we lay all of our experience without even knowing it to be there.

The crystal I had given to Rinpoche symbolised this realisation perfectly.

The mind and all its myriad manifestations is in a sense an illusion that masks the true essence of things. Like a rainbow that is produced when a light shines through a crystal.

When we are first moved to begin the job of refining our being, we might be inclined to investigate that rainbow and how we might make it more lustrous and clear. We might in our confusion be inclined to polish the surface that reflects the rainbow in the hope of making it brighter. Rather in the way that we might groom ourselves physically in order to appear more appealing to those around us. But in the end we come to recognise this to be nothing but an act of vanity.

So we might turn towards the crystal itself and polish that so it might always produce a more perfect rainbow. This is similar to the way that we might make efforts to refine our character and come in time to naturally project to the world a more virtuous and noble being at an inner level. We come to realise that the real lustre and radiance in our being comes from the heart and not from how we actually appear to the world.

Indeed we might come to the point where we are satisfied that our crystal is shining and bright enough, and that we are without taint or defilement. At this point we may well be inclined to think that we have done enough.

But what then if we were to take away the crystal entirely? Ah. Then what?

We are left with just the clear light that is the basis of all rainbows however they may appear. We come finally to recognise that all appearances are illusions, just a dance of light producing unfathomable fields of possibilities. They have in essence no real meaning but the one we attach to them.

Life is, in the final analysis, a dance, a pantomime. It is a story to be engaged in, either for our joy and appreciation, or our hardship and suffering, but in the end not one that can be clung to nor won. It doesn't matter what we do, as long as it is harmless to ourselves and others. And it doesn't matter what the world thinks of us, for it is not what we really are.

We should all learn to dance our dance with all our heart, but not get lost in it. You, me, Sayadaw, Dodrupchen Rinpoche, we are all just dancing the light. Playing our rainbows to the world. And in the end whether it is dull and lacklustre, or brilliant and lustrous, it is always coming into being from the same clear light that is the basis of all things.

Every day we wake up we have a choice. How well we reflect that light is entirely up to us. We have this life, and it is the most extraordinary field of infinite possibilities. It can be the source of wonder and miracles or confusion and despair, but when we all put our heads on the pillow and sleep at night, we each and every one of us rest in that clear, pristine light of pure awareness. What a shame we might never come to recognise it.

And when we die and our sense doors break down, when our consciousness falls away from the world of forms, all we are left with is the clear light and the fading impressions of all the experiences that have arisen from it and masked it all our lives.

Perhaps then we might come to recognise the perfection from which we all arise every instant of every day, instead of clinging to our confused idea of what we think we might be. There is a stillness and a peace that is beyond the mind's wildest imaginings, in the vast unfathomable spaciousness of that clear light.

It is the very "peace that passeth all understanding", for it will never be grasped by our mind until we finally break through the fog of our ignorance and pierce the veil of confusion that identifies only with the ego. To know it is to be beyond doubt, and to be beyond doubt is to be free of all fear.

Then fearlessness becomes the basis from which to dance our rainbow with all our heart, in the sure knowledge and acceptance of the fact that it is a gift that will not last forever and is certainly not something to get lost in.

I almost went back to Dodrupchen the very next day. There was nothing more I could explain to him. I had only to sit before him once more and let him know that I had understood. But then I knew he already knew. As it was we went back five days later and Jigme again took us in to see him. I had nothing to say.

I knew I had to continue my Vipassana to wear out over time the as yet unrefined aspects of my character but there was no sense of urgency. I knew I would go back to England and teach but it wasn't a mission I was on and it no longer mattered whether ten people or ten thousand chose to come and learn meditation. It just didn't matter. The world would roll on as it always had done and always will, whatever I chose to do.

I knew now something that I had sensed in my heart all my life. Something I had heard whispered in the wind since my earliest memories. I had always known it and all my confusion had only ever been caused by the fact that no one had pointed out to me that I knew. Until now.

My meeting was brief. Maybe ten minutes. But in that time I said all I needed to say. And once again Dodrupchen said everything there was to say.

Just before I left he told me.

"Please continue to do what you are doing. It is right that you teach what you teach. But in your own time please meditate for the liberation of other beings."

He knew I knew what he meant. And to this day it is my practice. The one I do behind the appearance of teaching meditation or healing, Chi Kung or alchemy. Tinker tailor soldier sailor...I am none of them any more than I am a meditation teacher, a healer or an alchemist. But the dance is the dance, so from time to time I am all of those things too.

I left Sikkim knowing I had a heart connection to this great master. I did return in time. A few years later I went back to attend the whole of the Dodrupchen puja and when it was finished I met with Rinpoche again. I had heard that he had been unwell during the winter and had spent most of it in silent retreat. I knew he would be exhausted from the ten day puja, and I wanted to give him a precious medicine that I had come across along my way.

As he had done with the crystal three years before, he took the bottle containing the medicine. He examined it and then put some in his hand and closed his eyes.

When he opened them he spoke to Jigme.

"Rinpoche says that this is a very rare substance. He thanks you for it. He says that there used to be some monks in Northern Tibet who made this substance but he did not know if they still did. They used to use it to heal all kinds of sickness and even cancer."

"Please tell him that I give it to him as a gift. It too has within it the clear light and the rainbow, just like the crystal. I pray that it may keep him healthy and strong for many more years, so that he can continue to hold the light for us all."

Then unprompted he put some of the medicine in a glass of water and drank it. He looked at me and smiled. He knew, and I knew he knew.

CHAPTER TWENTY-TWO

Alchemy

I had a dream one time while I was teaching Vipassana:

A young lad stood before me. He was no more than twenty-three years old. He had in his eye that eager glint, that heady mix of innocent vitality and enthusiasm in the face of the mysterious unknown.

The question he had asked me rolled around my head as it had done many times. If I had a penny for every time I had been asked this...

"I want to be a yogi and master the practice of alchemy," said the boy. "I feel I am ready. Will you teach me?"

I smiled to myself. Gone were the days when a yogi toiled for his knowledge and sweated to breathe life into it, today they want their cookies now!

"Have you any idea what you ask? What do you know about the four great elements?" I asked the young boy.

"Well I have been practising the meditation on the four elements for three years now. I think I know them quite well."

"Then you will know by now how the great work of the alchemist is done. So be gone with you and get on with it. And don't trouble me with your tiresome requests till it's done."

"But that's just it. I am asking you to teach me how to make the Philosopher's Stone."

"It is made out of mastery of the four great elements and consciousness itself. Are you not a master of these after three years? No? Then be gone, and get on with your work."

"Is that it then?" said the boy, "Just mastery of the four great elements?"

"Indeed."

"And how will I know when I have mastered them?"

"When the Philosopher's Stone appears."

"And when might that be?"

"When you have finally let go all desire for it."

"Huh?"

"Four times the world comes into being and is destroyed. Four cycles of folding and unfolding make the four ages of our world system. The cycle of Earth, Water, Fire and Air. When you have seen and understood clearly the coming into being of things and their undoing in each of the four cycles of Earth, Water, Fire and Air. When you have bellowed your furnace through each of these ages and when the elements are revealed to you in their final undoing, then you will know how to make the Philosopher's Stone.

Now in my reckoning an Aeon is the time it takes for the world to arise and settle, bring forth life and undo itself, and this undoing is done by each of the four elements in turn with the degeneration of the consciousness that vitalises it.

So if I am not wrong that is four Aeons. Now you have three years under your belt and your fire is not yet lit. I suggest, young man, that you have work to do."

And so it is. We live at the culmination of an age in which the efforts of man have turned tirelessly towards the ever swifter acquisition of the objects of his desires. Gone are the days of real toil in the pursuit of what is precious, to the point where little is valued and where the most precious of spiritual gifts is placed alongside one's material desires on the list of "Things I must have".

Today it seems that we give up little to acquire what we seek. The days of making sacrifices to win our heart's desire are long gone. We are so used to being able to gratify our desires with the simple purchase of their object that the idea of a lifetime's work, or many for that matter, in the pursuit of our aspirations is an alien concept to the minds of most.

I have been asked many times to teach the healing arts and the alchemical process to my students of meditation. I do not believe I am stingy with the teachings I share, I offer them up freely to everyone. They need only ask. But perhaps in doing so I have done them an injustice, for I have failed to instil in them the true sense of the road that is travelled on the way to spiritual knowledge.

We live in the West in a society lacking a culture of spiritual cultivation. Religion long ago took the place of genuine spiritual endeavour, and when even religious faith became too much of a commitment, intuition became the new god, giving everyone access to whatever truth suited their ideas of the world.

It is hardly surprising therefore that an aspiring yogi such as this lad would believe that the mastery of spiritual knowledge is something that can be taught like a university degree. "Sign up for the three year course in Spiritual Truth. The graduate study of the way of things." I can imagine such courses appearing in the syllabus of colleges before long, but reflect if you will on the chasm that lies between information and knowledge.

In many ways I had been a passenger on this great journey, waiting for this chance to take the helm. Towards the end of my time with Ada he told me that he had always known that one day I would go back to England to teach, and that I must be prepared to fly like an eagle and take up my responsibilities in my own country, as he had done in his. He told me that a time would come when I would have to go alone and work independently of my teachers. I knew that time was approaching.

It was during this time that I truly came to understand that no amount of theoretical or intellectual understanding would facilitate the transformation that experiential knowledge brings about. Indeed it is possible to grasp the path at an intellectual level, and it is often hard to spot where we are developing views and ideas in the belief that these views constitute actual wisdom.

For example, we can reason and intellectually grasp the notion of dependent origination, and in doing so think we have come to see the truth of it, but until we have actually seen it functioning both within us and in the world around us, it still only constitutes a view to which we may cling, and in this capacity it will not actually bring us to the absolute experience that cuts off at the root our ego clinging.

It is often very hard to review objectively the changes that have come about in us, indeed it may be many years of retrospective observation before we can actually know if we have brought about lasting changes through our practice. It is at this level that I found the practice of alchemy to be such a valuable teacher.

For if it is hard for us to spot the difference between intellectual understanding and transformative, experiential knowledge within us, in alchemy the difference is absolutely clear. The alchemical transformation either does come about and so can be seen in the materials transformed, or it doesn't. There is no middle ground.

No matter how much we may mull over the principles and grasp them intellectually, the process does not even begin until we actually light the fire and seal our crucible. And every step of the way we can observe and test the progress made.

There is a wonderful story about a man of great faith who upon getting sick went to visit a doctor he trusted completely.

"Doctor" he said. "I have become sick, but I know you are the greatest doctor of all. Please heal me."

The doctor investigated and duly gave a medicinal prescription.

"Ah you are so wonderful," said the man. "You have saved my life. How can I ever repay you?"

And he took home the prescription and placed it on his altar. Morning and evening he lit incense and candles and bowed down to the shrine as if he were showing reverence to a sacred text.

Needless to say, a week later his symptoms had not improved. So he returned to the doctor.

"Doctor, you are indeed the greatest doctor of all. And I have daily prayed to you and offered incense and bowed in homage. Yet still I am sick. I must have wronged you in some way."

"Oh my dear man," said the doctor. "You are indeed mistaken. It was no sacred text I gave you but instructions that you must actually follow. If you do not read the instructions how ever do you expect to get well?"

"Ah. Of course." Said the man. "Forgive me for troubling you. I am nothing but a fool. You are truly the greatest doctor. Thank you, thank you."

So he returned home, and every day, morning and evening after lighting incense and candles at his altar he recited the text one hundred and eight times, bowing between each repetition.

"One pill in the morning, two pills in the evening. After a week you will return to health."

A week passed and no change. On the contrary his condition worsened on account of not being properly treated.

He returned once more to the doctor to report the bad news.

"Oh you poor man. This is not a mantra I have written for you. It is a prescription for medication. You must buy these medicines and take them according to my instructions. One pill in the morning, two pills in the evening."

"Ah," said the man. "You are so wise. I have always trusted that you are the finest doctor. I know I will be saved. However can I repay you?" He bowed and left.

And in due course, having bought and taken the medicine prescribed he did indeed recover his health.

Now you may find this story foolish, but there are no end of people who study the texts, and receive teachings from many great masters, and debate amongst themselves, but never practice the path in such a way that they will come to know if the teachings are valid and true or not. What is more, like the foolish man in our tale, though they may hold in their hands the map that shows them the way, they never overcome their suffering, because they do not walk the path it points to.

We may be able to glimpse a way beyond suffering as we reflect upon the teachings of the great masters, but there is a great body of work between the peak experience, or the transcendent glimpse into the awakened state, and the real attainment of the wisdom that allows us to enter into and abide effortlessly in this realised state with full understanding of what it actually is.

We may come to a point where we think we are satisfied with our understanding, when actually we have not yet reached any real level of wisdom. If we are to honestly ask ourselves what do we really know to be true, the answer is actually not very much. In truth we cling to views as if they were truth, when actually they are nothing other than views. It is far more appropriate to open our mind and acknowledge that we don't know anything to be true, and then engage honestly in the process of experiential investigation.

I am sure Eckhart Tolle will testify to the long road that followed his own epiphany as he sought to fully understand and embody the realisations he had had. When it first happened, he was left in an almost unmanageable state for weeks on end, and it eventually took him some years to fully grasp what had actually happened to him.

It is without doubt that work previously carried out in former lives ripened him to the experience that fruited in this. There followed for him the real work of coming to embody this awakening in a realised way. This is the work of the Yogi. It is not the path of inspiration but the gradual path of the cultivation of our being at every level. It takes ardent discipline, honesty, commitment and patience. And always it is better to say, "I don't yet understand," than it is to assume that we do.

Over the next few years following my departure from Burma I continued to practice alone. I spent less and less time in Bali and began to teach in England more. It was in this time that the real depth of the path I had been on revealed itself to me. Not upon reflection, although that played its part, but as my own practice matured further and began to bed in.

During that time I travelled back to Burma often and began to practice alchemy in my spare time. It took great effort, patience and perseverance. By the time I could bellow the fire evenly, and put my mind one pointedly into the fire while it did its work, the purification I had been though that made this even possible had changed me.

With the purification of the material and mental bases, my greed had been purified too. The desire for what the work brought forth was gone. I came to see that the only way for the work to perform its function successfully was to have absolutely no desire for it to even succeed.

You see, the paradox is this: in order to acquire the most precious of things, what is most deeply desired, one must first forego any trace of desire for it. I saw in alchemy a perfect symbolism for the transformation process. Only in relinquishing our desire for its rewards are they finally revealed to us.

I remember the young lad who had asked me to teach him healing and alchemy. He was one of many. I had scolded him at the time, for I have always known that this is not really the knowledge we should seek. The real knowledge we need is that which I have hinted at in these pages. The knowledge that shows us the way out of suffering, so that we might walk that way for ourselves one day, should we choose.

To remove all traces of vanity and conceit from our path is perhaps the hardest challenge of all, for to put forth effort requires an aspiration to actually achieve something. Removing the greed and desire for personal gain is what transforms humanity's most destructive tendency – ambition, into one of its most noble – aspiration.

In the end I decided to give up my practice of alchemy. However helpful it may have proved to be, it is a process that is easily misunderstood. But I have little doubt that it served its purpose in bringing me to a final willingness to let go the remaining traces of ego that kept me from the final stage of the Path. It ripened me in a timely way. Perhaps it was a challenge I felt I needed to fulfil in some way in order to let go.

Observing the complete absence of desire for and attachment to the fruits of all that work, when they did come, brought about a profound change in me. What vanity had survived my practices of Vipassana had been finally undone by the alchemical work, both external and internal. I knew it was time to finally let go all ideas of what it was I thought I had to do.

CHAPTER TWENTY-THREE

Sister

I spent the next years settling back in England and teaching meditation on a more regular basis. Although Sayadaw had trained me in great depth, both practically and theoretically, it still remained the case that the most important work was to give people an introduction to the Dharma.

I wasn't the first to teach Dharma in my country, of course not. There were branches of various Tibetan, Thai and Burmese Buddhist schools and monasteries scattered around the country, and monks and nuns from these various traditions who were teaching meditation and Dharma.

But one of the reasons I had disrobed and left Pa Auk was that I didn't feel people would relate to me as a monk. I couldn't see a way to live as a monk in the West and function fluidly in the world. If I was going to teach I needed to be able to operate amongst people. I needed to find a way to live this Dharma in the context of the life that most people found themselves in.

When I began teaching, I suppose in a way I had cast myself as a bit of a maverick yet again. I had been influenced strongly by two Buddhist traditions as well as Taoism. The path I had followed was a fusion of all of these aspects and borne of my own desire to bring them into coherence. Although I was committed to offering the pith of all three of these aspects, there is a strong argument that says the Dharma should be presented within the context that the Buddha taught it.

The Buddha had made it quite clear that the Dharma pointed to a life of simplicity and eventually renunciation, and in time it indeed does. But most of the people I was teaching were coming to learn meditation to heal themselves or develop a more robust, flexible and organised mind, so that they could live the lives they had chosen more skilfully. Few of them were looking for a completely new way of life, but rather a way to refine the one they had.

So I had developed a system of teaching quite similar to what I had learned from Merta Ada. Although everything I had been taught and practiced at Pa Auk, and the Dzogchen transmissions I had received, informed and helped crystallize the teachings and practices I offered, the focus of my work was to steer people towards a more harmonious, considerate lay life. I found there was a real thirst for this.

Many people were coming to question the material, status-based, social structures that had come to govern modern life. Many were starting to recognise how it had caused an isolation and the loss of a sense of community and belonging. The folk aspect of life in England, which historically had played such a huge role in life, had gradually faded from view and it was missed, and in its place had arisen a grasping at status by which we might be compared to others.

Our obsession with celebrity today does not require anything admirable from our role models, merely that they are savvy or fortunate enough to get themselves noticed. Today our need to strive for acceptance seems to be based more on the image we might be able to project to the world than the character we actually possess as human beings.

But people were beginning to listen to the calling of their hearts. They knew something was missing and they had started to look outside the box for answers. Over time, more and more people began to come on retreat. Some sought to tame minds that had become fractured and disorganised by the pace of the life they were living, others sought to regain a measure of health that had been so compromised by this fragmented lifestyle.

I began to see that not only did the Dharma begin to answer some of the questions they were asking, but it gave them a sense of community again. A community that understood that above all else, it was a commitment to virtuous and considerate living that was the greatest contributing factor to the sense of peace and happiness we all seek.

People began to grasp the fact that they weren't dissatisfied because they didn't have what they needed, but because what they perceived to be their needs had become so great and so confused. Life at every level had become so complex and this complexity brought much instability. In many, a longing for more simplicity had begun to emerge.

Then one day I got a call from a nun who I had befriended at Pa Auk. She had become a close friend during my time practicing in Burma and also while I was away with Sayadaw in Taiwan. She herself had been teaching all over Asia for some years without a break and I had been worried about her health. I had extended her an open invitation to visit England for a rest.

The call came quite out of the blue, and she asked if she might visit for a month to take rest. I was delighted at the thought of seeing her again. She had been the person I felt most connected to while in Burma. She was about the same age as me and had been through Sayadaw's training just prior to my arrival in Burma. She had been my only companion during the most intense period of my practice and I was looking forward to catching up and sharing experiences.

George's family had a cottage with a small barn on their farm which they very kindly offered to make available for Sayalay's* stay.

We spent a couple of weeks renovating the barn and converting it into a small meditation room, so that when she came she would have a quiet place to stay and meditate.

She arrived in the spring and stayed over the period of the May full moon, which was the time that the Buddha had attained his enlightenment. It was wonderful that we would be able to be together for this time.

I arranged for some of my students to visit and cook for her, and stay and meditate if they wished. As it turned out Sayalay liked very much to cook and as often as not she prepared food for us.

We talked much over the first week or so, sharing our experiences of meditation and of teaching. It was clear that it was a rare chance for her to relax out of the public eye and free of responsibilities.

Then one day I came to the cottage to visit her after breakfast and she seemed very sad. I asked what was wrong and we sat down to talk.

"Sayadaw has asked me to ask you again why you didn't want to finish your practice at Pa Auk. I know he is still very sad about it."

I explained to her as I had done to Sayadaw, that I just knew I had to stop, and since then I had been happy to be where I was at.

Strictly speaking though, that wasn't true. I had been healing many people over the last year and my body was feeling weak and exhausted from it.

"Me too," she said. "I feel my body is very weak. It is very challenging to teach meditation and hold people when they face their instability. But I have the protection of the Sangha. You are very exposed, working alone as you do."

It was funny, in a way. I had felt a brotherly need to try to give her sanctuary and a place to rest and heal, and now I felt her own protective instincts towards me.

"Please, won't you reconsider? I know you think that you would not be able to heal people once you completely let go, but perhaps that is a good thing. You won't live long if you carry on doing what you do."

"But I also worry that I will lose my desire to teach. And I see how many people want to learn Dharma."

"But look at Sayadaw." she said. "He still teaches. You have to understand that once you let go your desire there will still be a willingness to do. That's what it is to be functional rather than volitional. People will still ask you for teaching and so you will teach. And if they don't then you will be able to take your ease. You must allow people's karma to bring them to Dharma, you cannot drag them there."

I thought about it. She was right. It was like the

old goatherd in Rewalsar had said, the will of man was the cause of all our problems. Who was I to decide if people needed to learn Dharma? If they wanted they could ask, and I was willing to teach as best I could. And if not me, then they would find someone else to teach them.

We sat for a while in silence. I knew what she was asking me was important to her. I equally knew that she was presenting me with an issue I had chosen not to face since I left Burma. Of all the milestones along the Path, the point at which the mind turns away from conditioned states to enter the experience and knowledge of the unconditioned, is the greatest of all, for it cuts off the karma that can lead to suffering rebirth.

The whole point of the Buddha's teaching is to lead us to this point. Nothing short will guarantee our freedom from suffering. Without reaching this stage our self-clinging is still capable of bringing ourselves and others to suffering.

Even while we are deeply committed to living virtuously our mind still maintains its capacity to fall into ignoble or selfish states. Our mind is merely an operating system. It has within it the capacity for extraordinary grace, compassion and love, but also extraordinary profanity and negligence.

Every mind has the same capacity although we may not express every aspect of it. Some express their anger and hatred, some greed and desire and others loving-kindness and generosity.

The whole of the Buddha's teaching stands upon the understanding that our mind is merely a conditioned phenomenon. When life works out favourably for us our mind will tend to react favourably, but when we encounter hardship or are challenged in our aspirations we tend to react less considerately.

My unwillingness to finally surrender my ego and take this final step was ultimately rooted in my rather naïve belief that if I kept my head down I should be able to work things out favourably for myself and others.

I still maintained my idea that I needed to stay this side of the river to teach. I was still stuck in the Bodhisattva ideal, that we refrain from taking our own enlightenment for the benefit of assisting others. But I knew also that there would come a time when my own students would be faced with the choice.

Would I be able to guide them across the river safely if I myself had not crossed? I knew inside the answer was no. So in truth I was hiding something else behind this argument. It could only be some kind of pride; an unwillingness to let go the idea of myself.

Then Sayalay spoke.

"You are very skilful at meditation and have great paramis. But you cannot lead people across the river of suffering until you cross it yourself. All you can do is teach meditation and Dharma. But the real Dharma is the Path out of Samsara*. It is not enough to show people what is the cause of their suffering. You must be able to show them the cessation of it. The Buddha taught us Four Noble Truths*. The truth of suffering and its causes are only the first two. The third is the cessation of suffering and that is Nibbana. The fourth is the Path that leads to the cessation of suffering. It is nothing short of that. You must teach all four Noble truths. That is what the Buddha taught us."

She stopped. As I looked at her, I could feel her deep love and compassion for me.

We sat and meditated for a while. I looked deeply at my unwillingness.

As we sat I became aware that Sayalay was sobbing quietly. I remembered how Sayadaw had shed a single tear the day I told him I was leaving. I knew she cared as deeply for me as Sayadaw had. I was moved beyond words.

Then she spoke through her tears.

"Burgs. I am sorry. I want to apologise to you."

"What do you mean? You have no reason to apologise to me."

"I do. I feel it is my fault you cannot go further. I came here to England to apologise to you, because it is holding me back too. I too, long for the highest peace in this life."

"Why is it your fault?"

"Did you review your past lives when you were with Sayadaw?"

"I did some."

"Do you remember your time in Burma, in Bagan?"

"I do. I remember two. One as a teaching monk and the other as a lay person."

"Do you know why you were a lay person in that life, when you had been a monk previously?"

"I remember the rebirth linking consciousness that caused the rebirth back in Bagan again. And of course, no one is born a monk. It is a choice we make for ourselves each time."

"Can you see if you went on to teach in the second life?"

"No I didn't."

"Do you know why?"

"I ran away from there."

"But why was that?"

"I became disappointed."

"Don't you think that perhaps that memory may have been what stopped you going on in this life?"

"I don't know. I hadn't thought of it like that."

"Something very strong must have occurred to cut off your previous aspiration to teach Dharma. Sit now and meditate...look into it deeply. Maybe you will see."

I sat and we meditated together. As I looked more deeply into the volition that had arisen in me when I suddenly decided to stop my practice, I could see more clearly now. It wasn't actually because of a vow to serve. That was just a view I had clung to. It was on account of karma. The door to any higher attainment had closed on me because I had not opened it to those I might have taught back in Burma.

I knew that following my life as a monk I had returned there. Yet something had caused me to give up my desire to teach and turn away, in spite of that aspiration being the reason for my rebirth in Bagan a second time. I left my practices and in time came to no end of suffering in the lifetimes that immediately followed.

All of it was because I had turned away from my commitment to the Path. It was a weighty karma indeed. I could see that it had been the cause for me cutting off my practice at the final stage in this life. And because of it I could see how much I was beginning to suffer even now. All the healing work I was doing was depleting me at a very deep level. I knew Sayalay was right. If I continued, I may not live much longer.

I reviewed again the time after my death in Bagan when I looked down over the scene of my cremation. This was the memory that had stunned me when I first visited there in this life with Ada.

The memory was strong.

As I was about to pass on from that life I saw that the people I had been teaching, for all their faith in the path would not go far enough to cut off their suffering without a teacher to guide them. I knew somehow that they would fall short and instead get lost in the practices of samadhi and not strive for insight. And because of that I could not see their sasana* lasting for long.

It had been this that had prompted my rebirth linking back to Bagan one more time. This was the karma that had brought me back to the same place again, with a strong aspiration to complete what I had begun. And yet in spite of it I had not fulfilled my commitment. I knew I had not taught in that next life but I hadn't yet seen why.

"Why are you apologising to me sister?" I asked.

"In that next life, you and I were to be married. It would have united our families and it was very important to our parents. We were very close and have known each other for many lives previously. But I rejected you."

I was stunned that she would say this to me. But it struck a deep chord in my heart. There was no past life in which I had seen myself married and in this life I had felt no inclination in that direction. Could it be because I was still carrying this rejection in me?

"If that is true," I asked, "then why did you reject me?"

"I don't know. Maybe some karma we cannot see. But I do know that because of my rejection you ran away from Bagan, and after that I don't know what happened to you. But I recognised you the first time we met in this life. I feel in some way I am responsible."

We sat in silence. I looked deep into this issue.

It was rooted in lust and attachment. I had been frivolous in my youth and become intoxicated in the pursuit of sensual pleasure. The intoxication was so strong that it even pulled me away from my deep commitment to teach Dharma. Sayalay hadn't rejected me because she didn't love me, but because she didn't trust me. I had been young, and indeed would have settled down in time but the combination of male lust and female jealousy is a powerfully destructive force and it drives us as humans as strongly as all our most noble aspirations; strongly enough even to undermine them.

When Sayalay had rejected me, my pride was deeply hurt. I rejected my home and family and ran away and fell into an ignoble life. So began my fall from grace. All the lifetimes of accumulating merit and keeping my virtue, all the depth of experience I had gathered in meditation and spiritual knowledge all were thrown away on account of lust and pride.

There are so many stories from the Buddha's time of those who were so close to freeing themselves from suffering but on account of negligence fell instead into untold suffering. It had taken me a long time to find my way back to a fortunate human life where I could reconnect to the seed of Dharma within me. I had the insight and had had to learn the hard way and yet still I was unwilling to relinquish the last part of my ego. However could I expect others to do it if I couldn't?

When people came to the Buddha for teaching he encouraged them to renounce their life of sensual indulgence and live simply with few needs. Only the most virtuous did he encourage to practice as lay people. But most he feared were not virtuous enough to live amongst sensual distraction without becoming lost and intoxicated in it.

Even those who knew how to live virtuously he encouraged to renew their good fortune by living piously, engaging in acts of merit and giving generously to the needy. He urged them to support those who had chosen the spiritual life, so that they might expect to meet with support themselves were they one day to choose such a path. He was careful not to allow them to fall into complacency on account of their good fortune and asked them often to reflect if they would be able to show the patience and forbearance that those less fortunate had to endure.

I was deeply committed to the belief that we in our age could free ourselves from suffering and find peace as lay people, but equally I knew we could not do it without in some way renewing the field of merit that we must have accumulated in the past to arrive at such good fortune.

And yet the truth was that I myself had not been able to keep my virtue in my youth, either in this life or in the past. Because of it I had come to grief and not fulfilled my highest aspiration.

"But do you not believe that it is possible to teach the Path as a married man or woman?" I asked. "I am deeply committed to finding a way to teach the path within this context."

"That is an important question." She replied. "Attachment to family and children is very strong in a woman, but not so much in men."

Somewhere inside I knew she was touching a very deep issue.

After Nancy had died, for a while I felt no inclination to form a bonded relationship with another woman. But in time I did. During my time in Java and Bali I had met an Italian girl. I fell very much in love with her and had considered moving back to England with her to start a family. She was with me at the time I started practising, and had begun meditating herself.

Eventually there came a time where I had to choose. I knew that I had to follow my path. It was a conviction I could not ignore. We were in Sardinia visiting her family, and had come to the airport from where I was to begin my journey back to Bali. I knew I had a choice to make.

In that moment I could have asked her to come with me. I had even started to look at houses in England as I was already considering moving back. But somewhere inside we both knew the next stage of the journey was one that we all must make alone.

I could have stayed with her for the rest of my life and not taken the next step, or I could have met her later on in my life when I had done what had to be done. But as it was, we met with the call to the path ringing strongly in my heart, and where I had to go next, I knew was a lonesome trail.

She knew this as much as I did. Without speaking we hugged deeply outside the airport.

"Goodbye Burgs. Bless you. Go and do what you have to do."

I kissed her forehead one last time and she stepped into her car. She turned and waved and drove off.

I watched her car as it drove around the loop. I felt the call to run after her and tell her I was wrong, that I didn't need to go; that I wanted to spend the rest of my life with her. But I didn't. I stood, and waved and watched her drive away.

It would not have been fair to ask her to stay. I had no idea how long my journey would take, and of course she longed as a woman to raise a family. I could not allow these two deep instinctual drives to come into conflict. I knew I would not have been able to let go deeply enough had I asked her to wait for me. And besides, even if I had, and then come back, would I have been the person she had been waiting for.

I had thought at times that I might have been able to do what the Buddha could not, and walk the final stages of the path with someone I loved by my side. But of course, in the end, I could see I was wrong. He had had to leave his home and family to go his way and eventually I saw that so must I. I learned in time, that letting go means letting go.

"Whatever was the reason for me rejecting you, "Sayalay continued, "I believe it is the reason you are stuck now."

I could feel her pain. It was a woman's pain. I could feel that her robes were her protection from it, but I knew the longing for motherhood was still not completely relinquished. I saw in her the greatest of all predicaments. How could a woman let go of her function as mother? Was it even possible? It is a deep instinctive drive, as much biological as it is emotional. I knew that for the Dharma to flourish I needed to present a way for people to follow the Path while fulfilling their function as householders.

This for me felt like the most important aspect to get right. But I knew that none of us succeed until we surmounted the destructive aspects of lust, greed and jealousy.

I saw Sayalay's pain and I knew she longed to let it go.

"I am tired", she said. "I am longing for peace in this life. I ask your forgiveness so that I can take my final leave."

Through her tears I could see the deep love that she had for me. I knew it was the love of a sister for her brother, but I could see she needed it to be cleansed of any attachment beyond that.

"Sister," I said, "whatever may or may not have happened back then, I can tell you from the deepest place in my heart, that I do not hold a trace of resentment towards you. I love you as my sister and always will. I know that whatever pain I experienced as a result of leaving Bagan that time, was entirely on my own account. If you did reject me, it was on account of karma. I must surely have wronged you in some way, and for that it is I who must apologise."

"Much time has passed since then," she said. "But this is the last attachment for me to let go. I long to know you are safe, and then I wish for this to be my final life."

I wanted to put my arm around her and comfort her, but her robes prohibited that. I knew we had shared many journeys over many lives. What was happening now was a letting go of our attachment to each other. Her pain was as deep as any I had ever felt myself. It was the pain of knowing that we had been unable to live virtuously enough to not cause suffering to others, even those most dear to us. That pain had taken its toll on us both over many lives and we both now longed for release.

"You are now and always have been my sister. That love runs deeper than any pain you may ever have caused me. I totally forgive you, and have done for a long time. I hope you can see that what I say is true."

I knew that for her, she was letting go the last traces of attachment and opening the door for her own final freedom. I was deeply moved for us both and wept with her. The idea that we have another half somewhere in the universe who might be our soul partner is a powerful archetype that calls to that part of us that seeks the union of the male and female. It is the notion around which the most fantasies are created, and the cause of more personal pain than any other.

Yet even this deep longing is rooted in the attachment to self, and will cause us to project our love singly upon another with clinging, and separate us from its highest expression that loves all beings equally.

There is no reason why we cannot meet with another in deep love and commitment, so that we can perform selflessly our function as husband, wife and parents. It is our highest function and the one which, if executed humbly, can renew our field of merit lifetime to lifetime.

And yet although all of us know in our hearts how we might fulfil this function virtuously, the power that greed, lust and jealousy has over us is hard to break indeed. It remains the area where on account of selfishness and pride we most easily come to grief.

We need only look at the huge number of failed marriages in our modern society to see how our selfishness has undermined our ability to honour our commitments to others.

Sayalay was Burmese. There is no such thing as divorce in Burma. Many don't meet their partner much before they are married, and yet there is within them an innate willingness and capacity to honour and respect each other. For them it is through marriage and parenting that they learn the true nature of humility, commitment and grace.

They learn how to meet, honour and respect each other as they share the function of providing a wing for their children. They never stop to think that they are married to the wrong person, who may not be the object of their desire or fail to fulfil some ego need. They do not consider it their partner's role to fulfil their personal needs, nor do they reject someone if they find their needs not met. They fully understand that karma brings people together, and that all challenges are an echo from the past and an invitation to evolve.

I could feel how much more painful it had been for Sayalay to let go than for me. She felt responsible for the hardships I had faced on my long wandering through the ages. I knew inside it was all my own doing and was able to take account of that.

I could see also that there was strong karma between us and that had things worked out otherwise we would likely have taught together in this life, not as husband and wife, but as brother and sister.

In a way it was an example I felt was needed, for the breakdown of the sacred nature of the relationship between man and woman and its descent into lust and jealousy is one of the many reasons for the degeneration of our age. I think we shared a sadness in the knowledge that we had failed in that capacity in some way.

We sat in silence as it grew dark.

If I was sitting before someone who might once have been a soul mate, I knew that we were in the process of freeing each other. And in that freeing there was a deep need to honour the journey shared.

In that moment I glimpsed what unconditional

love really was. I could see how the highest love is the one that clings not to others, but allows them to be free. While we cling to others with any trace of desire or need to possess we are unable to free that person from bondage to us. I sat with this realisation as it deepened within me.

I could see that there are no needs within us that we can expect another to fulfil, apart from the shelter and protection from parents in our childhood. The only way we can learn to love another completely is when we free them of our attachment and expectation, allowing them to be who they truly are, not what we want them to be. There is a deep truth in the saying: if you love someone, set them free.

The last two parts of the ego to be relinquished are lust and pride. I could finally feel in me a willingness to let them go. Equally I could see that we could not love others unconditionally, until we have learned to love ourselves, until that love needs nothing back in return.

I could now see that part of me that was doing what it was doing in search of love, in the search of the feeling of being good enough. But now I could see that there is no true path that seeks either reverence of others, or personal gain.

If we are to serve we will need to be willing to go unnoticed. The only gain to be accrued is from the merit that comes from living blamelessly and virtuously. There was no role left for my ego to play. If there was a tidying up of past karma to do, it would need to be done truly selflessly, functionally, free of the ego entirely.

Outside, the May full moon shone brightly. This was the night of the Buddha's birth, enlightenment and final entry into Parinibbana twenty-five centuries ago.

I looked back over the long road I had been down and the suffering I had been through since I last left behind my true commitment to virtue. I could see there was still enough pride in me, or had been when we were together in Bagan, to cause pain in others. Wherever I had got to, I needed to let go more.

And with that thought it became clear. To play our part in the ending of the suffering of others, was not just about trying to teach them Dharma, it was about showing them the way home.

And that means to remove ourselves from the bondage that causes us to bring suffering to any other being. If I had caused suffering to Sayalay, even if it was on account of her attachment, the karma of that was still blocking her final release and mine.

Greater still was the karma of not showing deeply enough the path to those who saw me as their teacher. I needed to fully embody the path now. It was no longer enough simply to be able to pass on the teachings.

"Sister," I said. "I am going outside to meditate. Can we chant together before I go?"

She opened her eyes. They were wet with tears.

"I am sorry. Please forgive me."

"And I am sorry too. Please forgive me."

We began to chant the Paritta.

It felt as if it was something we had done together for aeons.

As we finished I stood and walked outside into the night.

Outside it was a clear night, everything was silver

in the light of the full moon. I walked away from the cottage across a field until I came to a ridge looking out across the countryside.

I sat down for a while and rested in the stillness of the night.

I saw the long road I had been down stretched out over countless lives, some in this world, some in others. I was moved most by how personal it had all seemed, by how it had been my unique journey, in spite of the knowledge that it was ultimately free from self.

It was truly something special beyond imagining to come into being, in spite of all the pain we may bring upon ourselves. A gift and an honour that we do not even begin to fathom fully, let alone learn to appreciate. But I could see then, how in spite of the capacity of our heart to glimpse its most sublime potential, we will never come to realise that potential as long as we cling to the idea that it is personal, that is all about me, that its mine.

This final letting go, so violates our idea of self. We are so driven by our pride and greed that we will spend lifetimes stumbling around in the dark thinking that there is something personal to achieve that finally makes sense of it all. Perhaps that is the reason that even after first seeing Nibbana it may still be another seven lives before we are willing to completely let go into the deathless state.

Having spent aeons wandering around seeking a personal resolution to life without ever finding it, it is understandable that we might wish to savour the tail end of the journey and investigate for a while the experience of finally being free of regret and remorse.

We spend so long searching for the hidden meaning of life, when perhaps it is no more complicated than recognising that we come into being simply so that we can witness what it is to be alive. In our awakening we come to recognise and appreciate life for the miracle that it actually is. Just to glimpse it, smell it, taste it and feel it completely, with nothing in the way is the reason we come into being.

Why do we feel so strongly the need to take so much from it? Every day we wake up we are a success at life and the day we don't wake up we will be a success at death. As the Buddha said; "...in the seeing there is only the seen, in the knowing only the known." That is the gift of life, simply the ability to enter into it, to just know that we participated. And all of this is lost to us as we seek ways to prove to ourselves and others that we are special, that it is all about us.

I knew in that moment that I could disappear in a puff of smoke right there, and that once those who loved me had recovered from their loss, my presence here would go unnoticed. Like a pebble thrown into water, a ripple for a time before it settles back to its innate state of rest.

We had all got lost turning our ripples into waves, never stopping to see how much we have disturbed the universe with our presence. There are seven billion of us, that's a lot of waves, and a lot of disturbance to deal with.

I was ready to go quietly in this world and simply appreciate being a part of it. There was music enough in the wind, magic enough in the vision that rolled out before me in that still full moon night. There was no searching left to do. I was ready to come home. My heart gladdened with relief as I closed my eyes and let go.

It didn't take long. I entered quickly into

samadhi but knew that wasn't my resting place. I rested there for a while to gather my mind and emerged briefly to affirm my intention. I remembered back to when I realised that I had never made the aspiration to reach this unconditioned state.

I could see now that it was only ignorance that had allowed me to justify my position. The last part of the ego to be relinquished is pride. The desire, or felt need, to be someone special. That pride was gone. I was ready to lose sight of my idea of myself. The far bank of the river called as I closed my eyes once more.

I reviewed the arising and passing of things within me and around me, I turned my mind to their cessation. I let everything pass and felt no need to cling. What clinging I had previously been unable to see I saw now and relinquished, blissfully, effortlessly; and I followed it all to cessation.

And then my mind came to rest upon the non-arising of conditioned states. As my mind came to the unconditioned state and the cessation of formations, there was the faintest of clicks as I came to rest on the far side of the river, and everything stopped. I rested there for a moment then emerged.

I reviewed my mind. Though it still might rain, I knew I would not get wet. I closed my eyes and entered back into cessation this time staying there.

When I did emerge, there was just the coolness of the air on my face and the stillness of the night, the earth beneath me and the light of the moon. It was enough, it was complete, it was already perfect and it always had been. There was nothing to add and nothing to take away.

CHAPTER TWENTY-FOUR

Revisited

It wasn't until Sayalay had shown me that until we relinquish all pride, we are still not freed of our capacity to bring suffering to ourselves and others.

I had fallen into the timeless trap: the idea that the true hero is the one who is willing to sacrifice his own salvation to help others find theirs. Of course, I had failed to see this as the final attempt to flatter my ego: the idea of self as the hero and saviour of others.

And so I had wandered for many lives in my quest for the knowledge that would save the world. And for many lifetimes I had come to grief until I came to see that in order to find the warrior you must first kill the hero.

My insight had not been enough to see that it was necessary to complete the path before we would be equipped to guide others out of suffering.

It was like this. Imagine we were to take a journey to a magical land, to Xanadu, to a paradise where there was no more suffering. Through no end of hardship we strive earnestly towards our goal, and then one day we cross the last mountain pass and come to look down over the magical place that had so long been our destination. It is as if at that point we say:

"Ah-ha…finally now I know where it is. I must return to tell others the way here." And so we head back without ever having actually entered this magical realm.

Thereafter, on returning home we tell others of this magical place and encourage them to travel there with us.

"What is it like?" they will ask, "tell us all about it, how is it there?" to which we realise we have no answer, for we do not know how it is. We have merely glimpsed it from afar. We merely know where it is, but do not know what it is actually like. What testimony do we then have that will encourage others to make the journey themselves?

This is like the preacher who can only tell people how unsatisfactory their condition is, but cannot point the way to something that satisfies. And just because the preacher does not find his life satisfying, it does not mean that others do not. All he can do is share with others his own experience of suffering, but not his experience of peace or happiness that transcends it.

Surely it is not until we can testify to a peace that is beyond suffering that we might expect to be able to show others the way. It is one thing to teach people the truth of suffering, but without being able to teach the truth of the cessation of suffering and the path that leads to that point, are we really serving others or just pointing out to them their pain?

It is like a doctor who tells a man he is sick but has no medicine to give him. It might even be argued that he is better off not knowing he is sick.

To offer oneself up to the service of others with

the intention to deliver them out of suffering surely requires that we have realised for ourselves what the end of suffering actually is. This is not the work of the social worker or the one who delivers aid to the food camps of Africa. Though this is noble work of the highest order, it can only ease the suffering of others, it does take them beyond suffering.

The path of enlightened service was the work Sayadaw was doing to help others free themselves from all suffering. Until we fully understand the cause of suffering, we will never make sense of the confusion, chaos and hardship we encounter all around us. It will only be the cause of sadness and dismay but not real compassion.

Compassion understands fully why things have come to be the way they are and seeks the causal cessation of the suffering that arises in others. This causal cessation IS Nibbana itself, that which is beyond conditioned states and the suffering that is caused by our selfish clinging.

The idea of the Bodhisattva path is an often misunderstood notion. Today we are invited to huge arenas or convention centres to take our Bodhisattva vows and commit to deliver others out of suffering with no understanding of what this really entails.

There is a timely way of making such commitment, and to serve others is indeed the noblest way we can conduct our lives. But first we must look deeply at ourselves and ask if we are yet ready to be of real service. Many may choose to serve others to heal a feeling of lack of self-worth, and it is likely that this is what may prompt most of us to start to think less selfishly.

But for our efforts to bring forth significant benefits we must ourselves first be easy to serve and of few wants. So it is far from selfish to turn our attention to the serious job of refining our own character and raising ourselves up out of ignorance and confusion.

The Bodhisattva warrior understands that there is nowhere to apportion the blame for our hardships but in our own lack of understanding and the past deeds that this has prompted. He understands that only full accountability will open the door to our recovery from the wounds we carry.

To see the cause of our misery as the result of, for example, mistreatment in our childhood fails completely to recognise why we might actually have come to be mistreated and serves only to reinforce our sense of being a victim.

It does not mean that we should not open our hearts to those who have suffered hardship. Of course we must do so at every opportunity. When we fail to do that, we have truly lost all touch with what it is to be human.

But we will need a discerning eye of insight to find the root of our problems and understand why we are faced with them, for inevitably it will lie in our own misconduct in previous times.

In many ways it would have been more efficacious by design were the karmic energy of our deeds to fruit immediately after their doing, then we might not find it so easy to justify our sense of feeling the victim of misfortune. The mechanism by which these energies are accumulated means that most of the karma that fruits in this life has been produced in previous lives and what we accumulate now will not fruit until after this life ends. There is a saying that states;

"If you want to know where you have been and

what you have done, look at your body and how you fare. If you want to know where you are going and what you will become, look at your mind and what prompts you to act."

The Buddha says there are only four kinds of beings: Those born in the light heading into darkness; those born in the light heading into the light; those born in darkness heading into darkness; and those born in the darkness heading into light.

Whenever I read these words I remember the legless man on his box in Bandung, and the billionaire who came to see Ada who suffered a stroke at the loss of his fortune.

We are reaping now the fruits of our past deeds, good and bad, and sowing the seeds of our future good fortune or lack of it by our actions of body, speech, and mind. As they say, there is no sinner without a future and no saint without a past. When we understand this we begin to understand suffering. When we understand suffering we begin to see the way that leads out of it. And in the end it couldn't be simpler...

"Do good deeds, avoid doing bad deeds, and purify your mind. Such is the teaching of all the Buddhas."

Padmasambhava had not shown me the causal cessation of suffering that is Nibbana, he had shown me our true nature, the mind that does not suffer and is never defiled. A pure awareness, free from volition or even thought. It is the mind that does not identify with things or produce karma. This mind is there within the heart of all of us, from the most depraved to the most saintly. It is up to us to recognise it and abide in it.

307

Simply to come to know this awakened state of pure awareness is not to be free from all suffering, for we are still left to conquer our ego and lower mind and the tendency to identify with the conditioned forms it clings to.

Knowing the pure state of mind certainly dilutes the grip of the ego but it does not dismantle it completely. That dismantling is done in stages by the systematic investigation of its nature and the gradual letting go of the wrong views and habitual patterns it clings to.

I had met teachers who suggested it was not necessary to break down this ego mind but claim instead that we should just learn to recognise the higher mind, our Buddha Nature. It is a nice idea, but all of us except the most enlightened of beings continue to define ourselves by our egos.

The very work of spiritual practice is to dismantle its grip and free ourselves of it. A rare few may well be able to do this in one go, with the introduction to the pure state from an enlightened master, but for most it will be a long road of gradual surrender and letting go in stages.

I knew I was a talented yogi. I had had the introduction to the pure state of awareness from both Padmasambhava himself and Dodrupchen Rinpoche, but I had always known there was work to do on the ego. I could see how easily I could fall into complacency if I were to just take this blissful abiding in pure consciousness as my only practice.

It is only when we finally relinquish all attachment to conditioned states and the ideas we formulate about ourselves that we come to recognise and enter into the unconditioned state that is Nibbana.

I remembered back to my debate with the Abbot

of Tashi Jong before I began my retreat with George. He had said that the mind is only an elaborate fantasy, an illusion that we cling to that ultimately separates us from the awakened experience.

We had discussed the Tibetan tradition of mandala meditation, in which complex symbolic representations of the universe are visualised. I had met many people over the years who practised this.

But the visualisation of the mandala is not ultimately for the purpose of showing us how the world is, but for the purpose of showing us the mind's immense capacity to create fantastical illusionary states and ideas about life. The libraries of the world record all the philosophical views and ideologies that we as a species have dreamed up throughout history, but none of them have actually freed us.

The key to the path is not that we can formulate a view that answers all our questions. It takes us a long time to realise that there is no resolution in the mind. We do not visualise the mandala in an effort to create a perfect symbolic representation of the world, but to show us that it is only an illusion, as is the mind and all the views and ideas it dreams up.

The point of the exercise lies in the final act of dissolving the mandala into emptiness, or brushing it aside with a sweep of the hand so that we recognise that it was only an illusion all along. The mandala is an approximation for reality, in the same way that our thoughts and ideas are, but in no way does it constitute the experience of reality itself.

It is awareness that experiences reality directly and not the mind. While we are lost in the mandala, or equally lost in our thoughts we remain separate from the 'suchness' of our experience, and fail to awaken to it.

309

It is significant that these mandalas are traditionally made of sand and not carved into rock. The whole point is to see them blown away and dismantled into the grains of mixed colours from which they are made.

I had met so many people with extraordinarily complicated ideas of who they thought they were and how life might be. At the level of our lower mind we are nothing more than whatever we can dream ourselves up to be. It is helpful of course to have a positive and constructive image of our self, but in the end it is this self-image that separates us from all else and keeps us locked in our inner world.

In the end we must recognise that our entire mind is nothing but a mandala. We have spent lifetimes creating it and recreating it depending upon what we believe and how we have met the various experiences that come our way. But in the end our sense of being separate will not end until we see that it is our mind that is the mandala, our fantasy idea about the universe in which we live and our place within it.

If we stop at this point we will always find cause and justification for reinventing ourselves and reconstructing and tweaking the mandala. Some see God as the creator in the centre of the Mandala, others see themselves as God. Every one of us has built up our own unique worldview without any idea of whether it is true or not.

At a personal level perhaps it doesn't matter. As long as you believe in what you believe this becomes your reality. But this itself is what the Buddha called Samsara. The endless wheel of wandering on, inventing and reinventing ourselves in the tireless search for an idea of self that satisfies completely, but which never can.

We are never freed of this Samsara until the day we see that the mind is a mirage, a smoke screen that keeps us separate from the unconditioned state of awakening. It isn't just at night that we dream, we are dreaming ourselves into existence every second of every day.

Even within the context of our spiritual practice we can hang on to this illusion, believing that one day we will perfectly visualise the perfect mandala and come to the realised idea of ourselves. And yet, the moment we emerge from our meditation it is gone, like a dream that fades as we emerge from sleep.

It may well leave a lasting impression upon us, but that is only on account of our attachment to it or identification with it as 'my worldview' or 'my dream'. It's all the same. It's all only a fantasy.

True awakening is not reached at the point when we come to an idea about ourselves and life with which we are finally satisfied. Far from it. It is the point at which we finally lose all ideas of our self, the point at which this fantasy 'me' stops appearing right in the centre of all we experience, so that finally we are left free to experience the suchness of things, all things, just as they are.

This is what it is to wake up. It is called awakening and it is exactly that. To wake up from the illusion, the endless dream of self.

It is said: "When the fool wakes up, he becomes a sage. When the sage wakes up, he becomes an ordinary man." We are so busy trying to dream up the perfect idea of ourselves that we fail to spot that we are all just ordinary men and women fixated on the idea that we have to be special.

Padmasambhava had shown me the way of

awakening out of the illusion in which we live by introducing me to the pure state of consciousness that exists beyond all our ideas of self. Although he showed me this innate state as spontaneously present within all of us, he hadn't shown me the path that leads to the dismantling of the egoic fantasy that separates us from it.

It is by investigating the mechanism of the mind that leads to such attachment and desire that prompts these ideas of self, that we come to free ourselves of it. Sayadaw had taught me this way of investigation, and it was the Buddha's systematic path out of suffering that leads to the realisation of the deathless state of Nibbana.

Although this innate awakened state has existed within us all since beginningless time it hasn't in itself freed us of our self-infatuation. Indeed we have remained so intoxicated with our ideas about ourselves that we have never even noticed this stream of awakened mind that has travelled with us always. Only when we have brought to cessation the idea of self, do we realise the cessation of suffering. This is Nibbana.

I had recognised this innate awakened state many years before, but I had still managed to carry on reinventing myself. I looked back at the movies I had been in, the roles and pantomimes I had played.

I am a romantic rebel.

I am a ski-bum.

I am a fashion designer.

I am a shaman who hangs out in the wild with medicine men.

I am a healer who makes exotic medicines.

I am a Buddhist monk who knows the Dharma.

I am a meditation teacher.

I am awake.

Wrong. I am asleep. Asleep dreaming myself to be anything I am capable of dreaming myself to be.

Finally I saw. It is only when we lose all sight of our ideas of self that we awaken to the true experience of spontaneous presence. It really was as the Buddha said, "This self is a fantasy, it is an illusion, it is a conceit."

I could see that we are all held back by the same fear – the idea that the universe could exist without us in it. And yet the paradox is that the real universe will never reveal itself to us until we are willing to remove the idea of our self from the picture.

There it is. The ultimate Catch-22. In order to acquire what is most deeply desired we have to give up all desire for it. It's not about me, it's not about you, it's not about any of us. Life is quite simply an extraordinary, miraculous process that we are merely gifted the opportunity to witness and be a part of.

There is nothing to add and nothing to take away, no one to save, nor to condemn. We just sleep until it's time to wake up. No one ever said that our dreams should not be adventures, but just don't be so fooled by them that you miss the main event.

CHAPTER TWENTY-FIVE

One Dharma

Since my early days in Bali with Merta Ada, I had always had a strong aspiration to use my meditation skills to combine energy with medicines. I wanted to develop new substances that might work for us at the information level from which our sicknesses were arising. That was what motivated me to spend so much time practicing alchemy.

The meditation meditations on the material states of the body had shown me that consciousness and karma have a more powerful effect on our bodily functioning than what we eat and what medicines we take. I was convinced enough of this to know that we needed a new approach to disease and healing, as we entered an age where degenerative illnesses were increasing at exponential rates.

I could feel in the bodies of so many of the people who were coming to meditate with me that things were breaking down at an information level.

Our lives were so disconnected from nature and its cycles and our living environment so energetically dysfunctional that the software side of our being was beginning to literally pack up. It is because we have become so obsessed with ourselves, and so lost in our virtual lives that we have lost our connection to the natural world we live in and its rhythms.

We seem to never give ourselves a chance to allow the body's own intelligence to perform its reorganising and balancing role. We are incapable of getting out of the way for long enough for its higher intelligence to do its work.

Our ambitions are way out of whack with our physical capacity and so we are digging deep into our emergency reserves just to function at the pace we are asking of ourselves. I felt as if everyone was trying to compete in Formula One while they were only driving clapped out hatchbacks. It was a recipe for disaster.

If you combine that with the obvious conclusions we come to regarding the rate at which we are consuming our natural resources, it is clear that something has to give.

My dilemma was this: I had to try to suggest to people that they were going to have to live more simply, to reduce their consumption and be content with less, while impressing on them the equal need to start seriously the process of reconditioning their bodies and minds if they were going to cope with the challenges we all have to face.

I could see in these two issues an obvious conflict. That we weren't coping was a safety mechanism that in time would force us to re-think our lives. Even if we took away the affliction of serious physical degeneration, we were going to have to put the brakes on the speed with which we were consuming our planet.

If I was going to teach the way of reconditioning that would raise people back up to optimal health and energy, wasn't there a danger that they would just carry on as before taking their health and good fortune for granted, and continue to consume the planet at this extraordinary rate?

But the lessons I had learned from my practice of alchemy had shown me that the only way that we can reach the level of our full potential is by surrendering our greed and need for personal gain.

I had for some time been working with powerful energy medicine, and I offered it to anyone who asked. But I knew it wasn't here to heal our cancer or our HIV. It is here to help us on our way. To help raise up our light in the face of the difficulties we find in our lives.

Such things never have been, and never will be, a substitute for the work we all must do on ourselves, if we hope one day to come out of all the darkness, and rest in the knowledge that we have made a genuine connection to the light. That is the work of letting go our greed and selfishness and developing wisdom, compassion and love. Which in time transforms our misguided ideas of being the hero into the warrior that we are capable of becoming; the warrior who is willing to relinquish his grand ideas of himself and no longer be the cause of suffering in others.

The warrior, unlike the hero, is willing to go quietly among his fellow men, loving self and others equally. It is the fearless but patient work of the accumulation of merit and refinement of character that will incline us in time to let go our greed and search for higher meaning.

Thereafter, with that merit and character as the basis of our endeavour we will come out of our suffering, not with gritted teeth, but with a smile on our face and joy in our heart, knowing that we have lived well and are free from regret.

Then we may come to knowledge and vision, and come out of wrong view, to the honest and humble acceptance of who we are, coming finally to recognise the light that is perfect, that always has been perfect, and can never in any way be anything but perfect.

You are that light, and you always have been, and if you can't see it then it is only because of dust in your eyes. That dust is the ego that we cling to.

There is water that washes away that dust and brings clarity, and the end to confusion. It is the water of virtue, serenity, wisdom and the deep understanding of the nature of love.

And in the end it reveals one thing, and one thing alone, and above all else. For all the myriad ways that things come into being, and the countless forms they take within our conditioned world, there is after all, only love and not knowing it, and although that love is never known by the ego, it has always been known by the heart. If you haven't found that love yet, then go and find it, for it is the very reason that you came here.

If I am honest, there had been another reason why I left the forest, one I could not tell my teacher. There were things I had done in my past about which I felt a deep sense of shame, for which I had not as yet been able to forgive myself. I did not feel worthy enough to represent the truly virtuous path that Sayadaw stood for. If I was to teach, it would have to be as an ordinary man, no better or worse than the next, one who had made mistakes and was far from perfect.

As I began to teach back in England, it was this that I found increasingly difficult to bear. In my capacity as a teacher I was often looked up to. I felt a growing sense of shame that I was seen by others as perhaps someone of nobler qualities than they. I realised that there was nothing personal in what I had achieved, it was all merely a function of the Path itself. It would serve everyone as it had served me if they should choose to walk it.

The more people who came for instruction, the more I saw people facing their challenges with courage every bit as great as any I had found. I would often ask myself if I thought I would find the strength that I saw in others who battled to overcome life-threatening illness or deal with immeasurable loss.

I searched within the Dharma for the resolution to my shame, and indeed did find it to a point. I knew that whatever wrongs we had done in the past, although they may appear to be rooted in greed or ill-will, this greed and ill-will is not innate within any of us. Greed and aversion are not the roots of the chain of dependent origination, ignorance is.

One day, I had been teaching a silent retreat and had given a discourse on virtue and how it is the foundation for all progress upon the path to happiness. I took a walk in the break and my mind cast back over all the mistakes I had made in the past, some of which I had still not been able to forgive myself for.

As I walked I came upon a church. It was nestled unobtrusively beside a stream, and was quite deserted.

I walked inside.

The air was cool and still, and it smelt of stone, not unlike in the cave in Rewalsar.

I sat at a pew and looked up at the stained glass

window above the altar. It depicted the scene of Jesus' crucifixion.

My first reflection was how violent was the scene that was the very focal point of the Christian faith. It was a stark contrast to the image of the Buddha sitting in deep meditation. I began to reflect on its significance and reviewed the story of the last moments of Jesus' life on earth.

Only a few minutes before his death, he was in a state of despair. Tortured and abandoned by those he had tried to serve, he turned to God in dismay asking, "Why have you forsaken me?" It was clear that at that moment he could see the truth of suffering, but not its cause.

In the next few moments, as he experienced suffering in the extreme, he finally came to see its cause. It was not greed or hatred, it was ignorance. These people before him were confused and scared. It was in that moment that he saw the cessation of suffering, which was the moment of total surrender, out of which was born his capacity to forgive his tormentors.

His dying words were, "Forgive them, they know not what they do."

As he saw their ignorance all traces of blame were washed away, no unwillingness to forgive remained.

As I saw this I asked for forgiveness myself. I opened my soul to Jesus showing all the wrongs I had done. And in that moment I knew I was not judged. There was no trace of unwillingness to forgive. I realised that it is not by God or Jesus or the Buddha that we are judged, but by ourselves and others, who are equally confused.

I could see that there is no enlightened being that does not come to realise that ignorance is the cause of suffering. Hatred and greed, selfishness, jealousy and pride are not innate in any being; they are a by-product of our confusion and our ignorance. If Jesus was willing to forgive those who betrayed him and tortured him, then he would be willing to forgive me, as long as I was.

I could see then the point at which the mind of Jesus and the mind of the Buddha met. It was in their realisation of the truth of suffering, its cause and its cessation. Jesus had died in the moment following this realisation leaving us to look deeply into his message and the example of his life, for our own way out of suffering. But it was there.

We are all capable of killing the one who shows us our own suffering until we are willing to relinquish our pride and take accountability for ourselves. And it does not stop with shame or guilt.

It stops when we reach a point of humility that realises that all this suffering and pain we have caused and experienced, is only on account of confusion. As Jesus said, "They know not what they do."

He was dying; he was no more than thirty-five years old. He knew there would be no lifetime for him to share this truth with others, but in his total willingness to forgive, he showed us the way to be free.

The Buddha was thirty-five years old when he realised the truth of suffering and the path that leads to its cessation. He lived a further forty-five years before he died of old age at the age of eighty. And in that time he taught the way countless times to countless beings.

We who were born as Christians often look to the texts for the teaching of Jesus. We find the Sermon on the Mount, which implores us to right conduct,

321

but the real transcendent wisdom lies in the last words he uttered. "Forgive them, they know not what they do."

One night while at Pa Auk, I was practising my jhana meditations. Because jhana takes the fine material realm as its object and not the gross we become aware in stages of the beings that exist in these subtler realms. While I was first practising Metta jhana with Sayadaw in Taiwan and began to pervade the compound with loving kindness I started seeing previously unseen beings that exist around us. These beings take many forms, from the gross, miserable and suffering, to the sublime and exalted, from hungry ghosts to angels and devas, and the most exalted of all, known as the Brahma beings.

I had been deeply absorbed for hours when gradually a form began to emerge from the vastness around me. I was looking down on what I thought might be an enormous ancient temple. As I began to concentrate upon its form I was drawn down towards it. Suddenly I was overwhelmed with awe. It was not a temple but the head piece of a vast and majestic being.

I was now looking upon it from afar, yet it filled almost entirely the space before me, and sat in meditation so profoundly deep and unfathomable that I was almost terrified to behold it. Its face was so serenely peaceful and full of love. I knew in an instant that it had been in this samadhi for aeons. Whatever stillness, whatever love I had ever been able to glimpse in my own meditation paled utterly before it. As I looked upon it I thought I would die.

And then I saw! It was pervading the vastness of space with its unbounded love. This sublime being was pervading our whole world and the space in which it exists with its love. Although I knew it wasn't the original cause for the coming into being of things, I knew it was the source of the love that I had come to perceive behind their arising and passing.

What is more, I realised that there are countless beings in these higher planes that have attained to such lofty states of becoming, and turn the focus of their minds to the generation of boundless love and compassion for others such as us, who are still lost in the fog of confusion.

Indeed, what else might we aspire to do when we have reached such heights, but to rest in our bliss while we pour forth our love and compassion.

I knew that this Brahma would one day tire of even this exalted state, and feeling that he had done what might be done for the benefit of others, seek to take his own leave. Coming in time to the reflection on the truth of impermanence and dependent origination, he too would recognise that his own life also is conditioned and eventually must also come to an end. In time, even he would seek to turn away from the realms of conditioned formations and go beyond to the deathless state.

But in that moment I glimpsed the extraordinary field of potential that life affords us. Whatever our own personal attainments might come to be, I realised they are merely ripples in the field of infinite potentiality. We have both the capacity to create and destroy, and an extraordinary ability to wield our influence upon our domain and all that lies therein. I wonder how often we stop to ask ourselves if we are responsible enough to be exercising the potential with which we are so blessed, or whether our influence is for the benefit or detriment of others.

As Jesus looked down upon those who murdered him, there was only love for each and every one of them. He knew he could not deliver them out of suffering. That is something we must do for ourselves. But his willingness to forgive opened the door to us so that one day we might ourselves come to stop judging.

But it is each of us individually who must find forgiveness. Jesus, the Buddha, and all the great beings have never pointed the finger of blame, and though they may have shed tears of compassion there has never been anything but love for us all.

In that moment I felt so completely held, so completely and unconditionally loved.

It WAS true, there is only love and not knowing it. All the people who go running in the park on a Sunday morning, who turn up to church and pray, who cry in despair because they can't make sense of anything, all of us are longing for one thing and one thing only. We are longing to know that love. Keep your faith, and live in the absolute certainty that that love will never fail.

That this being had such mastery of itself to have sat in this state for the entire duration of our world system, holding the world and everything in it as the object of its unconditional love, was unfathomable. Even more so was that it was still there for all the chaos and confusion we as beings had come to produce.

I sat and thought for a while about the way we are asked to come to understand God as we grow up in our society. I thought back to all the church services I had sat through as a child, wondering who or what God might be. I wondered what might have happened had our ministers and priests taught us to train our minds so we could directly perceive the God to whom we prayed. Would they have glimpsed such a being as this and felt it to be the creator?

Or would they have gone beyond even this to fathom the extraordinary creative principle, at work always and everywhere, with its infinite innate intelligence, and its potential to perfect all things. Might they have called this God? Or might they have avoided the perceived need to label any of these things and been satisfied simply to have come to know them?

Perhaps then we would have inherited a living tradition of wisdom and knowledge and not solely relied upon the word of the texts and those saints of the past to whom we can no longer refer. In that moment I could see so clearly how we have gone so wrong. Ours was a religion of the word, and not of knowledge and vision.

What a terrible shame it is, that for all these centuries no one has ever given us the wings to fly and helped us develop the eyes to see the miracles we are supposed to take on faith.

The Buddha himself said:

"I do not ask you to believe in what so many others believe. I only exhort you to independent enlightenment, to use your own mind, developing it instead of letting it become dull. I urge you not to resemble beasts of prey, or stupid sheep. I implore you to be men with right views, men who toil untiringly for the acquisition of real knowledge which will never fail to prevail over suffering."

He was not saying that we should not revere and

respect those noble ones who have walked the path further than we have, but he was saying that faith alone would not be enough.

We should remember that all twelve of Jesus' disciples abandoned him and renounced their faith in his hour of need. These were supposedly saintly beings living under the guidance of their master. What chance then have we of standing firm when we are really challenged in this age of moral degeneration?

There is little doubt that Jesus himself came to know the God of whom he spoke, but what a tragedy that his life was cut off before he could teach us the path by which he had come to such knowledge. He bequeathed us his Sermon on the Mount as a treaty on virtue.

Such virtue is doubtless the foundation for any endeavour at establishing such states of mind that might directly see the truth. But sadly he did not live long enough to lay down a systematic path to the knowledge of such truth. And so we have been left with our prayers alone.

I remember seeing an old lady being read the last rites at the hospice where Dad died. I could feel the love and compassion of her priest but I knew...he didn't know. It was his faith alone that was the source of his love. And it is true that such faith will carry us far. It calls to the deepest longing in our hearts, the longing to be touched and to feel held by the beings we pray might watch over us. In such prayers, there is so much comfort. We can feel that energy so clearly in the majestic sounds of the Christian liturgy. You only need to listen to Allegri's Miserere Mei to be touched by this.

But in the end I came to the conclusion that for those of good heart it doesn't matter. They pray to their ideal of the perfected compassionate being and that ideal may be every bit as sublime in their mind's eye as the one that I beheld.

One thing I saw that night was that the being that held us with so much love was not easily shaken from its samadhi. This state of mind is a pervasive state and not an active one. It is pure, unbounded and unconditional love and it favours not one being over another.

I feel there is little chance that it will awaken and intervene actively in our lives, even when we die. Is it not enough that it has committed itself to provide the cover of such an extraordinary love while we flail around in the darkness looking for our way? How much more do we expect?

I know many of you will read this with mixed feelings, but it would have been wrong of me to tell my tale without sharing all of it. I have thought long and hard on what is the knowledge we seek and need. I know it is both the understanding of the way of things and the understanding of the true nature of love, and I do not think we have completed our journey until we have entered deeply into both of these things.

The Buddha was not wrong, he knew that faith and the knowledge of God, whilst a great comfort and protection, was not the cessation of suffering and so he did not teach such things. He was quite explicit about what he had set out to do. He taught the path to Nibbana, to the remainderless cessation of suffering, the unconditioned state.

Jesus was not wrong. He equally was clear about what he taught. He taught the path of loving-kindness and forgiveness, that if cultivated to its highest state will lead us to the knowledge of God.

I do not ask you to believe me. Some of you will

dismiss me as a romantic and I can only hope you enjoy this tale as the adventure that it is. But it is written for those of you who know in your heart the things of which I speak. It is an invitation to you to take up your own practice and seek such guidance that will open the way for you.

We have lost our ability to see. We are floundering in the fog of confusion and we do not know where to look. If you have patience enough and are willing to work hard, then there is a way. You need only follow each step in turn.

Start by asking yourself what you absolutely know to be true. Think hard on this until you come to the understanding that you don't actually know anything to be absolutely true, whatever views you might hold. Then let all views go and start with an open mind and heart, the systematic process of really looking into the way of things until it reveals itself in stages.

The first thing you can know for certain, and without doubt, is that everything you have ever perceived is impermanent and cannot be held forever. Use this as the spur that will push you on, let go your clinging to forms and views and allow your mind to open…and slowly but surely you will come to see. And once you have seen you will know.

CHAPTER TWENTY-SIX

Go Forth

I remember that last evening I spent with my Dad before I went off to teach. It was the last time I ever saw him.

"Do you remember the message I wrote in your birthday card the year you started Mad Rags?" He asked.

"Of course," I replied. "It said 'Go forth son. Bring golden opinions from all kinds of people' ".

"Well, will you promise that you will do that? Promise me you won't give up. I don't have the chance to make merit now. I wish I had known earlier in my life the things you have taught me. Perhaps then I could die without the fear of not knowing if I have done enough to get me to where I want to go."

I was choking on my tears.

"Dad, you have no idea how great is your merit. Everyone who has succeeded in their meditation or won their fight with sickness on account of the help I have given them, owes their debt of gratitude to you, not me."

"Don't be daft son, what have I done?" He smiled

"Do you remember the day you came to collect me from school after I was suspended."

"How could I forget?"

"Do you remember you stopped the car at Caesar's Camp on the way home? I thought I was in for a thrashing. But do you remember what you said to me?"

"I do. I told you to go and play your blues harmonica at the Grand Canyon, and you still haven't done it."

"Dad, it wasn't about the Grand Canyon. It was about permission. You gave me permission to follow my dreams that day. You could have said a thousand things; about how ashamed of me you were, or how shameful of me it was to not respect the opportunities I had been given, and you would have been right.

And if you had said those things, then out of shame I might well have become a banker or the barrister Granddad always wanted me to be. But you didn't say those things. You told me that if I wanted to play Blues at the Grand Canyon, then that's exactly what I should do.

It was in that moment that I knew I could seek the answers I needed without the fear of disapproval from others. I need never care about being an outsider or a maverick because I had my Dad's approval. And that is the only thing a young man ever really needs."

"Had you not given me acceptance and permission that day I would never have kept on tirelessly pushing the boundaries, pushing my limits, stretching my envelope, and none of those people I have helped might still be alive today. And so it is your merit and not mine, and it always will be.

And when death comes to you, as it soon will, you have a choice. You can either be terrified by the fear that you were not worthy of grace, or you can see that you have always been loved and never judged by any being that knows the truth.

Then you will see death as the biggest adventure of your life and enter into the unknown with the wild abandon that set me out on my quest, knowing that you have earned your colours and the ticket to where you need to go. I will never repay my debt to you and Mum, but what small merit I might make will always be yours."

He squeezed my hand feebly and sighed. His eyes were closed and there were tears on his cheeks. But I felt his heart skip a beat as it took its ease. He finally knew that he was safe. And I knew. And he knew I knew.

After some minutes he opened his eyes.

"You had better go, old boy. You have a retreat starting tomorrow. I'll be OK. Don't you worry about me. I'm not afraid any more. I am just so sad. I love this life so much. And I can't bear to lose that lovely lady that's your mother. And I still want to sit with you and learn so much. I am just so sad that I have run out of time."

Now my Dad is gone and the precious life he loved so much has come to an end. I know he is safe but I also know how much he wished he could have done more. He found the way late in his life and worked heroically to make his peace with himself.

In the end he won the greatest victory of all despite not recovering from his illness. But it was a hard fight and I know he would have preferred to have given himself more time.

So to all you brave souls out there who are

reading this, I have just one message for you. Go for it. Get out there and grab hold of your life and make it everything it is meant to be. Let it be a testimony to the love and gratitude you find along the way, because this human life is so hard to come by, so rare and so precious. Don't get to the end of it wishing you had done more. Go and find out what you are really made of, so that even if you fail to realise your dreams you will do so doing greatly and never stand amongst those timid souls who know not victory nor defeat.

Be willing to fight for the meaning you seek, be willing to pick yourself up time and time again and find the courage to stand tall in the face of your fears. Know that you and only you will ever turn it in to light. Go out and claim your life and make it yours in the face of all adversity and never, ever give up.

For it's the only fight worth truly giving your all for. Look deep into your heart and pay heed to its calling for it is only there that your truth lies. Look behind the world of appearances, to the truth that they conceal.

There is an eternal principle that governs all life and it is utterly reliable and always perfect and you won't learn it in your schools. Your heart knows the truth that this world has all but forgotten, so go and find it for yourself.

Besides, what else is there to do?

We have run out of time to delight in our sensual indulgence any more. Our greed has almost undone the very planet that sustains us. To continue to live the way we have done is fast becoming profane.

Do not wait for those around you to change. Go and seek your truth fearlessly. Do not wait for approval from others, ask only for their forgiveness, and never blame those who cannot understand you.

There is no room left in our world for greed and the ambitious desire for material status. They are false gods and we have worshipped them for far too long. There is only one thing left to aspire to and claim as your own, and it is the one thing that once grasped will never be taken away. That is the knowledge of the way of things and the entering into and living by this truth.

Your peace, everyone's peace, is right there, right in front of you, right now waiting to be claimed and owned. It is the peace of coming to love the being that you truly are, for what it is, as it is. Make your peace with it and forgive yourself for your mistakes as you make a deep commitment to not renew them.

Then find your sense of gratitude for the extraordinary gift and miracle that life is. Turn away from, and utterly relinquish all your sense of entitlement it is enough that this world even sustains your very existence.

What more can you ask of it? Perhaps then and only then will you refuse to be a part of its destruction, and enter into the way of gratitude, appreciative joy and love.

Do not despair in the face of the ignorance that you will see around you, but rest simply in the knowledge that you are doing your best to come out of it. Mahatma Gandhi, Martin Luther King, Nelson Mandela, even Jesus and the Buddha did not change the way of things, they simply held a candle by which we might see a way for ourselves, should we seek to follow.

I know there are many of you out there who are struggling to find your way. The old world values that brought us to this point are no longer valid.

You should not feel it is expected of you to strive in the material world as your forefathers did, for we have almost consumed the bounty of this planet in search of comfort and gratification at that level.

We will all have to learn to live simply and forego the cravings and longings for such things, if we are to sustain our existence long enough to find our way home. So go and find your meaning in the sustainable field of endeavour, the realm that will never cease to provide you with challenge and reward, in the quest for your own peace.

Accept yourself for who you are and strive earnestly to raise yourself up from that point. Waste not an instant waiting for your lucky break or your saviour to come and dig you out of your hole, but be willing to sweat your very blood to climb up to the mountaintop, in the knowledge that the victory won is wholly your own. And when you have claimed this, the greatest of all victories, be ready to give yourself utterly in service to those who are struggling in the darkness behind you.

Cry oceans of tears for the suffering you will see everywhere, but be sure they are tears of true compassion that has come to understand why it becomes that way.

Have no time for grief and pity, for however moved you might be by the plight of others the universe is always unfolding the only way it can.

In the final analysis you will find there is not, and never has been, a hair out of place and the only lessons we need are right in front of us at all times. See all of your challenges as an invitation to evolve, for when you can see this truth you will come to know the true nature of compassion.

We each of us have to work out our own salvation with dignity and diligence. The best you can do is hold your candle of love by which others may see the way. Be impeccable in conduct but do not preach what you have only just learned for it will still be many lifetimes before you have lived your truth enough to be called a sage.

Never seek to bend the minds of those who do not understand you. Send them only love and let your life itself set an example that might move mountains.

Learn to be of few needs and delight in simplicity. You will need little more than a quiet place to be. And while you are doing this work, you can sleep easy at night in the knowledge that you are no longer a part of the rank and file who chose not to step back and give our precious world a chance to rest and catch its breath while we do the very same.

Let your very being become an example and inspiration to those who lack the courage to give up their old ways. Go and make your life a vast field of merit through service and the loving care of those around you, so that when it is over you will know that you were a light upon this world for the brief period you were here.

Good luck to you, each and every one of you. Keep your faith and you will not fail.

And one day soon I'll be seeing you on the high plains, where we can run free together with the wind in our hair. And we will hold our hands up high knowing that we have done what had to be done. And we will shout it out to all the world.

"I'm alive, I'm alive, I'm alive."

Epilogue

There is an old Taoist adage in which a student asks his teacher;

"What did you do before your enlightenment Master?"

"I lived in the village, I sowed seeds and chopped wood and carried water."

"Only that sir? Just a humble wood chopper and water carrier?"

"Indeed."

"And what do you do now sir, now that you are enlightened?"

"I live in the village and sow seeds and chop wood and carry water."

"Only that sir?"

"Indeed my son, only that."

I have often reflected that if this master was to appear to us in this age, what might he ask us:

"So tell me please, what did you all do before you became intoxicated with your own creations and the creations of others?"

"Why sir, we sowed seeds and chopped wood

and carried water."

"And what now will you do, now that you have consumed your world with your intoxication?"

"Why sir, what else is there for us to do? We shall sow seeds and chop wood and carry water."

Some of you will delight in the idea of a return to such simplicity, that your movement upon this earth leaves no trace, and others will be horrified by the prospect. But there comes a time in every world system where human beings either learn to live as caring and responsible guardians of their planet or stop appearing there altogether. We are at that point of choice.

It is us, you and me, who are faced with this choice. It is not a choice faced by past generations, nor one future generations will face in the same way.

Have you ever stopped to ask why you may be here upon this earth at this time? Did anyone explain to you how you arrived here at this time in history and not at another time?

You could, in a different time and under different conditions have lived in the village, and chopped wood and carried water. But you didn't, you came here now. To this world at this time, at the end of the age of intoxication and the pursuit of pleasure.

It is no mean feat to appear upon the earth blessed with the good fortune many of you have.

The Buddha gave a discourse one time in which he explained how rare it is to appear upon the earth blessed with a fortunate human birth.

"Suppose you were to throw a yoke into the vast

340

ocean and set it adrift to float where it may," he said. "And suppose then there was a blind turtle that raised his head up above the surface of that great ocean once every hundred years. Greater is the chance of that blind turtle raising his head within that drifting yoke, than is the chance of achieving this fortunate human life."

Think about it for a moment. Here we are, somewhere down the line upon this fortunate human life of ours, upon this miraculous planet that supports such a life. Just a dot in the vastness of space.

How many aeons does it take for such conditions to appear? How long did we wait for the chance to appear here at this time? How great once was our longing to behold the extraordinary display of beauty that creation unfolds for us everywhere that we cast our eyes? How quickly did we forget the miracle of creation as we became intoxicated instead in our own creations?

Let us all take responsibility for our presence here and learn to live in a way that we may bequeath this blessed planet in all its miraculous beauty to those still to come, who like us have waited so long for their chance to behold it.

End Note

Two days before he died, Burgs' father, ever full of hope asked him,

"Will you promise to take me to Burma with you one day, son?"

In 2006 Burgs travelled to Burma with his brother Grant. He carried with him his Dad's ashes and released them into the Irrawaddy River in Bagan. It had been his last request.

Burgs continues to teach meditation
and chi kung in the UK and Europe.

For more information please visit
www.theartofmeditation.org

Glossary

Abhidhamma: the seven books of the Abhidhamma Pitaka, the third division of the Buddha's teachings, offer an extraordinarily detailed analysis of the basic natural principles that govern mental and physical processes. Whereas the Sutta and Vinaya Pitakas lay out the practical aspects of the Buddhist path to Awakening, the Abhidhamma Pitaka provides a theoretical framework to explain the causal underpinnings of that very path. In Abhidhamma philosophy the familiar psycho-physical universe (our world of 'trees' and 'rocks,' 'I' and 'you') is distilled to its essence: an intricate web of impersonal phenomena and processes unfolding at an inconceivably rapid pace from moment to moment, according to precisely defined natural laws. According to tradition, the essence of the Abhidhamma was formulated by the Buddha during the fourth week after his Enlightenment, and recorded by Sariputta.

Adhitthana: determination; resolution. One of the ten perfections (Paramis).

Anapanasati (Anapana): mindfulness of breathing. One of the practices the Buddha taught his monks so that they could cultivate their concentration and mindfulness.

Anicca: inconstant, unsteady, impermanent.

Arahant: a fully awakened being, who has freed themselves

Bodhisattva: a being striving to achieve full Awakening and Buddhahood in the absence of a teacher to show the way and bring forth the Dharma

347

in the time of darkness where the way out of suffering is not known. The term was used in the texts to describe the Buddha before he actually became Buddha, and applied from his first aspiration to Buddhahood undertaken before the Buddha Dipankara until the time of his full Awakening.

Brahma: 'Great One' — a sublime being existing in the higher fine material realms on account of highly developed states of samadhi and virtue. Such a life is immeasurably long, often extending beyond the time frame of the world cycle. This is the most exalted being in the conditioned universe. In many religions this being is referred to as God.

Dependent Origination: please see Appendix.

Deva: literally, 'shining one' — an inhabitant of the heavenly realms. These heavenly realms are pleasurable abodes and the destination of one whose strong and virtuous karma fruits at death.

Dhamma (Pali); Dharma (Sanskrit): this term has a number of different meanings. Firstly the Dhamma is the Universal Law that that governs life and all mind and matter. It is these natural laws that we should live in accordance with. Secondly it refers to the body of teachings that the Buddha left us. Finally Dhamma can refer to any state or phenomenon that occurs, mental or physical, or Nibbana itself.

Direct Perception: please see Appendix.

His Holiness Dodrupchen Rinpoche: still resides in his monastery in Sikkim, northern India.

Eight Samapati: these are the eight jhanas. The first four take the fine material realm as their objects and the fifth to eighth take the immaterial realm. It is the jhana consciousness which, if fruiting at death, leads to renewed existence in the Brahma realms.

Eightfold Noble Path: Right Speech, Right Action, Right Livelihood (which is our training in Virtue), Right Effort, Right Mindfulness, Right Concentration, (which is our training in samadhi) Right Thought, Right View (which is our training in Wisdom).

Four Noble Truths: these were the four realisations about suffering and its causes that the Buddha realised on the night of his enlightenment under the Bodhi tree. They are:

1. The Truth of Suffering
2. The Truth of the Cause of Suffering (which is clinging and the *Law of Dependent Origination*)
3. The Truth of the Cessation of Suffering (which is *Nibbana* and the remainderless cessation of the aggregates of clinging and their causes)
4. The Truth of the Path that leads to the Cessation of Suffering (which is the *Eightfold Noble Path*).

Jhana: a deep state of absorption samadhi in which the life continuum consciousness is momentarily interrupted leading to unification of the mind with its object and the momentary cessation of the sense of separation between subject and object.

Kamma (Pali); **Karma (Sanskrit)**: the Buddha famously said: "intention, I tell you, is Kamma. Having willed, one does Kamma by way of body, speech, & intellect" (AN 6.63). Our Karma is the result of past intentions of body, speech and mind. The Karma is the volitional force that prompts us to act and is wholesome or unwholesome dependent upon the virtue and blamelessness of the volition or otherwise.

Kasina: a word used to describe a set of ten meditation practices that are used for the development of Jhana concentration (samadhi). Each of the kassina meditations take a simple non-compound object such as earth, water or the primary colours.

Kuti: a meditation hut.

Pak Merta Ada: continues to run Bali Usada meditation retreats in Bali and across Indonesia.

Metta: the Pali word for Loving Kindness.

Nimitta: sign. This is the mind-produced sign that appears as the mind becomes deeply concentrated on its object. This sign varies from one meditation to the other, it may be a particular light or other sign and in each case it needs to be clearly identified and differentiated from the light that may appear simply as a by-product of the concentration and other mental states that arise in meditation. It is a spontaneously arising sign and not a visualisation that we seek to formulate actively with the mind.

OM AH HUM: the first three syllables of many famous Tibetan mantras.

Padmasambhava/Guru Rinpoche: the much revered founder of Tibetan (Vajrayana) Buddhism.

Pali: is the ancient spoken language that the Buddhist scriptures were originally recorded in.

The Ten Parami(s): please see Appendix.

Parinibbana: the causal cessation of the five aggregates of suffering when the arahant enters into Nibbana at death

Paritta: a protective chant in Buddhism that serves to prepare for practice and teaching, or to clear the space and mind of hindrances.

Peta (Pali); Preta (Sanskrit): a 'hungry spirit' — one of a class of beings in the lower realms, sometimes capable of appearing to human beings.

Puja : a devotional ceremony or ritual.

Rebirth Linking Consciousness: please see Appendix.

Saddu/Sadhu: the name for an Indian holy man.

Sangha: the community of monks and nuns who have taken refuge in the Buddha, Dhamma, and Sangha.

Samadhi: one pointedness or concentration leading to absorption and unification of the mind.

Samatha: the practice of serenity medittion where concentration is the focus. In Vipassana inisight is the focus rather than concentration.

Samsara: The round to conditioned existence that brings renewed becoming one liftime after another. It is this process by which we are bound until we finally free ourselves with the entering into the unconditioned state of Nibbana.
Sasana: The teachings on the Buddha. Also used to refer to the period of time during which these

teachings remain in tact and available to others.

Sayadaw (Burmese): venerable teacher; an honorific title and form of address for a senior or eminent bhikkhu (monk).

The Venerable Acinna (Venerable Pa Auk Sayadaw): has now retired from his position as abbot at the forest monastery. He now resides somewhere in the Himalayas of North India and continues to teach when requested. Pa Auk Monastery still continues to provide facilities for monks, nuns and lay yogis to practice according to the Sayadaw's teachings.

Sayalay (Burmese): an honorific title and form of address for a female renunciate.

Sutta: a word used to describe a single teaching or discourse of the Buddha.

Theravada: the 'Doctrine of the Elders' — the only one of the early schools of Buddhism to have survived into the present; currently the dominant form of Buddhism in Thailand, Sri Lanka, and Burma. It is sometimes referred to as the Theravada School, as contrasted with the Mahayana and Vajrayana Schools of Buddhism.

Vajrayana: the esoteric branch of Tibetan Tantric Buddhism.

Vipassana: clear intuitive insight into physical and mental phenomena as they arise and disappear born of wise attention in meditation. The way of attention that comes to see things for what they actually are in terms of the three characteristics (subject to suffering, impermanence and not self) and leads to the abandoning of wrong view and, over time, attachment and desire.

Appendix

Direct Perception

Much is made in the West of the importance of intuition as a spiritual faculty by which we may be guided on our life path. It is important to understand the difference between intuition and direct perception.

Intuition is a deep inner sense of knowing. It arises in a more direct way than normal reflective thought which is a normal mental process. Intuition is the subjective sense we get of something when we apprehend the information it presents to us at an energetic level. For example, someone walks into a room. You may have a deep instinctive feeling about this person which is not hinted at by their appearance, gestures or demeanour alone. This intuitive sense is coming from the information you are receiving in your energy field directly from the energy field of the person you are encountering. It reveals more to you than the person's appearance etc. would alone, but it needs to be understood that in the final analysis that intuition is still a deeper subjective sense of something and is not direct knowledge of it.

Direct knowledge is where the mind (heart base) apprehends an object directly and simply receives the information it is disclosing. In the above example where the same person appears in the room, by direct perception we apprehend the quality of that person's mind and consciousness directly through contact at the mind door. 'This person is greedy, arrogant, honest, etc.'. Through direct contact we know the state and characteristic of any object as it is. This is direct knowledge that appears in our mind door directly without any subjective evaluation or personal sense of it. While intuition is a deeply felt (and hence subjective) sense of something, direct perception is simply 'it is what it is'.

For example we might have an intuitive sense of what causes someone's cancer on account of how we feel when that person enters our own energy field. "I feel this is connected to your separation from your mother when you were five." In direct perception the dysfunctional materiality in the body is apprehended directly. "This cancer is produced by karma-produced materiality rooted in uncontrolled aversion." We simply perceive directly the object as it is.

The Buddha urged us to develop this faculty of direct perception so we might come to know things directly. He implored us to let go all attachment to views. Even a deeply held intuitive sense is a clung to view that is not known to be true. Attachment to views is one of the important causes for clinging to sense of self (the ultimate cause of suffering).

Rebirth Linking Consciousness

The stream of our awareness that gives the sense of continuity of personal experience is produced by a consciousness, which in Pali is called Bhavanga. It literally means life continuum. This consciousness arises from the heart base (in Pali 'hadayavatu'), and links one moment of active cognition with the next. Each time we perceive any object there appears in our mind a subtle response to it of either attachment or aversion. Some people like one thing while another will dislike it, and this response is conditioned by our previous experiences of such an object. The impulse of this response is registered in Bhavanga producing our subjective or personal experience of the objects that we encounter over time. The force of the attachment or aversion to the various objects we perceive in the life, forms the basis of Karma. As the Buddha said "It is volition I call Karma. Having willed, I act."

As such it is not the acts that we perform that constitutes Karma but the volition that prompts them; not what we do, but how we do it.

Over the course of our life the force of this volition is continuously registered in Bhavanga producing our unconscious store of reactions and impressions. It is this accumulation of Karma that conditions our behaviour and reactions to the multitude of experiences we encounter in our lives.

When we die of natural causes at the end of the life, the karma that supports our life and in particular the heart base becomes defunct. The life principle and the support for our consciousness thereafter withdraws; leaving our physical body to decay over time in the absence of the life supporting karma. It literally has run its course and expires. If our life is cut off prior to old age it is because of the untimely arising of disruptive karma. But whether we die in old age of natural causes or our life is cut off prematurely the process of dying is the same.

With the passing of the karmic support for our sense doors our awareness of the external world is cut off. Awareness then rests in Bhavanga and all the impressions stored therein present themselves according to the intensity of the volition (karma) behind them. There are many accounts of near death experiences where people describe a sense of their whole life flashing before them, and in a way this is what happens. Some impulses are rooted in greed, others anger, others in love or good will, or generosity. And so forth according to all the myriad ways we have responded to the experience of our life.

Consciousness can only take one object at a time and there will always be one impulsion that has registered with more intensity than any other. This is the one the mind will latch onto in the final moment of passing away. We call this the death consciousness, and the karma inherent in it becomes the link into the existence for which we are bound next, as well as being the basis of our character and the way others respond to us. It decides our destination and the conditions in which we come to find ourselves. It becomes also the basis of our very sense of self at the deepest level.

Some wholesome karma produces human existence, others deva life or heavenly existence. Unwholesome karma rooted in greed produces the kind of life the wretch who frequented the drains behind the kitchen was bound to and karma rooted in strong hatred or anger produces even more suffering in what we might call hell.

So while our prayers can well produce wholesome consciousness that might help us on our way we need to understand that it is the volition behind our prayers and not the prayers themselves that will produce wholesome fruit or not. The Buddha spoke emphatically on how virtue was the root of all success and Jesus taught us the Sermon on the Mount imploring us to live virtuously.

As he said himself, "As you sow so shall you reap."

Thus it is that virtue serves us more when we die than will the frequency of our prayers.

Once the mind has grasped the object of our death consciousness it becomes the very object of our Bhavanga consciousness for the entire duration of our next life despite the fact it may never become known to us, and is only renewed at the end of that life when we link into the next.

The object of Bhavanga is the first clue we get as to the nature of our previous life.

It appears momentarily in the mind door between each moment of active awareness but only so fleetingly as to be completely imperceptible to our conscious mind.

The first chance we get to catch the object of Bhavanga is the moment immediately following our emergence from absorption samadhi or jhana. During jhana the Bhavanga consciousness is cut off and it is this very cutting off of our subjective sense of awareness that opens the way to unification of the mind with its object. At this time we are in a profoundly deep and unwavering concentration. As we emerge from our absorption the very next object to present itself is the Bhavanga object that appears momentarily before our stream of active cognition continues. In this moment, with the powerful concentration of the absorption from which we are emerging, the mind is able at times to grab the object of Bhavanga and know it directly. Since this object is also the same object that our mind grasped as we passed away at the end of the previous life we may therein come to know both the karma that brought this life into being and hence the karma that fruited at the end of our previous life. The mechanism by which this process is carried out is complex and requires the ability to see the chain of dependent origination, but it comes to reveal the exact nature of who we were in the previous life and what kind of deeds we engaged in. Thereafter if our concentration is deep enough we can follow the process further to identify the Bhavanga object in our previous life and thereby come to know the karma that fruited at the end of the life before that. Our ability to go further and further back is determined by how strong our concentration is, for it is an exhausting practice that quickly can tire the heart if our samadhi is not sufficiently deep.

While I had been practicing the jhanas with Sayadaw I began to notice that an image had begun to appear quite regularly as I emerged from my absorption. It was always the same image. It was simply a peaceful scene looking across treetops as they swayed gently in the breeze. You may remember that this is the very same impression that we take to mind when beginning our practice of the air kasina meditation.

Eventually I came to recognise this as my Bhavanga object. I realised in time that I had practiced this meditation in my life before this and that was the reason that I had found meditation so easy to grasp in this life. I had the seed of it in my Bhavanga.

It was the delight I found and my attachment to my previous meditation on the air kasina that had come to mind when I died and re-linked me into the life I found myself in now. This was the understanding I finally came to when I began the meditation on dependent origination and was able to trace the causal chain of karma and its results back through my life and into lives before this.

Dependent Origination

This is the causal chain of interconnected forces that brings things into being. Furthermore it explains why it is that we cannot break out of the round of life, death and rebirth as an act of will. We are bound to the cycle of Samsara (wandering on) by the Law of Dependent Origination (Paticca-samuppada) and Karma. It is expressed in different forms in the Buddha's teachings but the most common formula is :

⚶ Dependent upon **Ignorance** (not knowing truth [impermanence, suffering etc.] or not knowing Nibbana), wilful/**volitional formations** (producing karma) arise (in the mind)

⚶ Depending on these wilful/**volitional formations** (which are clung to by the mind at death), **consciousness** (in particular the rebirth-linking consciousness) arises (at death)

⚶ Dependent on the **rebirth linking consciousness**, (karma produced) **mind and matter** arise

⚶ Dependent on **mind and matter**, the **six sense bases** arise in the body of our next life

⚶ Dependent upon the **sense bases, contact** (with other objects, external and internal, mental and physical) arises

⚶ Dependent upon **contact, feeling** arises

⚶ Dependent upon **feeling, desire/craving** (for the objects producing such feeling) arises

⚶ Dependent upon **desire and craving** (for objects), **clinging and attachment** (to such objects) arises

362

⅄ Dependent upon **clinging and attachment** (to objects appearing in the mind at death), renewed **becoming** arises

⅄ Dependent upon renewed **becoming**, **birth** arises

⅄ Dependent upon **birth**, thereafter inevitably follows **old age**, **sickness** and **death**, whereupon the whole process begins again and again and again.

This law of dependent origination is what the Buddha came to call the Second Noble Truth, the truth of the cause of suffering. We are bound to it for as long as clinging appears in the mind upon contact or recollection of all the myriad conditioned forms we experience and encounter throughout the life. This clinging is the very karmic force that produces the rebirth linking between one life and the next and the wheel of Samsara (or wandering on) as it is called.

The Buddha's Third Noble Truth, "the truth of the cessation of suffering" comes about with the non-arising of clinging. The Buddha's Noble Eightfold Path that leads to the non-arising of clinging and in turn the cessation of suffering is the Fourth Noble Truth. At the super-mundane level the path leads to the knowledge of the unconditioned (or deathless) state of Nibbana that cuts off all clinging to conditioned states and leads to the causal cessation of suffering with the non-arising of the five aggregates of clinging and their causes.

The Ten Parami(s)

Meaning perfection of character: also means skill. A group of ten qualities developed over many lifetimes, which appear as a group in the Pali canon. The ten paramis in order are:

1. Generosity (*dana*)
2. Virtue (*sila*)
3. Renunciation (*nekkhamma*)
4. Discernment (*pañña*)
5. Energy/persistence (*viriya*)
6. Patience/forbearance (*khanti*)
7. Truthfulness/self honesty (*sacca*)
8. Determination (*adhitthana*)
9. Loving Kindness/good will (*metta*)
10. Equanimity (*upekkha*)

It is the perfection of these paramis that ripens the mind for the understanding of higher spiritual truths and their realisation at an experiential level.

It is the highest perfection of Parami that ripened the Buddha's mind for his realisation of full knowledge of the path out of suffering.

The word Parami is also sometimes used to describe other skills and talents that sometimes appear in people in their life without any apparent teaching or training. This is on account of work put forth in previous lives.

Poorly developed cultivation of these qualities of mind, leads us to cling to self-supporting views, rather than engaging in open minded enquiry.

Burgs continues to teach meditation
and chi kung in the UK and Europe.

For more information please visit

www.theartofmeditation.org

Join the members area where
you will find Burgs' Beyond the Veil blog.